THE PHILOSOPHY OF T. S. ELIOT

The Persistence of Memory [Persistance de la memoire].
Salvador Dali, 1931. Oil on canvas, 9½ x 13" (24.1 x 33 cm). Collection,
The Museum of Modern Art, New York. Given anonymously.

THE PHILOSOPHY OF

T. S. ELIOT

FROM SKEPTICISM TO A SURREALIST POETIC 1909 – 1927

WILLIAM SKAFF

upp PHILADELPHIA 1986

UNIVERSITY OF PENNSYLVANIA PRESS

Acknowledgment is made for permission to quote from works by T. S. Eliot and others. A complete listing can be found at the end of this volume, after the Index.

Library of Congress Cataloging-in-Publication Data

Skaff, William.
    The philosophy of T. S. Eliot.

    Includes index.
    1. Eliot, T. S. (Thomas Stearns), 1888–1965—
Philosophy.   2. Philosophy in literature.   3. Skepticism
in literature.   4. Surrealism in literature.   I. Title.
PS3509.L43Z8655   1986   821'.912   85-31477
ISBN 0-8122-8017-2 (alk. paper)

Printed in the United States of America

Designed by Adrianne Onderdonk Dudden

TO PAUL FUSSELL

CONTENTS

ABBREVIATIONS AND TEXTS

KE   *Knowledge and Experience in the Philosophy of F. H. Bradley. London: Faber and Faber, 1964.*

SW   *The Sacred Wood: Essays on Poetry and Criticism. 2d ed. London: Methuen, 1928.*

SE   *Selected Essays. 2d ed. New York: Harcourt, Brace, 1950.*

UPUC   *The Use of Poetry and the Use of Criticism: Studies in the Relation of Criticism to Poetry in England. 2d ed. London: Faber and Faber, 1964.*

EAM   *Essays Ancient and Modern. London: Faber and Faber, 1936.*

PP   *On Poetry and Poets. New York: Farrar, Straus and Giroux, 1957.*

CC   *To Criticize the Critic and Other Writings. New York: Farrar, Straus and Giroux, 1965.*

Poems Written in Early Youth. New York: Farrar, Straus and Giroux, 1967.

The Complete Poems and Plays, 1909–1950. New York: Harcourt, Brace and World, 1952.

ACKNOWLEDGMENTS

I would like to thank James Breslin and Frederick Crews for their thoughtful reading of the manuscript and their many helpful suggestions. I am grateful to Richard Hutson for introducing me to the excitement of reading literature from a philosophical perspective, which he did so ably with the American Renaissance. I am indebted to Ulrich Knoepflmacher and Barry Qualls for teaching me the value of contextual criticism so well in terms of the Victorian Age that I was inspired to apply it to the modern period. I thank Georges Longree for a more sensitive appreciation of late-nineteenth and early-twentieth century French poetry and a stimulating introduction to the linguistic approach to poetic language. I remember with fondness my first experience of T. S. Eliot with Thomas Van Laan. The friendship and wise counsel of Phillip McCaffrey and Robert Miola have bolstered me through the latter stages of this project. Anne Bolgan's encouragement has been the least of her kindnesses. This book is dedicated to the one person who, through the lucidity, integrity, and ultimate sympathy of his vision of the human condition, has made it possible for me to continue as a humanist for as long as I have.

For their generous assistance I would like to thank the staffs of the Berg Collection of the New York Public Library; Rare Books and Special Collections of the Princeton University Library; and the Manuscripts Department of the McKeldin Library, University of Maryland.

THE PHILOSOPHY OF T. S. ELIOT

INTRODUCTION

T. S. Eliot is the first poet since Coleridge to have constructed a comprehensive philosophical system out of eclectic sources and then to have allowed those ideas to determine the nature of his verse and his principles of literary criticism, and to influence even the conduct of his personal life. In truth, Eliot's mind encompasses just about every important avant-garde intellectual movement of his time. His thought, as well as his poetry, is at the heart of the early twentieth century's creative impulse. This study presents Eliot's unique synthesis of contemporary philosophy, psychology, anthropology, and studies in mysticism, and demonstrates how it is responsible for the nature of his religious belief, the basic tenets of his literary theory, and the figurative, structural, and dramatic aspects of his verse. Although this system of thought pervades everything he wrote, Eliot never had occasion to state it directly and fully, not even in his dissertation in philosophy. When examining all of his prose, however, noting repetitions of key words, phrases, and ideas, one discovers an underlying dimension of meaning in them. By interpreting these concepts in terms of Eliot's reading, one can construct a coherent pattern of mind out of what would otherwise remain isolated pieces of a puzzle. Only then can Eliot's poetic enterprise be fully understood, and his literary achievement fully appreciated.

The approach of this study, therefore, is at once philosophical, literary, and biographical. I have adopted a unifying perspective on Eliot's poetry and prose that will enable me to reveal the relationship between a man's ideas and his art and life. Philosophical terminology itself has been restricted to those technical terms necessary for an understanding of Eliot's major theories and poems. At the same time, I have explained as specifically as possible Eliot's relationship to those thinkers important to his intellectual and artistic development. Finally, I have provided explanations, at times of a philosophical nature, for certain of Eliot's crucial ideas so that the reader can know precisely why Eliot thought in a certain way or proposed a certain theory. Often these arguments are merely implicit in Eliot's various writings and can only be surmised from a comparison of them all.

This book covers the first period of Eliot's life, from the beginning of his graduate work at Harvard in 1909—the initial stage of his mature thought—to the act to which his philosophical system inevitably led: his baptism into the Church of England in 1927. The study proceeds from Eliot's attempts to find intellectual explanations for the predilections of his personality in Chapters I and II, to his formulation of a general philosophy of mind out of this endeavor in Chapter III. Then Chapter IV traces his elaboration of this system into a philosophy of art and a philosophy of religion. From these more specialized philosophies, Eliot devises a theory of religious belief, as explained in Chapter V, and a theory of poetry, as explained in Chapter VI.

Chapter I, "Skepticism," presents the biographical and historical setting of Eliot's particular temperament—skeptical ever since childhood, by his own admission—and the intellectual formulation Eliot discovered at Harvard through which he chose to understand his personality: F. H. Bradley's idealism. Chapter II, "Mysticism," considers the religious impulse that began to make its strongest claim on Eliot's attention while he was a student at Harvard in the form of mystical visions. Eliot found his religious experiences to be in conflict with his skeptical temperament and sought some intellectual justification for them. After finding Henri Bergson's philosophy inadequate, Eliot modified Bradley's idealism according to suggestions from studies in mysticism so that it would accommodate his mystical moments. Chapter III, "The Unconscious," demonstrates how Eliot's reading in scientific psychology and theoretical anthropology for his dissertation on Bradley and for Josiah Royce's graduate seminar in philosophy now prompted him to elaborate the philosophical system he adapted from Bradley into a unified theory of the mind in all of its dimensions—metaphysical, psychological, and physiological—resulting in his concept of a collective-historical unconscious.

Chapter IV, "Primitive Experience," explains how further reading in anthropology and Classical studies, both during and after his formal education, helped Eliot move from a philosophy of mind to a philosophy of religion and a philosophy of art. He devised a theory of religious participation and the esthetic act based on the relationship between ritual as primitive behavior and the unconscious as the primitive mind. Anthropological investigations convinced Eliot that religion and art evolved out of primitive ritual. Thus he sought a poetic drama and a dramatic poetry because he believed that drama originated as ritual dance. Chapter V, "Mythic Consciousness," presents Eliot's theory of myth, which stems from his theory of ritual. Myths also form a part of the unconscious as patterns that turn the chaos of our world into a unified whole. Eliot decided that we can use myths to organize our everyday experience, in both art and life, through the mythic method. This literary technique suggested to him the self-conscious nature of the modern mind, and, in turn, a form of religious belief, mythic consciousness, that would transcend its skepticism.

Chapter VI, "A Surrealist Poetic," demonstrates how the well-known terms of Eliot's poetic theory—impersonality, objective correlative, unity of experience, wit—evolved out of the system of thought the previous chapters have developed. For Eliot, both the imagery and structure of a poem originate in the writer's unconscious and work to liberate the reader's unconscious. Thus Eliot's basic esthetic concepts can be fully explained only in terms of the collective-historical unconscious in all of its aspects, physiological, psychological, and metaphysical. By noting the crucial similarities, as well as the differences, between Eliot's poetic theory and practice and the esthetic and art of Surrealism, this chapter provides more insight into the true nature of Eliot's poetic than if it were considered in relation to Metaphysical verse, as is customary. Such a comparison between Eliot and Surrealism, in turn, explores the relationship between poetry and painting and points to various ideas and techniques that art of the early twentieth century in general may share. Not only do many of Eliot's images and those he admired in other contemporary poets resemble specific Surrealist paintings, but their syntactic structure itself facilitates the efficacy of metaphors based on visual properties.

Since this study traces the growth of a mind, its development must necessarily be sequential and cumulative, logical, and as far as possible, chronological. We must keep in mind, however, that it is virtually impossible to determine exactly when Eliot devised any given idea. Because Eliot was a man of letters rather than a professional philosopher, his thoughts find their way into print only when a certain book he is reviewing calls them to mind. He never wrote a treatise or series of books exclusively on his own nonliterary ideas. Furthermore, books of philosophy, mysticism, psychology, and anthropology that can be associated with one or another aspect of his thought were often read by him at the same time, many while he was at Harvard. We cannot be certain, for instance, how much he knew of Bradley before he read Bergson, and thus whether Bergson is an interlude or precursor in Eliot's movement toward Bradley. Likewise, anthropology was a continuing interest with him, and we can never really say when it first began to influence his thought. He read Jane Harrison and James Frazer during his seminar with Royce in 1913, mentioned them in a book review in 1919, and then discussed them enthusiastically in 1924. Thus dates can be given for the various aspects of Eliot's philosophy only in terms of periods of development which frequently overlap.

Eliot enters graduate school with a skeptical point of view in 1909, and he begins to express it through Bradley about 1913. He undergoes his first overwhelming mystical experience in 1910, turns to Bergson for an explanation in 1911, and then resorts to Bradley, whose system he is induced to modify by his readings in mysticism around 1913. His unified theory of the unconscious mind was developed from reading done in France as early as 1910, and for Royce's seminar in 1913; it is present in his dissertation in 1916 and continues to develop through 1924. The reading in primitive experience upon which his philosophy of art and philosophy of religion are based could have been done as early as 1911; the ideas are first expressed in Royce's seminar in 1913, continue to develop through 1919, and reach maturity from 1921 to 1925. Eliot's mythic method and mythic consciousness, evolving out of these previous interests, appear to develop in reviews from 1920 through 1927; yet the former depends upon the use of myth employed in the poetry as early as 1914, and the latter upon an analysis of the modern skeptical mind appearing in his dissertation in 1916. The poetic theory also begins as early as his dissertation and evolves throughout this period of his life. The evidence suggests, in the end, that Eliot's system of thought, in a rudimentary state, is formulated somewhere around 1913 to 1916; after that came an extended period of elaboration and clarification.

In the process of reconstructing Eliot's philosophical system and exploring its impact on his literary theory, this study examines several other issues of Eliot criticism as well. It proposes that

Eliot defined the modern consciousness by resolving into a new synthesis the romantic dichotomy of materialist science and emotional spirituality that plagued the nineteenth-century sensibility. It suggests that Eliot defined Modernism as a distinct artistic attitude by overcoming both the subjective irrationality of Romanticism and the collective rationality of Classicism. It considers influences on Eliot not previously treated, such as logical positivism, and considers the relationship between sources ordinarily thought to be independent of each other, such as Remy de Gourmont and Bertrand Russell; Bradley and Émile Durkheim and Lucien Lévy-Bruhl; Harrison, Gilbert Murray, and F. M. Cornford and scientific psychology. It discusses Eliot's enthusiasm for the modern ballet and the music hall, and shows how these art forms, along with the drama, contributed to the structure and content of his poetry. It proposes that the true nature of Eliot's religious experience was *not* a literal belief in Christian dogma, as has often been assumed, but a more complex psychological state. I hope that this broader contextual framework will contribute to our sense of the early twentieth century as a distinct cultural period and make clearer Eliot's place in it and contribution to it.

I. SKEPTICISM

I N the early autobiographical sketch "Eeldrop and Appleplex," Eliot characterizes himself as "a sceptic, with a taste for mysticism."[1] Such a seemingly incompatible combination was forced upon Eliot in part by history, maturing as he did at the close of the nineteenth century. Eliot was primarily a dialectical thinker;[2] perhaps inspired by Hegel's *Philosophy of History,* which he read while a student at Harvard,[3] Eliot tends to view history as moving according to a dialectic. Thus he finds Romanticism composed of a thesis inherited from the previous century and its own antithetical response. The "two directions" of Romanticism, he observes, are, on the one hand, "devotion to brute fact," leading to "the apotheosis of science," or skepticism, the nineteenth century's version of the eighteenth century's inclination to rely on reason and empiricism as the only criteria of truth; and, on the other hand, the nineteenth century's reaction to this scientific prejudice, "escape from the world of fact" through "vague emotionality,"[4] or mysticism. Eliot's skepticism also has a more personal source in his own childhood religious training. Eliot observed later in life that any attempt to convert him during his "pre-Christian state of mind" would not have succeeded, because he was raised in an atmosphere of the "intellectual and puritanical rationalism" characteristic of the fiction of George Eliot, who was "greatly admired" by his family.[5] He also recalled that his first poetic effort at the age of fourteen consisted of "a number of very gloomy and atheistical and despairing quatrains."[6]

Eliot identified his own skepticism with that of Henry Adams, who was also in a sense "born in it." As Eliot explains of Adams, this skepticism is a "product, or a cause, or a concomitant, of Unitarianism; it is not destructive, but it is dissolvent." For example, although Emerson eventually decided to stop performing the Eucharist because it did not "interest" him, he nevertheless did not judge his fellow townspeople who proceeded with the rite anyway.

To Eliot that attitude was typical of the majority of cultivated citizens in a "provincial" American city of his childhood. In short, the "Boston doubt" of Adams was also 'the St. Louis doubt' amid which young Eliot found himself, and Eliot would always admire the "austere grandeur"[7] of Unitarianism's skepticism, an "emotional reserve and intellectual integrity."[8] But as a twentieth-century man, Eliot possessed a more profound skepticism than the philosophical foundation of Unitarianism, British Empiricism, in which Hume questioned the validity of religion on logical grounds, and Locke denied the efficacy of art from a scientific standpoint. As Eliot observes of Adams, he belonged to a "later generation"; although much "interested" him, "he could believe in nothing." Like Eliot, also a member of a family of public servants, Adams did not believe in the wisdom of British diplomacy, in the appropriateness of American democracy, or even in the nineteenth century's credo, Darwinian evolution. As Gerontion, unable to find or believe in a sustaining faith, religious or scientific, fears that he and his world will be "whirled / Beyond the circuit of the shuddering Bear / In fractured atoms" (68–70) in an eruption of unrestrained cosmic motion, so with Adams: "wherever this man stepped, the ground did not simply give way, it flew into particles." Eliot observes that when Adams encountered the "speculations" of Jules Henri Poincaré late in life, "science disappeared entirely" for him.[9]

Poincaré's criticism of scientific method was just one symptom of that pervasive and indiscriminate skepticism with which the modern age began. The early twentieth century was a time when science itself, beginning with Einstein's relativity and culminating later in Heisenberg's uncertainty and probability, seemed to be renouncing its fundamental precept of objectivity. Like Adams's skepticism, Eliot's is also the product of a scientific tradition that had come to question the ability of science itself to find truth. But skepticism's uniformly destructive tendency also proved to be liberating, and thus constructive, as well. During the nineteenth century, scientific inquiry developed its own philosophy, Naturalism, according to which only material phenomena could be studied empirically and thus serve as a source of truth. Naturalism considered religious claims to be unverifiable, since they were thought to be made about nonmaterial entities and based merely on emotion, thus relative and private, impervious to objective investigation. But if in the twentieth century the scientific study of material phenomena was felt to be incapable at times of delivering truth, then intellectual integrity could no longer consist solely of a contempt for supposedly nonrational, nonsensory experience. Empiricism was thus extended in its application because a reluctance about entertaining intellectually certain kinds of experience seemed no longer justifiable. As a consequence, a number of studies of religious experience and mysticism appeared at the turn of the century, adopting an analytic or scientific methodology, significantly, to analyze a phenomenon that had previously been assumed incapable of rational study.[10] Romanticism had used mysticism and religious emotional experience as criteria for truth inaccessible to scientific method and criticism in order to overcome doubts posed by rational, empirical inquiry. Such a tactic proved to be inappropriate to the early twentieth century, with its movement toward an acceptance of the validity of mystical experience unprecedented since the empirical tradition began.

The scientific study of mysticism was tacit acknowledgment by the intellectual community of the possibility of adopting a mode of belief which the mere existence of science now did not immediately preclude. For Eliot, this belief had to be a synthesis of both poles of Romanticism, but in their modern form: first, the skepticism, not of scientific Naturalism, but implicit in any encounter of the mind with the world, and second, the perennial spirituality of human nature. As Eliot recognized, Adams satisfied his desire for "unity" by writing a study of thirteenth-century Europe.[11] For Eliot, however, that method of attaining unity, an escape into a past age when skepticism and this dissociation of intellect and emotion supposedly did not exist, was unacceptable. Eliot sought a unity possible in the modern world: a psychological and metaphysical order, a kind of belief, a mode of experience in which his pervasive skepticism could be accommodated and in which his mystical moments would no longer be vague and directionless.

1. A DEFINITION THROUGH BRADLEY

Eliot's intellectual development, then, begins with skepticism as one of his two basic psychic dispositions, and the one that would ultimately make possible the complete satisfaction of the other. In June of 1913 Eliot purchased his own copy of F. H. Bradley's *Appearance and Reality* (1893),[12] but he might very well have been familiar with Bradley to some extent before this time, and certainly

at least with Anglo-American Idealism of the later nineteenth century or its German original, for in "Spleen," published in *The Harvard Advocate* of 1910, "Life . . . Waits . . . (Somewhat impatient
of delay) / On the doorstep of the Absolute" (11, 13, 15–16). Although he encountered aspects of Bradley's thought in other philosophers and in other disciplines, only in Bradley's system did
Eliot find the potential for a statement of skepticism sufficiently
rigorous to suit his penchant for logical precision, and sufficiently
thorough to sweep away the philosophical assumptions of the entire nineteenth century. For Eliot, Bradley achieves a "perfection of
destruction" through a philosophical analysis that is "so purely
sceptical, that his greatness is due rather to a consummation of
dialectical technique than to a single vision."[13] Consequently, with
Bradley, we can only pursue his argument to its logical conclusion,
and "if it ends in zero, as it may well end in zero, we have the
satisfaction of having ascertained that certain questions which
occur to men to ask are unanswerable or are meaningless."

But these questions regarding the possibility of knowledge in
the world are so fundamental, and the response Bradley provides
is, in Eliot's view, so skeptical, that if you do agree to his theory of
the nature of judgment, then you arrive at a position which,

> according to your temperament, will be resignation or despair—the
> bewildered despair of wondering why you ever wanted anything, and
> what it was that you wanted, since this philosophy seems to give you
> everything that you ask and yet render it not worth wanting.[14]

Such a vision of epistemological nihilism, a philosophical 'dark
night of the soul', can be the foundation for religious experience,
in part by disputing the validity of any other belief that would
deny its possibility. Thus, if nothing can be certain, anything is
possible, for proof is unavailable, and everything must rest upon
belief. As Eliot observes, "wisdom consists largely of scepticism
and uncynical disillusion," and both "are a useful equipment for
religious understanding; and of that Bradley had a share too"
(*SE* 399).

Eliot explored Bradley's thought in *Knowledge and Experience in
the Philosophy of F. H. Bradley* (1916), his doctoral dissertation sub-
mitted to the Department of Philosophy at Harvard, begun while
he was a student in Cambridge and completed after he had mar-
ried and settled in London.[15] Bradley's philosophy is 'monistic' because he asserts that the ultimate nature of reality is *one* unified

whole, composed of all the various aspects or appearances of our world. It is 'idealistic' because 'Appearance', the world as we know it, is 'Reality' decomposed, separated by the mind into objects and persons, space and time; because the world is thus created by the mind, Reality is said to consist of ideas. Such a philosophy can be contrasted with our more customary view, which holds that Reality is 'dualistic', composed of mind and matter, and 'realistic', consisting of objects independent of the mind perceiving them. According to Bradley, our world of appearance, of multiplicity, comes initially to the mind as a unified 'immediate experience', or 'feeling': "the general condition before distinctions and relations have been developed, and where as yet neither any subject nor object exists."[16] Because Reality is a unity in which the mind cannot be distinguished from the world, such subsequent distinctions as 'self' or 'soul' in contrast to 'the world' are ideas merely, intellectual constructions of the mind, and thus not real. As Eliot summarizes, immediate experience is

> a timeless unity which is not as such present either any*where* or to any*one*. It is only in the world of objects that we have time and space and selves. By the failure of any experience to be merely immediate, by its lack of harmony and cohesion, we find ourselves a conscious soul in a world of objects. (KE 31)

Immediate experience does occur, however, as a single feeling, as a 'finite center'; and a self or soul can be thought of as a series, or history, of finite centers after they have been analyzed by the mind, that is, decomposed into self and other, and located in space and time. In fact, because the finite center provides us with our world, the self or soul can be considered as analogous to a finite center (KE 204). Eliot will call the finite center a 'point of view' (KE 147), suggesting the potentially personal or subjective element—the perspective on our world of the perceiving, or experiencing, subject—in an essentially impersonal, objective phenomenon—the occurrence, or creating, of our world in the mind. Further, the finite center, as immediate experience or feeling, is unified not only in terms of our world, since no divisions between subject and object are present in it, but also in terms of our ordinary mental experience, for no distinctions between ideas, emotions, and sensations are present either. As Eliot quotes Bradley, if our mental experience usually consists of "perception and thought," "will and desire," "the aesthetic attitude," and "pleasure and pain," then "feeling" is "the general state of the total soul not yet at all differentiated into any of the preceding special aspects" (*KE* 19–20).

Finally, Bradley posits that Appearance, Reality dissected by our mind into the world as we experience it, tends always to a higher state of synthesis similar to that state of feeling or immediate experience out of which it originated. Such a state of complete unity, a whole into which all of the divisions of this world, subject and object, mind and matter, person and person, and in addition, all possible points of view, will be re*solved*, Bradley calls the 'Absolute': "in the Absolute no appearance can be lost. Each one contributes to the unity of the whole . . . which comprehends and perfects them." Thus, "such a whole state would possess in a superior form that immediacy which we find (more or less) in feeling; and in this whole all divisions would be healed up. It would be experience entire, containing all elements in harmony."[17] Wilbur Long suggestively describes the Absolute as "an all-embracing unity that complements, fulfills, or transmutes into a higher synthesis the partial, fragmentary, and self-contradictory experiences, thoughts, purposes, values, and achievements of finite existence,"[18] that is, of our world as we live in it.

The skepticism inherent in Bradley's view of 'knowledge and experience' Eliot readily comprehended and emphasized. Above all, Reality is asserted to be either prior to our consciousness or after it; Reality is that from which experience comes or to which it tends, but never experience itself: "nowhere . . . can we find anything original or ultimate" (*KE* 146). Since our world is not an objective entity, separate from us, but occurs to each one of us individually as a finite center, each of our minds is a self-enclosed point of view that cannot be totally transcended (*KE* 145). As Eliot quotes Bradley, "regarded as an existence which appears in a soul, the whole world for each is peculiar and private to that soul. . . . No experience can be open to inspection" (*KE* 203). Even within our experience itself, therefore, knowledge of our world is indefinite, "varying and imprecise" (*KE* 139). Yet it is ultimately a matter of agreement, a coincidence of various points of view. When Reality becomes conscious, it is dissolved by the mind into objects and subject, and the object begins to develop "relations that lead beyond itself" (*KE* 23), linking it with other objects in our world. Such relations are provided by our particular point of view and that of other minds, and may not necessarily agree. A legitimate object or piece of information about our world is thus one with a sufficient number of acceptable relations, that is, one recognized by a sufficient number of points of view (*KE* 91, 98). As Eliot explains, "whether that object is 'real' or not depends simply on the number and kind of relations which, in a particular context we may for practical purposes demand: reality is a convention" (*KE* 98). Consequently, we can only view our world skeptically: we must "think of the world not as ready made, . . . but as constructed, or constructing itself, . . . at every moment, and never more than an approximate construction, a construction essentially practical in its nature" (*KE* 136). Ironically, then, because there is no "*absolute* point of view" from which a judgment may be made (*KE* 22), society, "social consilience", comes to determine what is real in our world (*KE* 44); that is, "the 'real world' of epistemology (to be distinguished from the Reality of metaphysics) will be an essentially indefinite world of identical references of an indefinite number of points of view, particularly those of other civilized adults with whom we come in contact" (*KE* 91); thus, "in adjusting our behaviour and cooperating with others we come to intend an identical world" (*KE* 143).

Ordinarily, in a dualistic, realistic view of Reality, simply what we perceive is the objective world. Such is our naive assumption about experience, and in more sophisticated form, the view of such New Realists in America as E. B. Holt and Ralph Barton Perry, and their allies in England, Bertrand Russell and G. E. Moore. [19] But the philosophical description of experience according to this view as expounded by these philosophers had its inconsistencies, not the least of which was its treatment of hallucinations, and a good portion of Eliot's dissertation is devoted to revealing various inadequacies in their theory. Eliot was attracted to Bradley's philosophy, therefore, not only on the basis of personal temperament, but also on philosophical grounds for valid solutions to certain basic problems. For Eliot, a hallucination *was* real, but from one and only one point of view: the person experiencing the hallucination. Because the rest of society did not experience the hallucination, it is said not to exist in our world. Already we begin to see Eliot seeking an adequate synthesis for the dialectic of private and public, personal and impersonal, individual and societal, which will serve him not only in his philosophical, but also in his religious, esthetic, and socio-political thought, and in his poetic theory and practice.

Such a philosophical skepticism will have implications for Eliot beyond metaphysics and epistemology. Because knowledge of our world is decided by a number of points of view confirming the same object or theory and conferring upon it a number of acceptable relations with other objects and theories in the world, "knowledge is invariably a matter of degree," and consequently, there are "degrees of truth and reality" (*KE* 51), the degree depending upon the kind and number of these points of view and relations. If, therefore, the unattainable Absolute is Reality and Truth, and contains within itself *all* of the points of view and relations of our world in a unified whole, then that object or theory that amalgamates the greatest number of the most disparate points of view and relations will be most true. As Bradley himself observes,

> to be more or less true, and to be more or less real, is to be separated by an interval, smaller or greater, from all-inclusiveness or self-consistency. Of two given appearances the one more wide, or more harmonious, is more real. It approaches nearer to a single, all-containing, individuality. . . . The truth, and the fact, which, to be converted into the Absolute, would require less rearrangement and addition, is more real and truer. And this is what we mean by degrees of reality and truth. [20]

This theory is a philosophical codification of one criterion Eliot will rely on throughout his life for what is ultimately valuable in the world, from the unification of the primitive and the modern mind achieved by James Frazer in *The Golden Bough,* to the uniting of seemingly incompatible experiences by metaphysical wit into a whole known as a conceit. As Bradley explains, "Truth must exhibit the mark of internal harmony, or, again, the mark of expansion and all-inclusiveness." [21] The tendency to unify, to establish and then resolve a dialectic, is in fact an essential quality of Eliot's mind, undoubtedly accounting for the appeal Bradley's philosophy had for him, and for his own quest to synthesize the two poles of Romanticism into a single modern frame of mind.

A corollary of the theory of the degrees of truth is no less significant to Eliot. A theory will, of course, be true according to the number of points of view it integrates. Naturally, then, as Eliot observes, any metaphysical theory will try to integrate all existing points of view into one idea (*KE* 163). But "any assertion about the *world,* or any *ultimate* statement about any *object in* the world, will inevitably be an interpretation" (*KE* 165), because we lack any absolute point of view which would guarantee certainty. Such an interpretation involves "a change of point of view," or "a transmigration from one world to another, and such a pilgrimage involves an act of faith." Because "a philosophy . . . can ultimately be founded on nothing but faith," "the notion of truth, *literal* truth, has so little direct application to philosophic theory" (*KE* 163; my emphasis). The claim of nineteenth-century Naturalism that science is capable of explaining every aspect of our world, of describing the nature of Reality and attaining an absolute Truth, is therefore suspect, because "materialism itself" is merely an interpretation (*KE* 164), just one point of view of our experience. Through Bradley, Eliot finds philosophical confirmation of his suspicion that not only religious doctrines but also scientific theories must depend simply upon faith for endorsement when they make ultimate assertions about the nature of reality. Consequently, there can be for Eliot no *literal* belief in any dogma, scientific or religious. In order to participate in organized religion, therefore, he would have to discover some kind of belief, some mode of certainty, not ultimate perhaps, but sufficient, other than that which depends upon the metaphysical assertions of religion or science.

2. ROYCE'S CHALLENGE

In *Knowledge and Experience,* then, Eliot is intent on constructing a thoroughly skeptical view of the world using Bradley's philosophy as a basis and simply extending its inherent skepticism to its logical conclusion. One possibility for certainty which Eliot presents only to reject, the theory that social interaction does not merely determine the convention of what constitutes our world of experience, or Appearance, but actually can supply a partially certain if incomplete idea of Reality itself, derives from the one Idealist with whom Eliot came in contact at Harvard, Josiah Royce. Eliot was a student in Royce's seminar, "A Comparative Study of Various Types of Scientific Method," in 1913–14, the academic year immediately following the summer during which Eliot presumably read intensively his newly purchased copy of *Appearance and Reality*. In the papers that he presented, Eliot explored a few of the crucial issues of epistemology from the standpoint of Bradley's idealism; these skeptical arguments he would later incorporate, in modified form, into his dissertation. Like Bradley, who was his British counterpart, Royce represented the enlightened and polished twilight, as Eliot was to recount later, of the Hegelian Idealism that was the "orthodox doctrine" of American university philosophy departments at the turn of the century, and that had "begun to turn manifestly mouldy." As Eliot proceeds to explain, this idealism was an "inheritance" from an era when philosophy instructors were usually "retired non-conformist ministers," the more prepared of whom studied in Germany and endorsed the "Ethics of Kant" and the "Mysticism of Schleiermacher."[22] Far from "mouldy," as Eliot knew, Royce himself was sufficiently aware of the fallibilities of his own doctrine, and those of his opponents, to do able battle, especially with the Pragmatism of William James and the positivism of the New Realists. Eliot had only the greatest respect for Royce, referring to him in later years as "extraordinary,"[23] "great,"[24] a kind of patriarch of American philosophy (*KE* 10).

The primary difference between the idealism of Royce and that of Eliot is one of emphasis and destination: Royce attempted to move away from skepticism, and Eliot wanted to move toward it. Royce maintained that we 'intend' a common world of external objects through ideas about that world; the intended ideas of various people involve 'interpretations' of reality, and any conflicting intended ideas are to be resolved by the 'community' at large. That there is a valid interpretation to be had is ensured by the existence of the Absolute, for Royce an Eternal Knower, whom the community strives to emulate when it interprets. Thus, because the community is a historical entity, it becomes the temporal embodiment of the Absolute, as the Church is the community of God embodying his revelation over time. This 'ideal community' of human purpose Royce identifies with Reality. The individual, in turn, attains his most complete definition and fullest possible life in dedicating himself to the Community, to values and causes outside himself, through an act of loyalty.[25]

Royce's idea of Community—a collective whole to which one is inextricably related and to which one must in some way conform—when modified by a similar theory in Emile Durkheim eventually became a crucial concept in Eliot's thought, both psychological and literary. But in Royce's seminar Eliot was testing the viability of a complete metaphysical skepticism; despite Royce's efforts to the contrary, he denied any possibility of establishing a common world of everyday experience that we all shared with ultimate certainty. As Harry T. Costello records an exchange during one meeting of the seminar, Royce, responding to one of Eliot's papers, said that "an interpretation could, in everyday life, be tested by asking questions until mutual understanding was attained," while Eliot replied that "no interpretation helps another. Interpretation adds to and thus falsifies the facts, and presents a new problem to disentangle."[26] Our world only consists, Eliot would maintain at a later meeting, of "a monadology of points of view, each point of view carrying with it its own interpretation and valuation of the real world."[27]

When he came to write *Knowledge and Experience,* Eliot modified Royce's claim that we can derive a partial certainty about the nature of our world through a mutual interchange of knowledge between members of society into the assertion that society does indeed *in practice* determine the nature of reality, for we come to believe that we experience a world consisting of objects when we "feel obscurely an identity between the experiences of other finite centers and our own" (*KE* 143). But an "obscure feeling" cannot substitute for philosophical certainty based on logical analysis; "we have theory as well as practice" (*KE* 159), Eliot observes, and *in theory,* "the identity between one man's world and another's does not consist . . . in one world which is the world of right perception" (*KE* 144). Thus, following Bradley's lead, Eliot both accedes to and then subverts Royce's claim, concluding that Truth in our world, in our experience, is not only incomplete, but also impossible.

That Bradley's skepticism would lead Eliot to a state of "despair," therefore, is not difficult to appreciate, for this skepticism is so thorough that it casts doubt even on philosophical endeavor itself. Bradley argues that "philosophy . . . is itself but appearance. . . . Metaphysics has no special connexion with genuine religion, and neither of these two appearances can be regarded as the perfection of the other. The completion of each is not to be found except in the Absolute."[28] If philosophy is merely Appearance, it will always remain in an incomplete state, unable to achieve that unity which would eliminate uncertainty, resolve all discrepancies, permit total inclusiveness, and render it True. As Eliot is astute to point out,

> Bradley's universe, actual only in finite centres, is only by an act of faith unified. . . . The Absolute responds only to an imaginary de-

mand of thought, and satisfies only an imaginary demand of feeling.
Pretending to be something which makes finite centres cohere, it
turns out to be merely the assertion that they do. (*KE* 202)

Thus, Bradley's system is not immune to its own pervasive skepticism, inherent in which is its own potential self-destruction.

But ironically, the integrity of its doubt preserves and ensures
the utility of Bradley's philosophy as a whole. If nothing, not even
a universal and comprehensive skepticism, is certain, anything remains a possibility, and not merely through faith, but through a
renewed empirical search. Such an investigation will not be conducted according to the materialistic prejudice of Naturalism,
which through Bradley has already been called into question, but
according to a new, more open and all-inclusive empiricism which
will not discount any part of experience, even if mathematical formulas do not apply. As Eliot once observed, "Bradley is thoroughly empirical, much more empirical than the philosophies that
he opposed" (*SE* 403). In an empirical spirit, then, Eliot surmises
of the promised unity, coherence, and harmony of the Absolute
that "this assertion is only true so far as we here and now find it to
be so" (*KE* 202). Through this appeal to experience, despair can
now be transformed at least into the "resignation" that accompanies any search for something real, something true in our world;
consulting our own experience, Eliot confesses, "we feel that there
are truths valid for this world though we do not know what these
truths are" (*KE* 164). By destroying all of our ordinary assumptions about the nature of reality, Bradley's philosophy has cleared
the way for the recognition of a more valuable truth. As Eliot
observes, "the virtue of metaphysical analysis is in showing the
destructibility of everything, since analysis gives us something
equally real, and for some purposes more real, than that which is
analysed" (*KE* 157). Further, Eliot stipulates that "all significant
truths are private truths" (*KE* 165), and that "the only real truth is
the whole truth" (*KE* 163). "Feel," "more real," "private," "whole":
Eliot seems to be suggesting that the confirmation in the "here and
now" of the existence of Bradley's Absolute lies in the possibility of
reaching immediate experience. Such a confirmation, being experiential rather than analytic, would not offer a philosophical certainty, to be sure; but it would be a kind of certainty perhaps more
reliable, if less logically precise, than metaphysics could provide.
Such a confirmation Eliot found through mysticism.

Four Quartets, the rose garden has accumulated, as Louis Martz has shown,[9] a number of personal memories and literary associations. But the initial experience, perhaps only an uncanny exhilaration, happened to Eliot as a child. Living next to the Mary Institute, a girls' school in St. Louis founded by his grandfather and attended by his sisters,[10] Eliot recalls, later in life, a high brick wall that separated his family's backyard garden from the schoolyard. When the girls were playing, he listened from the other side.[11] To a shy and lonely child the laughter of the girls suggested gaiety, companionship, and relief; their bodiless voices promised a salvation from the constraint of his family life. As Eliot grew older, he continued to look to women for spiritual fulfillment; but like Dante, who looked both to and beyond Beatrice, Eliot sought redemption on a philosophical and religious plane also. The "first world" (21) of the rose garden, then, has both biographical and theological primacy, and Eliot's mystical moments begin, however faintly, in his childhood. Eliot must surely have been reflecting upon his own life as well when he once observed of Traherne that "his chief inspiration is the same curious mystical experience of the world in childhood which had also touched Vaughan."[12]

Fascinated by the mysticism of the saints whom his mother portrayed in her poetry, and curious about his own moments of heightened emotion, Eliot avidly read a number of philosophical, psychological, and sociological studies of mysticism and religious experience while at Harvard. Among those that had a marked influence on him were W. R. Inge, *Christian Mysticism* (1899), William James, *The Varieties of Religious Experience* (1902), and Evelyn Underhill, *Mysticism* (1911).[13] During his Harvard years Eliot apparently had his first mystical experience of overwhelming intensity. In the manuscript poem "Silence," dated June 1910, Eliot records a powerful vision in which he felt the everyday world of experience split apart and its distracting claims upon his attention recede. All of reality assumes for him a state of stillness, at which he feels a kind of terror. Eliot was both awed and troubled by this intimation, and his reading must have assumed a greater urgency.[14]

Despite the tendency in Unitarianism to value personal religious experience as sincere and genuine, the scientific rationalism and social utilitarianism of Eliot's own Unitarian upbringing would incline him to regard these mystical moments with some suspicion and doubt. Refining that skepticism inherent in Unitarianism into which Eliot was born and giving it a historical dimension was the critique of Romanticism by Irving Babbitt, whose course in French criticism of the nineteenth century Eliot took during the academic year 1909–10.[15] Babbitt argued that Romanticism's reliance upon instinct, intuition, and spontaneity was irresponsible, misleading, and destructive because man's nature is not entirely good, as Rousseau posited. Private vision and emotional impulses require discipline, restraint, and intellectual enlightenment before they can be trusted to lead to personal fulfillment and social stability.[16]

In light of Babbitt's polemic, Eliot must have been disturbed by the fact that his own mystical experiences and emotional elations, being spontaneous and private, had no connection with any authority outside of himself. Further, being confused and indefinite, despite their intensity, these moments bore no relationship to any religious orthodoxy which could serve as a sanction for them. Since they were not religious in imagery or message, could their source be divine? In addition to Babbitt's critique of vague emotion and private inspiration, the prevailing logical positivism of the New Realists at Harvard's philosophy department, and Eliot's own skeptical predilections, also must have prompted him to seek some philosophical answer, some intellectual system which would explain and validate these mystical moments by integrating them into a comprehensive view of the world. Such a philosophy he thought he had found in Henri Bergson.

1. A POSSIBLE JUSTIFICATION: BERGSON

Eliot observed later in life that the only time that he had ever been converted through the inspiration of another person was temporarily to Bergsonism.[17] Eliot spent the academic year of 1910–11 in France, and in January and February of 1911 he attended Bergson's lectures at the Collège de France.[18] Paris offered Eliot, as he reminisced, a stimulating intellectual environment. The older generation, Anatole France and Remy de Gourmont, continued to write with great erudition, and "provided types of scepticism" for the younger generation to accept or reject. Emile Durkheim and Lucien Lévy-Bruhl introduced new sociological theories, while Pierre Janet reigned over psychology. Alfred Loisy taught the history of religions in "scandalous distinction" after his excommunication, and "over all swung the spider-like figure of Bergson."[19] Indeed, Bergson had a wide influence during the early years of the twentieth century, not only in philosophy and psychology, but also in such disciplines as sociology, anthropology, Classical studies, and comparative religion. Coming at a time when academics were anxious to have a philosophical justification for their distrust of Naturalism, Bergson's thought enjoyed its great appeal through its attack on science. Bergson contended that our experience does not merely consist of material phenomena, that these phenomena are in fact not indicative of the true nature of reality at all, and therefore that the mathematical and chemical formulas that science employs to analyze the physical world are actually only partial and inadequate conceptions of truth, explaining only a portion of reality.

What made Bergson's philosophy even more persuasive to an audience that was anxious to escape the materialism of science and yet at the same time dependent upon its empirical method as a criterion for truth was that Bergson frequently incorporated theories and evidence from biology and the other sciences into his philosophical arguments, a procedure Eliot termed the "use of science against science."[20] This use of scientific discovery made Bergson's philosophy appear empirically reliable at the same time that it was attacking the traditional guardian of empiricism for its encroachment upon what Bergson claimed to be nonmaterial aspects of the world. Thus, Bergson's critique of scientific materialism provided an epistemological and metaphysical justification for certain kinds of experience which the nineteenth century believed to be merely emotional and of dubious value. One such experience students of religion thought rescued by Bergson was mysticism. As Evelyn Underhill writes of the "Vitalists," "Bergson, Nietzsche, Eucken," their philosophy "possesses the merit of accepting and harmonizing many different forms of experience; even those supreme experiences and intuitions peculiar to the mystics; . . . it leaves in the hands of the mystics that power of attaining to Absolute Reality which they have always claimed."[21]

Bergson's thought is termed Vitalism because he argues that the true nature of reality is the process of life itself and not an intellectual construct extrapolated from it; life, in turn, is not a product of the universe, but rather, our universe is a manifestation of life. To Bergson our everyday experience is actually static and segmented: time is merely a series of individual moments; objects are really portions of space partitioned off by our intellect. By contrast, life or Reality is a dynamic and amorphous state, or 'duration' (*durée*), in which all the appearances of Reality lose their isolating dimensions and interpenetrate. Instead of points past, present, and future, for instance, all time is simultaneous. Any phenomenon in space and time is implicit in every other phenomenon. Further, Reality is in a constant state of flux, a perpetual state of becoming, or in 'creative evolution' (*évolution créatrice*), continually renewing and extending itself. Duration is thus a unity, consisting of all possible times and places, and at the same time constantly changing. A 'vital force' (*élan vital*) is said to provide the impetus for this motion.

Bergson explains that we are ordinarily unaware of this true nature of reality because we usually exercise only the rational side of our mind, which partitions time and space into static segments and analyzes these isolated fragments in terms of scientific formulas. But Bergson argues that we can quite easily reach duration and bring it into consciousness through 'intuition', civilized man's self-conscious use of a primitive instinct of duration latent in his psyche. Thus, Bergson contends that science and rationality do not present us with the true nature of our universe at all, but take us further away from Reality. They merely analyze the material appearance of life through mathematical insight; only through intuition can we gain a true sense of the Reality creating these phenomena.[22] In its emotional nature and promised unity, then, duration serves as the analogue for the collective consciousness postulated by the sociologist, the ritual experience observed in primitives by the anthropologist, and for the mystic, his way to God. Bergson himself encouraged the application of his thought to mystical experience, asserting that "philosophy introduces us thus into the spiritual life."[23] Some twenty years after Eliot heard his lectures, Bergson was to record his approval of Underhill's applying his ideas to mysticism, and then to proceed himself to relate his theories directly to mystical experience; he came to associate the vital force with God.[24]

2. THE HISTORICAL CRITIQUE: BABBITT

Eliot's allegiance to Bergson's philosophy was short-lived. By 1913 he was criticizing various aspects of Bergson's thought in essays he wrote at Harvard, often using arguments derived from Bradley.[25] In addition to adopting this new philosophical orientation, Eliot

again relied upon Babbitt's historical perspective to understand the
nature of his own mystical experiences and to reveal the inade-
quacy of the explanation supplied by Bergson. Babbitt's arguments
seemed more compelling to Eliot now that they were corroborated
by the antiromantic polemic of Maurras and Benda which he had
subsequently encountered in France.[26] But this time when Eliot
employed Babbitt's version of intellectual history, he observed the
theory from Bradley's philosophy that there can be no absolute
historical knowledge because we can never escape our own contemporary point of view from which we perceive our world
and our past. Thus, a given period of history will be perceived
in a unique way by all other periods, making any imaginative
work with a historical setting a revelation of its own era to a
much greater degree than of the era depicted.[27] Eliot proceeded to
reconsider the saints of his mother's poetry and their mysticism
from a historical perspective, keeping in mind that the documen-
tary value of her poetry resides in its "rendering of a state of mind
contemporary with the author," evident in both subject and
treatment.[28]

What Eliot found lurking beneath the mysticism of Charlotte
Eliot's *Savonarola* was the romanticism of the nineteenth century Babbitt so despised. Furthermore, when Eliot compared his
mother's drama to what he considered to be its ideological successor, Shaw's *St. Joan,* he uncovered a line of descent from the liberal theology of the early nineteenth century to the evolutionary
philosophies at the end of the century culminating in the Vitalism
of Bergson and Rudolf Eucken: "this Savonarola is a disciple of
Schleiermacher, Emerson, Channing and Herbert Spencer; this St.
Joan is a disciple of Nietzsche, Butler and every chaotic and imma-
ture intellectual enthusiasm of the later nineteenth century. . . .
Joan is a Life-Forcer *déclassée.*"[29] Although Eliot recalled in later
years that "Herbert Spencer's generalized theory of evolution was
in my childhood environment regarded as the key to the mystery
of the universe,"[30] Eliot, like Henry Adams, was unable to believe
in "Darwinism" and "Evolution":[31] those philosophies of the nineteenth century which grounded themselves in the process of time.
Consequently, Bergson's intuition, derived from these doctrines of
perpetual change, also seemed suspect. Babbitt himself perceived
"a long series of philosophers from Rousseau to M. Bergson," noting that "we can get a glimpse of reality, says M. Bergson, giving a

new form to the Rousseauistic strife between head and heart, only by twisting ourselves about and 'intuiting' the creative flux."[32] Eliot's repudiation of the Romantic mysticism inherent in this line of thinkers was, however, more complicated philosophically than Babbitt's insistence that the emotions be governed harmoniously by the intellect through the development of an 'inner check'. The external authority Eliot sought to validate his mysticism was correspondingly more profound than Babbitt's humanistic recourse to the classics of world culture as a guide for the intellect to follow. Eliot did not wish to stifle or extinguish the emotional spontaneity of his mystical experiences as Babbitt's kind of discipline would have required. Eliot only wanted to direct and refine them by integrating them with some larger impersonal order, and to discover this order by understanding their nature and origin.

Examining the strain of Romantic thought from Schleiermacher to Bergson and the Vitalists, Eliot discovered that metaphysical concepts and theological terms had ceased to be used as if they had "definite meanings": this lack of precise meaning permitted them, instead, to be employed only for emotional stimulation. In short, Eliot perceived "the tendency of words to become indefinite emotions." As he explains, "compare a medieval theologian or mystic, compare a seventeenth-century preacher, with any 'liberal' sermon since Schleiermacher, and you will observe that words have changed their meanings. What they have lost is definite, and what they have gained is indefinite" (SW 9). Liberal theologians of the nineteenth century minimized the importance of Christianity's claims regarding history or the natural world and often imaginatively reinterpreted them in an effort to preserve their faith from being discredited by scientific discoveries. No doubt these theories were customarily perceived by these theologians to be conclusive because of their own bias in favor of scientific criteria. Any disruption of science's view of material phenomena, including Creation, miracles, an afterlife, even God, was imaginatively reexplained without any reference to the supernatural. In their reinterpretation of theological doctrines, the liberal theologians emphasized the emotional aspects of religious life in order to keep their religion immune to the rational critique of science. But such an interpretation required that theological concepts become vague and indefinite in their meaning, since any reference to the material world or to a system of thought involving the supernatural would open them to empirical attack. As a consequence, these terms were used for emotional evocation, and religious experience became primarily mystical.

When Eliot speaks of the "Mysticism of Schleiermacher,"[33] then, he is implicitly criticizing this movement by Romantic theologians toward a purely emotional basis for religion, away from any metaphysical system within which the emotion could be intellectually justified, for Schleiermacher considered himself to be not a mystic, but a theologian. Schleiermacher said to his congregation that he did not "hold the conceptions and doctrines of God and of immortality, as they are usually understood, to be the principal things in religion. Only what in either is feeling and immediate consciousness, can belong to religion."[34] As he elaborates:

> The usual conception of God as one single being outside of the world and behind the world is not the beginning and the end of religion. . . . Similarly, the goal and the character of the religious life . . . is not the immortality that is outside of time, behind it, or rather after it, and which still is in time.

These are merely "ideas"; we must seek, rather, "the immediate consciousness of the Deity as He is found in ourselves and in the world," thus attaining "the immortality which we can now have in this temporal life." To achieve this religious experience, people must "strive to annihilate their personality and live in the One and in the All"; they must strive "in the midst of finitude to be one with the Infinite and in every moment to be eternal."[35]

Such words as "One," "All," "Infinite," and "eternal" used in this way, if provocative, nonetheless have no relationship, in Eliot's eyes, to any coherent philosophical system, religious or secular, that could endow them with any definite intellectual meaning. They arouse for him, therefore, merely 'indefinite emotion'. Throughout his life Eliot would continue to object to what he perceived to be the contemporary legacy of this Romantic malady. He compares Lancelot Andrewes's scrupulously precise use of words to the "vague jargon" of the modern world that substitutes for "exact ideas"; "when all dogma is in doubt except the dogmas of sciences, . . . when the language of theology itself, under the influence of an undisciplined mysticism of popular philosophy, tends to become a language of tergiversation" (SE 305). In fact, Eliot never was to be reconciled to the use of Schleiermacher's Romantically spiritual 'infinite' and 'eternal' in religious discourse.

Criticizing revisions in the new Prayer Book years later, Eliot would continue to object to the Romantic tendency to capitulate to science's encroachment upon religion by resorting either to vague, emotionally evocative terminology or to the reinterpretation of theological concepts in order to make them conform to scientific ideas. As a substitute for 'incomprehensible,' 'infinite' merely "throws a mathematical cloak over theology," and as a substitute for 'everlasting,' 'eternal' fails to give a true sense of the nature of time. For Eliot the substitutions render the English language "vaguer."[36]

Following this line of Romantic mysticism into the twentieth century, Eliot extends his objection to an indefinite and emotional use of theological concepts by nineteenth-century theologians to a similarly vague and evocative use of metaphysical terms by their successors, the Vitalists. Because Rudolf Eucken employed Hegelian concepts for their emotional effect rather than for their relevance to a system of thought, while all the time assuming that his words had definite meanings, he appeared to Eliot to be not so much a philosopher as a philosophical spectacle when Eucken lectured at Harvard as a visiting professor in the academic year 1912–13:[37] "no one who had not witnessed the event could imagine the conviction in the tone of Professor Eucken as he pounded the table and exclaimed *Was ist Geist? Geist ist . . .*" (*SW* 9). For Eliot, steeped in Idealism himself through Bradley, Eucken lacked a sufficient awareness of the ideas of the philosophical school from which he was deriving his terminology, and thus was not always cognizant of its implications: recalling one of Eucken's pivotal aphorisms, "*es gibt keine Privatwahrheiten* (there are no private truths)," Eliot comments that "I should reverse the decision" (*KE* 165). Likewise, Bergson, Eliot believes, devises a deliberately vague terminology which at once replaces traditional religious conceptions which Bergson feels have been discredited while at the same time maintaining a similar emotional impact. Adopting an orthodox Christian perspective, Eliot observes that the "potent ju-ju of the Life Force is a gross superstition," and that Shaw's *St. Joan* is among the "most superstitious of the effigies which have been erected to that remarkable woman." Eliot is frustrated that this vocabulary, lacking a sufficient intellectual and historical basis, is capable of emotionally "deluding the numberless crowd of sentimentally religious people who are incapable of following any argument to a conclusion."[38]

Just as Eliot detects "a certain opposition to ecclesiasticism"[39] in both *Savonarola* and *St. Joan,* which through their liberalism pretend to be defenses of the Church, so he perceives a similar threat to orthodoxy in Bergson's concept of intuition, which appears to be a defense of religious mysticism. Because Bergson defined intuition as a faculty distinct and separate from the intellect, Eliot perceived this intuition to be the Romantics' undirected emotional self-absorption, which to him could lead only to private vision and self-worship. Noting that John Middleton Murry, in his view of intuition and intellect, is a follower of Bergson, who is the culmination of a philosophical tradition founded by Descartes,[40] Eliot came to oppose Murry and his Romantic mysticism under the label of Classicist. For Eliot, Descartes with his *cogito ergo sum* would be the first Romantic philosopher: according to the Cartesian standpoint, one is to "build a moral hierarchy . . . on the fact of *one's own existence* as the primary reality."[41] Eliot finds both Descartes's epistemology and his ontology, the spirit as self-consciousness within a body of matter, to lead directly to the dialectic of Romanticism: Descartes is among the "ancestors of materialism as well as of absolute idealism, of doubt as well as of irrational faith, of the antinomy of faith and reason."[42] Bergson and Murry simply continue the Cartesian self-reliance and dichotomy of mind. When Murry, as quoted by Eliot, observes that if people "dig *deep enough* in their pursuit of self-knowledge—a piece of mining done not with the intellect alone, but with the whole man—they will come upon a self that is universal," he is expressing at once a version of Bergson's search for the all-encompassing duration and, in Eliot's words, that "form of pantheism" which is Schleiermacher's search for the Divine: as Eliot again quotes Murry, "the man who truly interrogates himself will ultimately hear the voice of God."

But for Eliot, such a portrayal of mystical experience as merely self-communion is unacceptable. The practice of mystical contemplation, he replies, was the subject of several Catholic handbooks which demonstrate that these Catholic mystics were not, except for a few heretics, "palpitating Narcissi; the Catholic did not believe that God and himself were identical" (*SE* 16). Both Bergson's intuition and Murry's 'inner voice' derive from a Romantic philosophy which strives to isolate the emotions from the intellect and from the world. As Eliot argues, "Romanticism is a short cut to the strangeness without the reality, and it leads its disciples

only back upon themselves" (SW 31). Eliot required a philosophy
which would not dissociate but integrate the intellect and the
emotions, thus giving his mystical moments an intellectual dimension. In turn, because thought would play a role in mystical experience, mysticism could then be related to some 'outside authority', or order, an institution with a history, such as the Christian
Church, which would sanction it, give it direction, and thus prevent it from remaining vague and indefinite. The philosophy Eliot
seeks will come from a modern sensibility "infinitely more disillusioned" than the undisciplined emotion of Shaw's religion or the
pessimism of Hardy's; "it may be harder and more orderly; but
throbbing at a higher rate of vibration with the agony of spiritual
life."[43]

3. THE PHILOSOPHICAL CRITIQUE: BRADLEY

If Babbitt, along with Maurras and Benda, provided the impetus
for Eliot's historical critique of Bergson, Bradley supplied the point
of view for his philosophical critique. In comparison to Bergson,
Bradley's philosophy proved to be "harder" because it is more logically rigorous; "more orderly" because it finds a place for both the
emotions and the intellect; more "disillusioned" because its skepticism questions all knowledge, not just scientific; yet more "spiritual" precisely because, by its abolishing all certainty, all forms of
experience are made possible. Bergson and the Vitalists questioned the ultimate validity of scientific truth by opposing it with
emotional experience of a reality posited to be more fundamental than the material world. For Eliot, such a metaphysically indefinite appeal to emotion derives from the Romantic school of
German Idealism beginning with Kant, and he observes that by
contrast, Bradley's philosophy, despite its reliance upon Hegel,
is nevertheless "unaffected by the emotional obliquities which
render German metaphysics monstrous."[44] Whereas Bergson's critique of science is really based on the nineteenth-century opposition between the intellect and the emotions, Bradley's critique of
science forms a part of an overall criticism of knowledge in general. Furthermore, Bergson reveals a nineteenth-century prejudice
toward scientific truth within his philosophy itself: thus Eliot observes, Bradley's is a "*purer* philosophy" because "Bergson makes
use of science—biology and psychology—and this use sometimes
conceals the incoherence of a multiplicity of points of view, not

all philosophic." Eliot finds such a confusion of points of view to
be a nineteenth-century malady of misuse of words dictated by
emotion:

> The vast accumulations of knowledge—or at least of informa-
> tion—deposited by the nineteenth century have been responsible for
> an equally vast ignorance. When there is so much to be known, when
> there are so many fields of knowledge in which the same words are
> used with different meanings, when everyone knows a little about a
> great many things, it becomes increasingly difficult for anyone to
> know whether he knows what he is talking about or not. And when
> we do not know, or when we do not know enough, we tend always to
> substitute emotions for thoughts. (SW 9–10)

This confusion Eliot finds characteristic of the "mixture of
genres" that is Bergson's writings. When "the admirers of Bergson"
claim that he is "an artist," Eliot explains, "they mean precisely
what is not clear, but what is an emotional stimulus." What results, "the undigested 'idea' or philosophy, the idea-emotion" (SW
66–67), is unacceptable to Eliot because, in its emotional vague-
ness and logical imprecision, it contains a number of unrelated
points of view. According to Bradley, any multiplicity of points of
view cannot lead to a true vision of Reality, but only to the plu-
rality of our world. If immediate experience resembles the unity of
the Absolute, and comes to us as a finite center or point of view,
only a single point of view would have the coherence and comprehensiveness characteristic of immediate experience to be a satisfactory approximation of Truth.

Likewise, Eliot finds Bergson's opposition between intuition
and the intelligence, accepted by Murry, to contradict Bradley's
idea of Reality as the unity of immediate experience subsequently
separated into the world as we experience it, into objects, selves,
emotions, and thoughts. Noting that Murry believes that mathematics should be reduced to a "science of quantity," dealing only
with the material aspects of reality, Eliot replies that it should instead be considered a "science of relations,"[45] because when immediate experience is dissolved by the mind into objects and intellect,
the intellect begins to perceive relations between objects which are
not merely physical, but also logical, and experiential, and thus
emotional. As Eliot contends, both the intelligence and intuition
are "mysterious" because Reality is apprehended and the world

created according to Bradley by one and the same faculty: we merely "complicate our ignorance by calling it 'intuition'; . . . the term 'intelligence' is adequate," because truths at times can be "grasped immediately by inspection."[46] Thus, while Bergson's attempt to find a place for both the intellect and the emotions in our quest for knowledge only continues the Romantic dichotomy between empiricism and intuition, Bradley's philosophy asserts that the intellect and the emotions are originally one faculty and, furthermore, essentially inseparable from the objects of the world to which they react and attempt to understand. Bradley's philosophy, therefore, provides Eliot with the possibility of finding an intellectual dimension to his mystical moments which, as unifying experiences of the mind, can never be purely emotional.

From the standpoint of Bradley's thought, Eliot even found Bergson's very attempt to devise a philosophy based on intuitive knowledge suspect. Philosophy, as the search for a fundamental explanation of the world, necessarily involves the use of the intellect; it is the self-conscious application of mind to reality. Any philosophy, such as Bergson's, that claims that Reality and Truth are discovered through intuition is inherently self-contradictory because philosophy as intellectual explanation cannot be derived from intuition defined as a purely emotional, spontaneous, unconscious, and nonrational faculty. As Eliot explains, "our philosophy should spring from our point of view and not return upon itself to explain our point of view. A philosophy about intuition is somewhat less likely to be intuitive than any other."[47] By claiming to explain the world through a theory of intuition, Bergson has already transcended the intuitive point of view and adopted an intellectual point of view. Thus, "an *élan vital* or 'flux' is equally abstracted from experience, for it is only in departing from immediate experience that we are aware of such a process" (*KE* 19). A philosophy such as Bradley's, which claims that in the unity of immediate experience or Reality both intuition, or emotional experience, and intellect are one entity, avoids this self-contradiction.

In addition to this Romantic conception of a nonrational intuition, another potentially self-destructive aspect of Bergson's Vitalism also derives from the nineteenth century: the evolutionary idea that the essential nature of duration, of Reality, is movement and change. If Reality is flux, what then, is the character of Truth? The "Bergsonian stream flows so rapidly and turgidly," Eliot wryly observes, punning on "turbidly," that with creative evolution, truth can no longer be stable and constant, and in fact ceases to be truth at all: what troubled Eliot about Murry's "fluid world is that Truth itself seems to change, either imperceptibly or by sudden mutations." That contention he found unacceptable.[48]

Eliot was not the only thinker with such reservations, and he is certainly following the lead of his early influences. Babbitt was quick to note the consequences of a Bergsonian fluctuating truth in criticism and ethics: "any attempt to base judgment on the flux is about as promising an undertaking as to seek to found a firm edifice on the waves of the sea."[49] As helpful as Underhill thought Vitalism was in securing an intellectual foundation for the intuitive, nonscientific activity of the mind essential to mystical contemplation, nevertheless she also decides that "the great defect of Vitalism, considered as a system, is that it only professes to answer half" of the question of the nature of Reality. With his emphasis on the constant 'becoming' of the world, Bergson might accurately portray the immanence of God, Underhill believes, but not his transcendence. As John Ruysbroeck asserts, whom she quotes, "tranquility according to His essence, activity according to His nature." Because "the mystics have always insisted that 'Be still, be still, and *know*' is the condition of man's purest and most direct apprehension of reality,"[50] Underhill concludes that Bergson's philosophy is finally inadequate in explaining mystical experience.

When he read those words in Underhill, Eliot, judging from his own mystical experiences, must surely have concurred. He was, after all, eventually to characterize such moments as 'still points'. Bradley provided him with philosophical support. As Bradley observes, "you cannot be a Christian if you maintain that progress is final and ultimate and the last truth about things."[51] Bergson's duration, from which all material phenomena emerge and in which all are blended together, is analogous to Bradley's Absolute, in which all the Appearances of our world tend to be unified; both are asserted to be the ultimate nature of existence. In contrast to the creative evolution of Bergson's duration, however, Bradley argues that

> there is of course progress in the world, and there is also retrogression, but we cannot think that the Whole either moves on or backwards. The Absolute has no history of its own, though it contains histories without number. These, with their tale of progress or de-

cline, are constructions starting from and based on some one given piece of finitude. They are but partial aspects in the region of temporal appearance. . . . And the question whether the history of a man or a world is going forwards or back, does not belong to metaphysics. For nothing perfect, nothing genuinely real, can move. [52]

From this philosophical standpoint, Eliot wrote in an essay at Harvard that Bergson's duration is "simply not final,"[53] and Bergson was abandoned as a possible justification for mystical experience. But Eliot did retain Bergson's idea that memory mingles with and directs our conscious perceptions. He appears to have written "Rhapsody on a Windy Night" (1911) according to this doctrine, allowing the succession of imagery to be determined in part by a process through which present perceptions recall and are then transformed into past images. [54] Most important, Bergson's attempt to integrate intuition into a philosophical explanation of existence indicated to Eliot that an intellectual justification of such a seemingly emotional experience as mysticism might after all be possible. Thus, Eliot began his study of Bradley receptive to its potential for validating mystical contemplation. Moreover, both philosophers, despite their ultimate differences, based their thought on the same fundamental tenet that Reality is previous to the multiplicity of our ordinary consciousness as a unity in which all the elements of our everyday world are harmoniously fused. Eliot was, therefore, prepared by Bergson for what could be perceived in Bradley as an analogous philosophical system purged of all of what Eliot felt to be its nineteenth century Romantic fallacies. Above all, however, Bradley provided a logically rigorous system of thought which made one pair of terms often associated with mysticism more than merely emotional stimulus. As Underhill muses, "over and over again—as Being and Becoming, as Eternity and Time, as Transcendence and Immanence, Reality and Appearance, the One and the Many—these two dominant ideas, demands, imperious instincts of man's self will reappear; the warp and woof of his completed universe."[55]

4. ELIOT'S RAPPROCHEMENT: STUDIES OF MYSTICISM

The studies of mysticism written at the turn of the century that Eliot read suggested repeatedly that Bradley's monistic philosophy is directly applicable to mystical experience. William James, for instance, observes that

> mystical states in general assert a pretty distinct theoretic drift, [and] point in definite philosophical directions. One of these directions is optimism, and the other is monism. We pass into mystical states from out of ordinary consciousness as from a less into a more, as from a smallness into a vastness, and at the same time as from an unrest to a rest. We feel them as reconciling, unifying states.[56]

James notes of "absolute idealism" and "absolute monistic identity" that mysticism is "relatively in favor of all these things—it passes out of common human consciousness in the direction in which they lie."[57] Underhill speaks of "that 'only Reality,' that immaterial and final being which some philosophers call the Absolute, and most theologians call God."[58] She contends that "in Idealism we have perhaps the most sublime theory of Being which has ever been constructed by the human intellect, . . . a manifestation of that natural mysticism, that instinct for the Absolute, which is latent in man."[59] W. R. Inge chooses to explain how Christian mystics cope with the problem of evil in Idealist terms: "the problem among the speculative writers was how to reconcile the Absolute of philosophy, who is above all distinctions, with the God of religion, who is of purer eyes than to behold iniquity." Inge substantiates his point with a revealing footnote: "compare Bradley, *Appearance and Reality,* where it is shown that the essential attributes of Reality are *harmony* and *inclusiveness.*"[60] In addition to associating Bradley's Absolute with God, Inge recalls Bradley's theory that the self is simply a construction of the intellect, one of its countless circumscriptions of the comprehensive unity that is Reality, when he notes that in mysticism "the false self must die. . . . It is a process of infinite *expansion,* of realising new correspondences, new sympathies and affinities with the not-ourselves."[61] In fact, much of Inge's terminology used to discuss mysticism seems to derive from Bradley: "the unity of all existence is a fundamental doctrine of Mysticism"; because "there are other circles with other centres in which we are involved," "we can only achieve inner *unity* by transcending mere individuality," at which time is "felt" the "*immediacy* of the communion."[62] Surely Eliot's readings in mysticism pointed him directly to Bradley's idealism and must have made it appear *the* philosophy of mystical experience.

But Inge's vocabulary is not used with quite the logical rigor that Bradley brings to bear on his use of 'finite center', 'unity' of the 'Absolute', 'feeling', or 'immediate experience'. Bradley himself actually objected on philosophical grounds to the equating of the Absolute with the God of Christianity. Traditionally, God is like man, "a thinking and feeling being" who has "a private personality"; thus, man is capable of entering into a "relation"[63] with God, as the finite objects of Appearance, once partitioned off from the unity of immediate experience, acquire relations with each other. But at the same time, God, as an omnipotent and omniscient being, is supposed to be capable of joining us to him in his infinite unity: "the consummation, sought by the religious consciousness, is the perfect unity of these terms," of a personal with an all-encompassing God, and then of finite man with infinite God. But God cannot be both finite and infinite, personal being and impersonal unity at the same time. Further, in order for God and man to merge, their relations as two finite beings must cease, and God must become all-inclusive and thus impersonal: "the harmony of all these discords demands . . . the alteration of their finite character. The unity implies a complete suppression of the relation, as such." But if God cannot relate to man as another being with thoughts and feelings, then he is not the God of the Bible. As Bradley concludes:

> If you identify the Absolute with God, that is not the God of religion. If again you separate them, God becomes a finite factor in the Whole. And the effort of religion is to put an end to, and break down, this relation—a relation which, none the less, it essentially presupposes. Hence, short of the Absolute, God cannot rest, and having reached that goal, he is lost and religion with him.[64]

By the same token, a "future life" is, according to Bradley's system, impossible, because "the Absolute would not *consist* of souls."[65] If our self, our personality, is merely an intellectual formulation composed of the relations between the Appearances of our world, when we merge with the Absolute, we will lose these superficial distinctions in its harmony. A consistent skeptic, Bradley notes that "a personal continuance is possible, and it is but little more"; he advises that "it is better to be quit of both hope and fear, than to lapse back into any form of degrading superstition."[66] Above all, Bradley observes that his Absolute cannot be a transcendent entity, like heaven: "the total universe, present imperfectly in finite experience, would, if completed, be merely the completion of this experience. And to speak of transcendence into another world is therefore mistaken."[67]

This skepticism of Bradley's regarding the specificity of religious doctrines is reflected in the simplicity of those few ideas that Eliot will come to adopt as his own theology. In ethics, Eliot will endorse Original Sin, but as the idea of the inherent fallibility of human nature. In metaphysics, he will treat the supernatural as an essential and necessary concept, and the Incarnation as, in the words of "Burnt Norton," a "perpetual possibility" (7), an ambiguous phrase signifying at once that the miracle itself might have actually occurred, and that in any event its religious significance, its saving grace, is always available to man. But Eliot will never speak of an afterlife, or even of God as a personal being. In an early review of a book on theories of religion by Clement Webb, Eliot confesses that "we may not sympathise with his demand for the personality of God or with his demand for individual immortality."[68]

At the same time, however, Eliot did not accept Bradley's dismissal of the Christian religion and its God. For someone who had experienced mystical states and was now in search of some intellectual foundation for them, Bradley's opinion that "the essence of religion is not knowledge," nor does it consist "barely in feeling," could not have been welcome. And for someone who was annoyed by Romanticism's quest for substitutes for religion, Bradley's contention that "religion is rather the attempt to express the complete reality of goodness through every aspect of our being"[69] was certainly too close to Arnold's "the Eternal not ourselves that makes for righteousness," despite Bradley's tart repudiation of this phrase in *Ethical Studies* (1876)[70] which had Eliot's approval (*SE* 400–401), to be at all satisfactory. Probably influenced by his reading in mysticism, Eliot saw in immediate experience and the Absolute a significance for religious experience denied by Bradley.

Scholars of mysticism such as Underhill, James, and Inge, however, were not the only thinkers to perceive a religious dimension in Idealist philosophy. A. E. Taylor, a disciple of Bradley and an admirer of Royce whose work Eliot praised on two separate occasions,[71] observed in 1924 of his own monistic *Elements of Metaphysics* (1903):

> I have always wished my book to be understood in a definitely theistic, indeed, in a definitely Christian sense. I have never disguised

it from myself that when I speak of the "Absolute" I mean by the word precisely that simple, absolutely transcendent, source of all things which the great Christian scholastics call God.[72]

Reviewing the history of Idealist philosophy, Eliot observes that Kant was the first "exponent" of "'religion without revelation'" who "deeply influenced later German theology" (*UPUC* 135); and if his Idealism encouraged a pantheistic view of God at times contrary to orthodox Christianity, as with Hegel, nonetheless the tradition as a whole attempted to preserve religious feeling rather than destroy it. Lotze, after all, asserted that for him the Absolute was indeed God. Inge quotes Lotze, in fact, to substantiate the mystic's claim that the way to God is embedded in our own psyche: "within us lurks a world whose form we imperfectly apprehend, and whose working, when in particular phases it comes under our notice, surprises us with foreshadowings of unknown depths in our being."[73] Thus, Eliot feels that despite their potential unorthodoxy, Kant, Hegel, and Lotze are not "so despicable as some enthusiastic medievalists" portray them to be, and are, when compared to the British utilitarians who were followers of Bentham, "catholic and civilized and universal" (*SE* 398).

Despite Bradley's contrary view, therefore, a number of philosophers have found reasons to perceive the Absolute of Idealism as a kind of deity. Eliot too will associate the Absolute of Bradley with God.[74] Unlike orthodox theology, however, God as the Absolute cannot have a specific identity, and thus be an anthropomorphic deity. Unlike Romantic theology, in turn, God as the Absolute will not be all created things, that is, the universe, and thus a pantheistic deity. Rather, the Absolute will be for Eliot, as it is for Bradley, a state of unity and comprehensiveness toward which the universe tends, and which does not at all resemble the Appearances of our world, since they are all reconciled and transformed in its harmony. God the Absolute becomes for Eliot this undefinable whole, a metaphysical boundary which mystical experience approaches but cannot attain: "the absorption into the divine is only the necessary, if paradoxical, limit of this contemplation" (*SW* 170). If mystics are really attempting to reach the Absolute, and if Bradley's Absolute can be viewed as God, as Eliot's readings in mysticism imply, then Eliot has found an intellectual system which logically explains his mystical moments. But merely to postulate philosophically the existence of the Absolute is not for Eliot confirmation of its actual existence. Consistent with his extended expiricism, Eliot requires some experiential proof to validate Bradley's philosophy, and such a proof turns out to be, paradoxically, mystical experience itself.

Bradley's philosophy in itself actually provides a way, however limited, through which its idealism can be empirically verified. To be sure, there can be no direct experience, no actual consciousness, of the Absolute by a finite soul. Because the Absolute is a unity of all the components of the world as we know it, including ourselves, no personal identities can survive in its pervasive and transforming harmony; as Bradley notes, "we can hardly say that the Absolute consists of finite things, when the things, as such, are there transmuted and have lost their individual natures."[75] Nevertheless, our world comes to us as a finite center of immediate experience or feeling which has a similar unity to that of the Absolute. Bradley observes that, of course, "this indiscriminate totality is inconsistent and unstable," and "its own tendency and nature is to pass beyond itself into the relational consciousness," separating itself into objects, thoughts, and their relations. But Bradley insists that "still, none the less, at every moment this vague state is experienced actually. And hence we cannot deny that complex wholes are felt as single experiences."[76] In other words, we really do have a sense of the harmony characteristic of the Absolute: as Bradley asserts, "feeling . . . supplies us with a positive idea of nonrelational unity."[77] According to Bradley, such a sense of unity is even "exemplified most easily in an ordinary emotional whole" which "comes to us as one," where "its diversity, at least in part, is not yet broken up into relations" between the emotion isolated by the conscious mind as an object and the object or event that accompanied it in its original unified state. Bradley concludes that "from such an experience of unity below relations we can rise to the idea of a superior unity above them. Thus we can attach a full and positive meaning to the statement that Reality is one."[78]

Eliot will concur: we do indeed have knowledge of "feeling and the transition from the merely felt to the objectified," for this transition is neither "saltatory" nor "wholly unconscious" (KE 26). Considering our resulting sense of immediate experience, Eliot admits that we are prompted to the notion of an "all-inclusive experience outside of which nothing shall fall" (KE 31). Thus, for Eliot, Bradley's Absolute attains a degree of empirical verification, and his mystical experiences, in turn, acquire a philosophical justification. Eliot will consider his mystical moments to be those times

when he is able to sense immediate experience. As a member of
the Church years later, when speaking of a mystical moment, Eliot
will allude to the state of unity present in immediate experience, at
which time all the diverse contents of the mind are reconciled to
form a harmonious arrangement: "you may call it communion
with the Divine, or you may call it a temporary crystallization of
the mind" (SE 358).

Not surprisingly, however, before he adopted the Christian religion, Eliot found his mystical "experiences of finite centres . . .
mad and strange" (KE 168), for they entail a loss at once of personal identity and the familiar arrangement of the world as we ordinarily experience it. But in Bradley's idealism he discovered, not
only a metaphysics capable of explaining his mysticism logically,
but also a philosophy that ensures it an intellectual as well as an
emotional dimension. In immediate experience intellect and emotion are not as yet separate faculties; as Bradley explains, immediate experience is "a whole . . . where will and thought and feeling
may all once more be one."[79] Mystical experience as immediate experience is, therefore, both intellectual and emotional at the same
time. Mysticism is thus capable of the kind of discipline which an
outside authority such as the Church might offer. In a Christian
frame of mind, Eliot would be able to approach immediate experience with a system of ideas which would prevent the encounter
from being merely fearful and enigmatic, and ensure that it would
be, in addition, enlightening and enriching. Such assurances can
only come from an impersonal source, and such a defining of experience only from a religious institution: "the distinction," as
Eliot observes, "is between the individual as himself and no more,
a mere numbered atom, and the individual in communion with
God" (SE 402).

Bradley's philosophy actually suggests one method of mystical
contemplation traditionally employed by Christian visionaries: the
'negative way' to God, counseled by St. John of the Cross, for instance, who provides an epigraph for Sweeney Agonistes. According to Bradley's system, to commune directly with God would
certainly be impossible, because one would undergo total annihilation in the unity of the Absolute. But one can approach this
unity of the Divine by moving back through consciousness to its
harmonious beginning in immediate experience, in which all Appearances of our world are present as a unified whole. This negative way to God does not involve the metaphysical destruction of

our existence which would occur if we were subsumed into the Absolute, but it does involve the psychological surrendering of our ego, our personality, our self, which is itself a construct of the mind, a product of our consciousness as it dissolves immediate experience into the components of our reality. Thus, when Eliot asserts of "mere experience at the beginning and complete experience at the end" that "immediate experience, at either the beginning or the end of our journey, is annihilation and utter night" (KE 31), he has in mind this loss of self, an act of humility and purgation analogous to St. John's 'dark night of the soul'. The difference is that, whereas the annihilation of immediate experience is temporary and occurs within life, that of the Absolute is final and can only result in life's end, or in a new beginning.

The studies of mysticism that Eliot read actually explain this negative mystical approach to the Divine in terms of Idealism. Considering God as the Absolute, Inge observes that "complete union with God is that ideal limit of religion, the attainment of which would be at once its consummation and annihilation."[80] William James notes that, philosophically, the way to God has to be negative, for "whoso calls the Absolute anything in particular, or says that it is this, seems implicitly to shut it off from being that—it is as if he lessened it." Eliot reasons that, as one must approach the Divine purged of attachments to the temporal world, so must one approach immediate experience void of all distinctions and relations that violate its unity. Likewise, James concludes that "like Hegel in his logic, mystics journey towards the positive pole of truth only by the 'Methode der Absoluten Negativität.'"[81] So convinced is Eliot, therefore, that Bradley's philosophy explains his own mysticism and that of Christian practitioners, that even in his dissertation he explicates a line of poetry of mystical import in terms of Bradley's idealism while simultaneously suggesting a religious perspective. In saying that her companions are shadows, the poet, Eliot explains, is indicating that her world, her experience, is inferior to that of other people, because it is "vague, less of an idea." At the same time, however, she is also indicating that it is superior, because her shadows are the premonition of another reality, another world, which, if it had been "realized," if the everyday world had come to be transformed into it, would have been a "higher type" of experience. The ordinary world is "less real" in comparison, and is considered "to 'mean'" this superior reality (KE 55–56).

In modifying Bradley's thought to accommodate religious experience, Eliot has arrived at a position aptly described by A. E. Taylor's final assessment of Idealism in *Elements of Metaphysics*:

> Our conclusion may in a sense be said to involve an element of Agnosticism, and again of Mysticism. But it is only agnostic in holding that we do not know the precise nature of the Absolute Experience. It implies no distrust of the validity of knowledge, so far as it goes, and bases its apparent agnostic result on the witness of knowledge itself. Similarly, it is mystical in transcending, not in refusing to recognise, the constructions of understanding and will. [82]

By defining God as the Absolute, Eliot is able to retain his allegiance to skepticism: God indeed exists, but one can say nothing about him. By defining mysticism as a sense of immediate experience, Eliot retains his allegiance to philosophical endeavor: mystical experience may be an undefinable state of wholeness, but this unity contains within itself a rational as well as emotional dimension. Religious experience continues to gain in definition and creditability when Eliot broadens his philosophical system to include the concept of the unconscious.

III. THE UNCONSCIOUS

W HILE Eliot's reading in religious mysticism was suggesting to him that his own mystical experiences actually
were intimations of the immediate experience described
in Bradley's philosophy, the same books also proposed that these
states of feeling were related to another level of experience, the
unconscious, and explained by another realm of thought, psychology. Inge, for instance, employs the same spatial metaphor for the
mind used by both practitioners and psychologists when he states
that mysticism involves "sinking into the depths of our inner consciousness, and aspiring after direct and constant communion
with God." To elaborate, Inge quotes a psychologically explicit
statement by Jean Paul Richter: "we attribute far too small dimensions to the rich empire of ourself, if we omit from it the unconscious region which resembles a great dark continent."[1] William
James directly relates mystical experience to the findings of psychologists investigating hysteria during the late nineteenth century
from whose work psychoanalysis will develop: "religious mysticism is only one half of mysticism. The other half [is that] which
textbooks on insanity supply. Open any one of these, and you will
find abundant cases in which 'mystical ideas' are cited as characteristic symptoms of enfeebled or deluded states of mind." Unlike
religious mysticism, however, the "voices and visions" of insanity
are "a *diabolical* mysticism, a sort of religious mysticism turned
upside down," for "instead of consolations we have desolations;
the meanings are dreadful, and the powers are enemies to life."
Nevertheless, James concludes that both kinds of mysticism erupt
from the same portion of the mind:

> It is evident that from the point of view of their psychological mecha-
> nism, the classic mysticism and these lower mysticisms spring from
> the same mental level, from that great subliminal or transmarginal
> region of which science is beginning to admit the existence, but of

which little is really known. That region contains every kind of matter: "seraph and snake" abide there side by side.[2]

Underhill will also emphasize the dualistic nature of the unconscious mind: "in this depth of being, in these unplumbed levels" of his "subconscious or subliminal personality," man "finds, side by side, the sources of his most animal instincts, his least explicable powers, his most spiritual intuitions: the 'ape and tiger,' and the 'soul.'"[3] But Underhill proceeds to describe other aspects of the unconscious, depicting its nature and origin in a way prophetic of the view Eliot would adopt of this psychological concept:

> Included in the subconscious region of an average healthy man are all those automatic activities by which the life of the body is carried on: all those "uncivilized" instincts and vices, those remains of the ancestral savage which education has forced out of the stream of consciousness; all those aspirations for which the busy life of the world leaves no place. Hence in normal men the best and the worst, the most savage and the most spiritual parts of the character, are bottled up "below the threshold."[4]

Such early views of the unconscious as the source of both mental aberration and spiritual fulfillment seem to foreshadow the two directions that depth psychology would explore in the early twentieth century through Freud and Jung. But Eliot seems to have first learned of the theory of unconscious mental phenomena through their immediate predecessors of the late nineteenth century in France who also studied the behavior of hysterical patients. Having been aware of Pierre Janet during his student year in Paris,[5] Eliot read his *Neuroses et idées fixes* (1898) and *Obsessions et psychasthénie* (1903) while at Harvard[6] and made use in his dissertation of observations Janet reported of hysterical patients (*KE* 115), later reflecting that he had followed the developments of the clinics of Théodule Ribot and Janet (*SE* 49). Perhaps Eliot reveals that in his mind depth psychology is inextricably related to the kind of philosophy which interested him at this time when he recalls, in the same breath, that he had read books "from Vienna" and heard a lecture by Bergson (*SE* 49). Certainly Underhill inadvertently suggests the underlying purpose for such an interest when she herself speaks of "the researches of Murisier, Janet, Ribot" as "attempts to find a pathological explanation which will fit all mystic facts."[7] The terms of the contrast that W. M. O'Neil draws between Janet and Freud coincidentally reveal the extent to which Eliot would integrate the former, rather than the latter, into his thought:

> Briefly put, Janet's view was that the neurotic lacked sufficient mental energy to hold his psyche together in a state of integration; as a result parts of it functioned in disassociation from the rest. Freud's view by contrast, was that there were diverse mental energies which were in conflict with one another. Dominant forces repressed those at variance with them and in the neurotic this repression was so ineffectually achieved as to render the mental situation unmanageable and intolerable.[8]

The concept of the unconscious is, of course, not unique to the twentieth century; it has existed in some form at least since the ancient Greeks.[9] From the beginning of Christianity, mystics have traditionally spoken of their experience in the spatial metaphors characteristic of modern theories of the unconscious. St. François de Sales, for instance, says that "this root is the depth of the spirit, *Mens,* which others call the Kingdom of God."[10] William Law's account of the unconscious mind bears an uncanny resemblance to Bradley's theory that all of experience comes to us as a finite center, and that the harmony of this immediate experience is similar to that of the all-inclusive Absolute:

> There is a root deep in thee from whence all these faculties come forth as lines from a centre, or as branches from the body of a tree. This depth is called the centre, the fund, the bottom of the soul. This depth is the unity, the Eternity, I had almost said the infinity of thy soul, for it is so infinite that nothing can satisfy it, or give it any rest, but the infinity of God.[11]

The various ideas of the unconscious current at the turn of the century reflect psychological speculation from the beginning of the nineteenth century on, as codified by Carl Gustav Carus in *Psyche* (1846) and, more popularly, by Eduard von Hartmann in *Philosophy of the Unconscious* (1869), each author revealing the influence of German Idealism.[12] In the course of his dissertation on Bradley's thought, Eliot will differentiate three kinds of unconsciousness which correspond to the three categories defined in these works: (1) the metaphysical unconscious; (2) the physiological unconscious; and (3) the psychological unconscious.

The *metaphysical* unconscious, as appropriated from philosophy, is the fundamental substance, entity, process, or mode of the universe, from which we and our world derive our existence. Because it is actually existence itself, we cannot be conscious of it, but if it ceased to be, so also would we. In Bradley's system it is immediate experience before the beginning of consciousness and the Absolute at the end of consciousness. The *physiological* unconscious consists of those bodily functions which sustain us as material beings and have a significant effect on our behavior, but of which we are not aware: the flow of our blood, the operation of our nervous system, the scheduled secretions of our glands, the chemical reactions in our cells, the physics of the atoms. The *psychological* unconscious consists of those feelings, perceptions, and ideas which pass out of consciousness to be stored in our memories and sometimes recalled in dreams, and also of those impulses and desires of which we are usually unaware but which constantly influence our behavior and occasionally erupt into consciousness. The psychological unconscious will be refined and divided by Freud into the individual unconscious, the source of abnormal mental behavior, where asocial and self-destructive urges are suppressed only to haunt us in the future, and by Jung into the collective unconscious, the source of our religious longings and fulfillment, where myths and symbols common to all of humanity are stored only to resurface to ensure our salvation. The collective unconscious will be further subdivided by sociologists into a repository of beliefs and values, even our very conception of reality, instilled upon us by our society before we can be aware of their artificiality, and by anthropologists into a repository of the primitive impulses and customs present throughout the life of mankind before we even existed.

Significantly, Eliot perceived all of these various modes of the unconscious to be interrelated and interdependent: his reading in scientific psychology, sociology, and anthropology, as well as in Bradley's idealism and studies of mysticism, all seemed to overlap conceptually and thus point to a unified theory of the mind. Eliot went on to propose that this composite unconscious is both collective and historical in nature. Eliot's view of the unconscious is nothing less than fundamental to his sense of experience and will determine the nature of his thought and practice, not only in religion, but in literature as well.

1. THE CONTRIBUTION OF
SCIENTIFIC PSYCHOLOGY

When Eliot first discovered the concept of the unconscious, he thought of it not only as a psychological but also as a metaphysical phenomenon—as immediate experience, which imperceptibly brings us our world. Through scientific psychology, Eliot explored the implications of the unconscious as a physiological phenomenon as well. At the time Eliot was at Harvard, experiments performed during the late nineteenth century by scientific psychologists indicated a direct connection between physiological conditions and mental phenomena, suggesting that events of the mind depend upon, even correspond to, various states of the body. Such evidence gave renewed vigor to the old philosophical question of the relationship between the mind and the body. The numerous psychologists and psychologically oriented philosophers to whom Eliot refers in his seminar with Royce, in his dissertation, and in book reviews he was simultaneously writing—Samuel Alexander, Theodor Lipps, G. F. Stout, E. B. Titchener, James Ward,[13] and Wilhelm Wundt[14]—were debating other philosophers on both this issue and the resulting dilemma of the proper subject matter of psychology in general. A. E. Taylor's chapter entitled "The Problem of Soul and Body" in *Elements of Metaphysics* consists, in fact, largely of a comparison of the diverse theories of these thinkers on the relationship between the mental and the physical, based on the findings of scientific psychology.[15] Out of this debate Eliot evolved his theory that the psychological unconscious and the physiological unconscious are continuous.

During the 1880s William James and Carl Georg Lange had expressed the view, influential in subsequent theoretical discussion, that emotional experience does not occur in the mind without accompanying changes in the physical condition of the body, and that these physical symptoms actually consist of the only possible description of a given emotion.[16] In Royce's seminar Costello records Eliot arguing that the mental events which psychology describes are "probably not independent" of the physical things "to which they refer." Royce asks how Eliot's contention compares to the "James-Lange theory" and to "Behaviorism," and Eliot replies that he is proposing an "amended behaviorism." As he explains, in Costello's shorthand, "in James' theory you have an illusion to explain. For me the emotion is real but there is a point of view from which it is reducible. Psychology reduces to physiology."[17]

Eliot's assertion that emotions are inseparable from the objects which accompany them recalls the unity of Bradley's immediate experience, and Eliot proceeds to elaborate these remarks made in Royce's seminar in *Knowledge and Experience*. The James-Lange theory, having its philosophical basis in realism rather than in idealism, cannot explain illusion or hallucination other than to say "the child 'thinks it sees' a bear." Because the world for James and Lange is composed of real objects and subjects perceiving them, a person cannot be said to perceive an object that does not exist. Their materialism stems from this realist premise: since real objects are material objects, they will cause physical changes in the body when a subject perceives them. According to idealism, on the other hand, the world is not a separate entity from the mind experiencing it. For Eliot, therefore, from the child's point of view he or she actually *sees* a bear, although the bear, unperceived from any other point of view, lacks sufficient relations to be termed 'real'. But because Eliot, after Bradley, insists on "the unity and continuity of feeling and objectivity" (*KE* 115), of an emotion and the physical object that provoked it, he is sympathetic with James's and Lange's contention that the mental event, the perception and the ensuing emotional response, does not occur without accompanying bodily processes. Thus, he concludes that, with reference to the frightened-child paradigm, although he cannot support the James-Lange theory, nevertheless he does not believe that there is "any priority of image over emotion, or vice versa," that is, the physiological process of perceiving an object and the emotional response associated with it are "inextricably related" (*KE* 116), indeed simultaneous. Further, because the hallucination, however real to the perceiver, lacks sufficient relations to qualify as a real object, since no one else can perceive it, it "can complete itself only backward, i.e., the experience has its relations in the direction of neural process, not in the direction which the image intends" (*KE* 113), that is, not in the direction of the real world that we all share. Thus, hallucinations "dissolve into the physiological process; and nothing 'went on' which cannot be described by the neurologist" (*KE* 122): the objects we experience mentally either exist in the real world or must be explained solely through physiology.

By adopting the limited materialism inherent in the James-Lange theory, and at the same time by criticizing its (and Alexis Meinong's and Bertrand Russell's) realist position on hallucination with an idealist metaphysic, Eliot arrives at his conviction that *all*

mental events and their physical basis are continuous. The materialism Eliot employs in his theory of psychological-physiological
continuity is restricted by the idealist system into which it is integrated: the materialism that may be considered to be "at the basis"
of idealism from one perspective actually encompasses "only one
aspect of the situation" (KE 153), because idealism substitutes the
subjectivity of an ideal world that we experience for the objectivity
of a real world that we perceive, eliminating the realist basis of materialism altogether. Our mind, as Eliot explains, is both "absolute," being a point of view that is inherently unavoidable, and at
the same time "derived," having a "continuity" with the "nonmen-
tal," and thus having an "origin," along with other minds, in an
"indifferent material." In this way, idealism ensures the unity of the
body and the soul while still maintaining that the world occurs in
the mind, for both are ultimately physical entities. By accepting
the materialist premise of the James-Lange theory, that minds are
physiological in origin, but now devoid of its realist implications,
idealism accounts for the operation of the world as if all of our
minds possessed a common reality: from a biological perspective,
all minds share a "common medium" and can be considered "objects"; because their "physical structure" and "environment" are
similar, we can conclude that their "content" is similar as well
(KE 145). Eliot proceeds to argue that, if the mind itself is matter,
a part of the body and the physical world, then all of its experience
must be the result of this material foundation: when we attempt to
consider any mental event, any perceptual "idea," as an object, it
either asserts itself as a part of our experiential reality or "melts
back" into the "different" reality of its physical origin. Perceptual
experience, therefore, reduces to "ideas in relation with the nervous system on the one hand, and with the intended reality on the
other" (KE 76), that is, both to our physical nature and to the
world we subjectively experience and yet all seem to share. Thus
Eliot concludes of minds and their experience that "their objectivity is continuous with their subjectivity, the mental continuous
with the merely mechanistic" (KE 145): "the body is in felt continuity with the spiritual self" (KE 155). Consequently, the physiological unconscious, consisting of those bodily processes that
make our thoughts and feelings possible, is continuous with the
psychological, both conscious and unconscious.

Although the James-Lange theory posited the inseparability of
the mind and the body, Eliot could not wholeheartedly defend it

for the
y more
ording
jects as
a single
ely felt,
consid-
feeling
ate, but
ect that
oth as a
ives ap-
different
t notes,
   cannot
that fre-
does the
ny emo-
KE 204),
re those
lic" and
nscious-
is either
nich has
ntinuous
onsisting
nus con-
   that the
logy, ac-
ychical'"
ss, there-
mediate
must in-
er to ex-
ilable to
ncludes,
"disposi-
us, there
disposi-
which is

because, at the same time, James still insisted that states of consciousness, sensed through introspection, are the primary subjects
of psychological investigation. Despite James's implicit if uninten-
tional endorsement of a materialistic view of mental phenomena,
he still endorsed a *philosophical* psychology of 'faculties' of the
mind, such as 'will', 'attention', and 'disposition'. The materialism
inherent in the James-Lange theory became the principle postulate
of the subsequent Behaviorism associated with John B. Watson,
which at the same time rejected its method of introspection. Watson argued that only objective behavior rather than subjective
mental states could be studied by psychologists,[18] thus encourag-
ing a *scientific* psychology of psycho-physical processes. Eliot
agreed with Behaviorism's tenet that these psychological faculties
are not real, but on the basis of idealism rather than on Behaviorism's professed materialism. For idealism, there are not subjects
perceiving an objective world, only finite centers from which the
world of self and other evolves. Because reality occurs internally in
the mind rather than through the perception of an external world,
the contents of the mind must be either (1) the real world itself,
corroborated by relations supplied by other points of view, or (2)
hallucinations, occurring only to one point of view and capable
merely of physiological relations, or (3) ideas, developed by considering reality from points of view additional to our own. Subjective mental states, immune from other points of view, lack
sufficient relations to qualify as real, as objects: such conceptual
"ideas," rather, inhabit a "half-way stage" between existence and
"meaning" (*KE* 80–81); thus, 'will' lies half-way between object
and subject, between reality and physiology, and 'attention' is a
"half-object" also, because any description of attention can consist
only of the physiology of the person and the reality that he is perceiving (*KE* 81–82).

Eliot's ensuing analysis of the nature of ideas and 'half-objects'
enables him to evaluate the relative merit of faculties of the mind
studied by philosophical psychology, physiology studied by scientific psychology, and metaphysics studied by philosophy, and in
turn arrive at a complete picture of mental experience. Eliot reasons that, if reality comes to us as a single point of view or finite
center, we must develop ideas about reality by contemplating it
simultaneously from an additional point of view. In order to develop a philosophical psychology, therefore, we consider ourselves
not only in terms of reality, objectively, but also subjectively, from

which additional point of view we see our behavior no
actions in the real world but also as the activity of ment
our mind which cause us to perform those actions. W
ideas, as Eliot observes, by moving from one point of v
other or by assuming more than one point of view simu
a posture that creates "our assumptions, our half-objec
ments of imagination" (*KE* 147); thus, half-objects are li
that they exist solely from an "external-internal" poi
(*KE* 162). Consequently, faculties of the mind are act
rather than objects in the material world; yet, because
itself is also matter, they can be further analyzed into t
cal origin. For this reason, Eliot considers the psycholog
nation of the mind to be inferior to the physiological to
that the foundation of "structural" psychology "resolves
physiology (*KE* 85). At the same time, however, Eliot r
value of the mental process that produced such half-obj
and attention. This transcending of the point of view or
ter, which brings us objects of the real world, to othei
view, thus generating ideas, produces the half-objects o
ogy which, if inferior to the objects of the real world, ne
cannot be produced by scientific investigation. As Elio
in order to have the discipline of psychology, we must "
the faculty of the will, although we realize that it is "me
ance." The result will not be a scientific but rather a "p
cal" psychology, because science "deals with objects o
relations of objects" (*KE* 81). The "changing" of point of
essary to produce ideas and other kinds of objects, in
volves a leap which science cannot take, and which m
must take"; by its "attempting to bind together all points
one" (*KE* 163), metaphysics tries to give us a better i
Absolute. Such a task is doomed from the start, becaus
observes, the Absolute does not belong to any of the ty
ject that he has defined: "it is neither real nor unreal r
nary" (*KE* 169).[19] But the ability to explain the nature
nonetheless, lies beyond the scientific explanation su
physiology, for metaphysics at once incorporates and trai

Eliot will, therefore, refer to his philosophy as an "
behaviorism, because the *emotional* and *logical* componei
sciousness remain "real" for him despite the fact that
psychology "reduces to" physiology. To be sure, psy
faculties cannot explain the nature of reality and the m

as scientific analysis of material phenomena. Eliot obta
emotional experiences of the mind a foundation ultim
secure than either of these views by itself could provide.
to Eliot's idealism, the "aspect of mere existence, in all
well as feelings, is what we call immediate experience."
point of view or finite center, "so far as feelings are n
they are neither subjective nor objective" (*KE* 24). Wh
ered from an additional point of view, on the other hand
becomes a distinct object of consciousness, no longer p
another object in the world, now separated from the
accompanied it and from the subject that experienced
unified center: "internal and external are thus not adj
plied to different contents within the same world; they ai
points of view" (*KE* 204). Yet we continue to believe, E
that there is "something private" about feelings, "that
'know' them from the outside," although we must confe
quently "an observer understands a feeling better tha
person who experiences it" (*KE* 24). Eliot decides that
tions may be better understood by others than by myself"
because "so far as feelings are objects at all," they must s
properties common to all objects: they are "equally p
"equally independent of consciousness" (*KE* 24). Our
ness, the "world" studied by the psychologist, therefor
the real world itself, "that part of the external world
previously been content of that consciousness," thus "
with the whole external universe," or an hallucination,
of "physiological and psycho-physical conditions," and
tinuous "with the history of that subject." Eliot conten
"latter relation is the subject-matter of psychology: psyc
cordingly, deals with the personal rather than with the '
(*KE* 75). Psychology is not the study of our private feeli
fore, because our feelings once differentiated from
experience have already become public; and psycholog
evitably deal with the public world of physiology in o
plain mental experiences that are merely private, una
other points of view, such as hallucinations. As Eliot
what is subjective is not what is "mental," and what is
tion" is finally a disposition of the "whole organism."
can be no difference between a "psychical" and a physi
tion, because any disposition "must rest upon somethii
actual, and this must be a physical structure" (*KE* 79).

For Eliot's idealism, then, the mind's experience becomes available to the public because of the very dissolution of the originally private unity of immediate experience into subjects and objects of our shared world, including emotions when separated from their objects, and at the same time because as physical beings our mental life is continuous with our physiology, and matter is a public phenomenon. By contrast, the Romanticism of the nineteenth century, and that espoused by Murry, and that unavoided in Eliot's view by Ramon Fernandez, considers the world to be private and subjective, asserting personality as the "ultimate, the fundamental reality in the universe." Eliot observes that such a position must be adopting a theory of reality similar to that of traditional psychology. The mind appears to possess, for Fernandez, a "primary reality," that is, psychology assumes a prominent position over ontology. As a consequence of assuming reality to be a subjective phenomenon and personality a private entity, the Romantics "make man the measure of all things." Feeling considered as merely private in origin, however, offers no certainty for the truths it proposes. Thus, there are, like Eliot, thinkers who would find an "extra-human measure," an outside authority, an objective assurance. Feeling considered as public in origin, on the other hand, will supply a kind of certainty. Eliot, among others, recognizes this security in a "revealed religion," a public institution which evokes and thus sanctions certain kinds of emotion. But feeling is also public in origin if it derives from an impersonal material. The physiology of Behaviorism thus assures that mental events are objective: as Eliot notes, the term 'personality' designates for both Aristotle and Watson "something outside."[21] Significantly, both the physiological basis of feeling and the Church's ability to generate feeling are associated in this way, supplying Eliot with an impersonal criterion for truth and reality, and an impersonal source of religious experience.

2. A UNIFIED THEORY OF THE MIND

By integrating scientific psychology with idealism, then, Eliot finally moves from the idea that the mind and the body are inextricably related to a composite theory of the unconscious, incorporating the metaphysical dimension of existence as well. The psychological unconscious functions as a unified state resembling feeling or immediate experience in that it too precedes consciousness which dissolves it into subject and object, thought and emotion. If mental activity depends upon our physical nature, then the psychological unconscious must be continuous with the physiological unconscious, or the nervous system. At the same time, immediate experience as the finite center which makes possible our existence and provides us with our world is the metaphysical unconscious. The psychological unconscious, therefore, if not exactly the same entity, is nevertheless continuous with the metaphysical unconscious also. To begin with, Eliot observes that our *conscious* feelings, or emotions, resulting from the dissolution of immediate experience, cannot be independent of that finite center from which they originate: "the objectified feeling of psychology does not exist apart from the rest of feeling which is merely felt, no matter how negligible that rest of feeling may appear" (*KE* 27). Thus, in a metaphysical explanation of the mind, "we must accustom ourselves to 'feeling' which is not the feeling of psychologists, though it is in a way continuous with psychological feeling" (*KE* 16). By the same token, Eliot will next make a similar distinction between the psychological unconscious and the metaphysical unconscious, to which the former's *unconscious* feelings also owe their existence:

> Experience, we may assert, both begins and ends in something which is not conscious. And that this 'not conscious' is not what we call 'unconscious' should be sufficiently obvious. For what we term unconscious is simply an element *in* experience which arises in *contrast* to other elements in experience. It refers either to certain supposed mental entities which guide or influence our conscious action. (*KE* 28)

Nevertheless, Eliot goes on to confirm that the metaphysical, psychological, and physiological unconscious are inherently related:

> Undoubtedly our mental life is directed by many influences of which we are not conscious, and undoubtedly there is no clear line to be drawn between that of which we are conscious and that which as 'feeling' melts imperceptibly into a physiological background. (*KE* 28–29)

In turn, therefore, the physiological unconscious is continuous with the metaphysical unconscious. As Eliot compares the original finite center to the resulting soul, located in time and space after the finite center yields its unity to the experience of our world, the point of view from which each soul is a world in itself must not be confused with the point of view from which each soul is only the function of a physical organism, a unity perhaps only partial, capable of alteration, development, having a history and a structure, a beginning and apparently an end. And yet these two souls are the same. And if the two points of view are irreconcilable, yet on the other hand neither would exist without the other, and they melt into each other by a process which we cannot grasp. (KE 205–6)

Thus, Eliot has developed a unified theory of the mind in which the metaphysical, physiological, and psychological unconscious are all distinguishable and yet continuous. Eliot is able to achieve this unification of the components of our mental life because he has a broader, more eclectic idea of immediate experience that will accommodate the various kinds of unconsciousness than the concept's originator, Bradley. Eliot understands the term "unconscious" in its psychological sense and merely draws a distinction between this meaning of unconsciousness ("mental entities") and immediate experience as the metaphysical unconscious ("the whole" of our world): "the unconscious, in short, denotes something within experience, as the conscious does, and neither of these terms will represent the whole" (KE 29). Eliot's point is that, were it not for the metaphysical unconscious as immediate experience, there would be neither consciousness nor the subliminal nor physiology. Eliot is arguing that the psychological unconscious cannot be synonymous with immediate experience simply because it is just one part of it. Eliot still maintains that immediate experience is the "'not conscious'," but an unconscious that transcends mere psychological unconsciousness.

Bradley, on the other hand, explicitly considers Hartmann's theory of the unconscious in relation to immediate experience only to ignore the three kinds of unconsciousness Hartmann posits. Like Eliot, Bradley understands the term "Unconscious" in its psychological sense ("psychical"), but then proceeds to argue the contrary position: that the psychological unconscious is separate from immediate experience. He maintains a strict correlation between immediate experience and the finite center that Eliot does not observe in relation to unconsciousness, and argues that the psychological unconscious cannot be part of immediate experience because it is not within the sphere of consciousness at any given moment, that is, because "man cannot be directly aware of it."[22] "Outside that of which a man is aware there is," Bradley agrees, "a larger world of experience. But he cannot experience [this unconscious] content immediately." As long as the "[finite] centre exists, there is a world within it which is experienced immediately, and a world without it which is not experienced at all. . . . [T]his world[,] the region of the Unconscious, . . . is outside his immediate experience."[23]

Eliot and Bradley are arguing opposite positions. Eliot asserts that the psychological unconscious is not synonymous with immediate experience because it is *only a portion* of it, while Bradley contends that the psychological unconscious is not immediate experience because it lies *entirely outside* of it. For Eliot, the psychological unconscious is still a part of immediate experience; for Bradley, it is not.[24] Yet, while maintaining his restricted view of immediate experience as finite center, Bradley goes on to suggest the possibility of a kind of unconsciousness on the psychological level:

> If we like to take 'consciousness' as the state in which we experience a not-self, we may thus ask if there ever was or ever is an experience which is in this sense wholly subconscious. In such a state there would be feeling, but there would not be an object present as an 'other'. And we should so far not be aware of any distinction between that which is felt and that which feels.

What results is a preconscious sense of unity between the individual and his world and its objects: "by feeling, in short, I understand . . . an awareness which, though non-relational, may comprise simply in itself an indefinite amount of difference. There are no distinctions in the proper sense, and yet there is a many felt in one."[25] Bradley speculates that modern man might very well experience this unconscious feeling of wholeness between the self and the world not only as a child but also as an adult. We might very well share this feeling, Bradley implies, with the earliest of mankind:

> Was there and is there in the development of the race and the individual a stage at which experience is merely immediate? And, further, do we all perhaps at moments sink back to such a level? . . . For myself I think it probable that such a stage of mind not only, with all of us, comes first in fact, but that at times it recurs even in the life of the developed individual.[26]

That modern man shares with the history of the human race this unconscious experience is a conclusion toward which anthropology and folklore, in Eliot's eyes, supplied overwhelming evidence.

3. A COLLECTIVE-HISTORICAL PHENOMENON: DURKHEIM, LÉVY-BRUHL, FRAZER

From a basic conception of the nature of the unconscious as metaphysical, physiological, and psychological, Eliot proceeds to specify its properties as both 'collective' and 'historical'. These characteristics were vividly suggested to him and given concrete definition by his reading in the early anthropological studies of Émile Durkheim and Lucien Lévy-Bruhl, which, considering their theoretical aspects, Eliot would categorize as sociology and social psychology (SE 49), and in the studies of comparative mythology and ritual by James Frazer, whose implications were eventually corroborated by the Classical studies of Jane Harrison, Gilbert Murray, and F. M. Cornford, and later by Jesse Weston's study of folklore.[27]

Philosophically, of course, the unconscious is already collective and historical for Eliot in theory. According to Bradley's idealism, although our individual experience can in its entirety be considered a single point of view, it is actually composed of a series of finite centers or points of view. These perspectives, being diverse and irreconcilable, comprise our fragmented world of multiplicity. Such points of view as naturalism or religion shape and arrange our experience according to their orientation by providing certain relations between the elements of reality. For instance, when the unified feeling of a finite center dissolves into our world, we experience (1) a distinct object, a rose with its whiteness and sweet smell; (2) emotions that we feel in response to the object, such as delight over the rose's beauty; and (3) relations or ideas that link the object (and its accompanying emotion) with others in the world according to various points of view; biology tells us that the bee depends upon the rose for nectar, Christianity that the rose symbolizes the Virgin Mary. Our own overall point of view is unique and subjective because it consists only of a limited number of these perspectives; some are variations of naturalism and religion, others are less readily recognized and codified. These several points of view or perspectives that compose our particular world are gathered, along with the various histories of experiences that occur to us in that world, in the timeless unity of immediate experience before it disintegrates into our everyday world of selves and objects in a continuum of time, of society and history. The unconscious as immediate experience is collective, therefore, because, as the integration of all those points of view that provide us with our world and determine our experience, it precedes the individual and is thus impersonal, communal. It is historical because, consisting of the histories of all the selves, objects, and events that occur in our world, and yet immune to time and change itself, it establishes the simultaneous existence of the time schemes of every point of view included in our experience and maintains them as a unified whole.

Interestingly, the sociological theory that Durkheim developed to explain how customs and beliefs, especially religious rituals and myths, remain stable and perpetuate themselves in primitive societies over numerous generations is analogous to Eliot's interpretation of Bradley's philosophy. Eliot based one of his papers for Royce's seminar on the possibility of comparative religious studies[28] in part on Durkheim's *Les Règles de la méthode sociologique*[29] and "Représentations individuelles et représentations collectives."[30] In a book review a few years later,[31] Eliot recommended the last chapter of Durkheim's *The Elementary Forms of the Religious Life*[32] as the best summary of Durkheim's thought.

For Durkheim, our mind organizes our experience according to certain fundamental categories known as 'collective representations' (*représentations collectives*). Because our consciousness actually consists of collective representations, they determine the very nature of our world. Since we never conceive of reality apart from them, Durkheim observes that "their stability and impersonality are such that they have often passed as being absolutely universal and immutable."[33] Durkheim contends that we do not acquire these categories by reasoning them out as individuals; we are, in fact, not aware of them at all, for they are unconsciously instilled in us by the society in which we live. Society thus functions in our mind as a pervasive and comprehensive unity from which all of our experience comes: "since the universe does not exist except in so far as it is thought of, and since it is not completely thought of except by society, it takes a place in this latter; it becomes a part of society's interior life, while this is the totality outside of which nothing exists."[34]

Durkheim recognizes that this concept of totality is the same as that utilized by philosophers, "theorists of knowledge,"[35] when they postulate such an entity as the Absolute. But for Durkheim the idea arises from social experience: "the concept of totality is only the abstract form of the concept of society: it is the whole which includes all things, the supreme class which embraces all other classes." In its social form, this totality, of which all the collective representations form a part, Durkheim calls the 'collective conscience' (*conscience collective*), which Eliot translates as "social consciousness" (*SE* 49). In its ubiquitous and inclusive nature, the collective conscience is analogous to the unity of the Absolute and of immediate experience, from which our world evolves. As Durkheim notes, "if the world is inside of society, the space which this latter occupies becomes confounded with space in general."[36] Time is, thus, similarly a function of the collective conscience. Recalling Bergson's terminology, Durkheim continues to observe that "the rhythm of collective life dominates and embraces the varied rhythms of all the elementary lives from which it results; consequently the time which it expresses dominates and embraces all particular durations. It is time in general, . . . impersonal and total duration."[37]

Significantly, Durkheim perceives a continuity between the metaphysical, sociological, and theological ideas of totality when he admits that, "at bottom, the concept of totality, that of society and that of divinity are very probably only different aspects of the same notion."[38] Eliot, of course, also associated the unity and comprehensiveness of the Absolute with the Divine. Now, following Durkheim's lead, Eliot assimilates the collective conscience instilled by society as the sociological unconscious into that continuity linking the Divine as the Absolute to the metaphysical unconscious as immediate experience, to the physiological unconscious, and to the psychological unconscious. Durkheim's concluding description of the nature and function of the collective conscience indicates how readily the concept could assume metaphysical, mystical, and theological significance for Eliot:

> The collective conscience is the highest form of the psychic life, since it is the consciousness of consciousnesses. Being placed outside of and above individual and local contingencies, it sees things only in their permanent and essential aspects, which it crystallizes into communicable ideas. At the same time that it sees from above, it sees farther; at every moment of time, it embraces all known reality; that is why it alone can furnish the mind with the moulds which are applicable to the totality of things and which make it possible to think of them.[39]

Eliot's contention in his later writings that society should by nature embody the religion of its people unconsciously, beyond any deliberate and overt religious profession and observance, is an ap-

plication of Durkheim's concept of the collective conscience as a
kind of sociological Absolute, a social immediate experience, unconscious and thus everpresent and all-powerful. Such a theory at
once reinforced and added a new dimension to Royce's emphasis
on the Community as the arbiter of the Absolute, and to Babbitt's
ethical criticism of self-reliance as inevitably misguided, of the individual alone as hopelessly wayward.

In addition, Durkheim's sociological analysis of human thought
corroborated Eliot's idea that logic has a dialectical function, serving as a means of transcending all the divergent points of view to
approach the philosophical unity which is, in Eliot's opinion, the
goal of metaphysical speculation. For Eliot, the logical analysis of
the world performed by metaphysics could approach the unity of
the Absolute because logic is an inherently impersonal order, not
dependent upon any single point of view, through which all points
of view can be related. Similarly, Durkheim observes that "logical
thought tends to rid itself more and more of the subjective and
personal elements which it still retains from its origin." But, as
metaphysical speculation for Eliot cannot ultimately formulate a
successful synthesis of all the various points of view of intellectual
inquiry, so logical thinking for Durkheim can never reach such a
complete objectivity: "really and truly human thought . . . is the
ideal limit towards which we are constantly approaching, but
which in all probability we shall never succeed in reaching."[40] At
the same time, however, Eliot believes that the logical analysis of
metaphysics by its very nature strives for the unity of divergent
points of view characteristic of immediate experience and the Absolute. Likewise, Durkheim also contends that the very nature of
logical thinking derives from the collective conscience:

> Impersonal reason is only another name given to collective thought.
> . . . In a word, there is something impersonal in us because there is
> something social in all of us, and since social life embraces at once
> both representations and practices, this impersonality naturally ex-
> tends to ideas as well as to acts.[41]

Durkheim's effect on Eliot, then, was to emphasize that the impersonal and the unconscious are at the same time the collective,
at once consisting of and affecting the experience of all the members of a given society. Lévy-Bruhl, in turn, confronted Eliot with a
collective unconscious that he shared with all the previous members of the human race. The sociological theory of Lévy-Bruhl is
similar to Durkheim's to the extent that he also postulates the exis-

tence of collective representations in order to explain how customs and beliefs in primitive societies endure beyond the lifetime of their individual members. But whereas Durkheim, adopting a purely sociological perspective, wants to account for the origin of these collective representations in society by formulating an all-embracing collective conscience, Lévy-Bruhl, on the other hand, becomes the social psychologist, examining how these collective representations are possessed by the mind of a given member of the society. Thus, while Durkheim discovers the collective aspect of the unconscious, Lévy-Bruhl makes possible the revelation of its historical dimension by comparing the nature of primitive thought to that of modern man.[42]

Eliot's paper for Royce's seminar on the possibility of comparative religion as an intellectual discipline[43] was also based in part on Lévy-Bruhl's *Les Fonctions mentales dans les sociétés inférieures.*[44] In this book, Lévy-Bruhl asserts that when a primitive mind perceives an object according to a collective representation, a mental process occurs, which Lévy-Bruhl calls 'mystical participation' (*participation mystique*), in which the perceiver and the object perceived are felt to be one. Lévy-Bruhl proceeds to use this law of participation to account for primitive peoples' belief in the occult, according to which certain objects can effect physical changes in other objects a great distance away without ever moving themselves. As he explains:

> In the collective representations of primitive mentality, objects, beings and phenomena can, in a way incomprehensible to us, be at one and the same time themselves and something other than themselves. In a fashion no less incomprehensible, they emit and receive mystical forces, properties, qualities and actions which are felt outside themselves, without them ceasing to be where they are.[45]

Eliot himself was fascinated with this concept of mystical participation, particularly with the ability, in this frame of mind, to think of oneself as two things *simultaneously* while never losing consciousness of the separate identity of either object. According to his understanding of it, Lévy-Bruhl differentiates clearly between a pre-logical mentality, that of the Bororo of Brazil, and a logical mentality, that of civilized man. For Lévy-Bruhl, the Bororo's claiming of the parrot for his totem is not

> merely the *adoption* of parrot as an heraldic emblem, nor a merely mythological kinship or participation in qualities; nor is the savage *deluded* into thinking that he is a parrot. In practical life, the Bororo

never confuses himself with a parrot. . . . But he is capable of a state of mind . . . in which he *is* a parrot, while being at the same time a man."[46]

In Royce's seminar, however, Eliot criticizes Lévy-Bruhl's contention that this process of thought renders the primitive mind inherently different from our own: as Costello records Eliot's words, "Lévy-Bruhl draws the line between the crude mentality of primitive [man] and his own [mentality] too sharply." Eliot perceives an analogous desire for explanation present both in comparative studies of scholars of religion as 'interpretation', and in primitive peoples in a more rudimentary form as their mystical participation. Because an interpretation of behavior can only be made from an additional point of view, Eliot is skeptical that a sound comparison can be made between the religious practices of different peoples. As Eliot observes, there is a "distinction between interpretation and a fact, a point of attention which has only one aspect or a definite aspect which places it in a system."[47] A fact is, therefore, the single appropriate point of view, in this case that of the primitive people engaged in the religious custom. Like interpretation, 'explanation' also introduces a foreign point of view; in comparison, Eliot notes later in the seminar that "description is more sophisticated than explanation" because it attempts to adopt a point of view as close as possible to the object observed, but it also is "as bad as explanation" because the additional perspective is nevertheless present. Just as the modern mind interprets experience with the intention of explaining it, Eliot observes that "primitive consciousness luxuriates in the feeling of explanation," indeed has a "craving for explanation."[48]

Eliot has now established a hierarchy of mental activity: "explanation is more primitive, description more sophisticated,"[49] with interpretation somewhere in between; but all three persist in some form in the modern mind. As Eliot notes, for primitive man, explanation of events was supplied by "superstition,"[50] specifically, the occult influencing of one object by another according to mystical participation. For modern man, on the other hand, "explanation is often by cause and effect."[51] Eliot contends, however, that "any attribution of force or volition is participation,"[52] and thus he proposes that explanation in terms of participation and of causality which are analogous mental processes. As Costello summarizes Eliot's argument:

Causality is . . . due to a double process of participation, that between effect and cause and that between the object and us. Later these
two sorts of participation get separated into cause and volition, in-
variable sequence and act of will. But both are ideal constructs.[53]

For Eliot, cause, or "necessity," is "hypothetical," simply an abstraction which the mind formulates in order to explain why one
object, for instance, moves another object in the world. Like cause,
the will, as Eliot proposes later in his dissertation, is also merely
an idea, a half-object which the mind fabricates out of experience
as a separate object when it observes that the body has, for instance, moved an object in the world. But the primitive mind cannot distinguish between object and idea such that it can formulate
an idea entirely separate from the objects or events that might suggest it: "[to the] primitive, [there is] no mere fact and [there is] no
mere idea."[54] Thus, the primitive perceives the world as a series of
mystical participations in which both animate and inanimate objects are capable of effecting change in it: "will is not a character of
consciousness purely, and it is not at all a character of things as
such; it arises only in a conflict, and is in the primitive mind cog-
nized as a character of object as naturally as of subject" (KE 81).
Lacking the ability to formulate distinct ideas, that is, half-objects
existing somewhere between the reality of objects and the entirely
solipsistic, the primitive mind does not distinguish objects from
its own thoughts at all: Eliot surmises that "externality" was probably considered to be "force" or "spirit" before it was perceived to
consist of objects, because "primitive life . . . is immersed in practice and incapable of the degree of speculative interest necessary
for the constitution of an object" (KE 151). Thus, the primitive
does not experience the world and the mind separately, but rather
a single unified whole in which objects and his thoughts are
indistinguishable.[55]

In Royce's seminar, Eliot's critique of comparative religion,
which began with the futility of interpretation of the meanings of
primitive rituals by scholars and concluded with the fallibility of
the concept of causality as explanation, was throughout an application of Bradley's idealism. Causal explanations separate the
world into objects and abstractions, a world which Eliot assumes
to be most real when it is least divided. In this way, causality actually moves farther away from the Truth than the more unifying, if
more fanciful, notion of mystical participation. What makes Eliot's

critique so effective, indeed even possible, therefore, is that he had come to recognize that Lévy-Bruhl's description of primitive mentality is very near to being a characterization of immediate experience itself. When Lévy-Bruhl explains the mystical participation inherent in collective representations, he might just as well be describing immediate experience: primitive peoples' "mental activity is too undifferentiated for it to be possible to consider the ideas or images of objects by themselves, independently of the sentiments, emotions, and passions which evoke or are evoked by these ideas and images." Whereas the thought process of modern man is "more differentiated," the "mental activity among primitive peoples is not a pure or almost pure intellectual or cognitive phenomenon," but consists, rather, of "more complex states where the emotional and motivational elements are *integral parts* of representations," which are "coloured and pervaded by them."[56]

In his dissertation, Eliot actually conflates the historical, as primitive mentality, with the metaphysical, as immediate experience. In order to prove that the conception of Reality as immediate experience is philosophically superior to Russell's Reality of 'sense-data' and 'universals' from which he constructs the external world, Eliot at one point posits that these concepts are late developments in the progress of the human mind, not on the basis of logical argument, but on the basis of historical evidence: he *quotes* Lévy-Bruhl to the effect that the primitive mind does not think in terms of pure abstractions and generalities (*KE* 105). For Eliot, therefore, immediate experience in its psychological form acquires a historical dimension and can be said to have actually existed at a certain time in "the development of consciousness in biological evolution," and in the course of human history as well. Regarding "primitive consciousness," Eliot observes that when we examine an inferior state of mental activity, either an animal, child, or unexerted adult mind, we do not discover the constituents of a mature, evolved consciousness; they are present simply at a lower level. "We do not find feeling without thought, presentation without reflection: we find both feeling and thought, presentation, redintegration and abstraction, all at a lower stage" (*KE* 17).

If mystical participation can define immediate experience, and explain how the psychological unconscious functions, then the primitive mind must live on in our own. Our mind becomes a composite of the archaic and civilized consciousness of human history: Eliot observes that throughout the evolution of man or during the development of a child there occurs a "systematic al-teration of values, with an outer expansion and an inner elabora-tion of content, which we find to be continuous with the values and content of our own experience" (*KE* 85). For Eliot, "one seeks, among savages, an internal kinship, not one of resemblance"[57] which interpreters of primitive religious practices fail to supply, because the primitive mind lies just below our own consciousness. Even Lévy-Bruhl is guilty of such interpretation: he explains that he will use the term 'mystical participation' "not with allusion to the religious mysticism of our own societies, which is something quite different, but in the narrowly defined sense in which 'mysti-cal' is used of the belief in forces, influences and actions impercep-tible to the senses, but nonetheless real," that is, to "an occult power."[58] Although aware of the difference between 'mystical' and 'occult',[59] Eliot makes no such distinction when he refers to mysti-cal participation: "the mystical mentality, though at a low level, plays a much greater part in the daily life of the savage than in that of the civilised man."[60] Significantly, Eliot describes mystical par-ticipation as if it were synonymous with religious mysticism: "the union of the worshipper with his god, the identity of the individ-ual and his totem."[61] If primitive mentality is continuous with the modern mind, then for Eliot primitive mysticism can only be the crude forerunner of our own. As Eliot discovered from his reading in religious experience and anthropology, descriptions of primitive and modern mysticism not only resemble immediate experience, but also each other.

In light of Lévy-Bruhl's social psychology, Eliot was able to as-sociate the unconscious with a particular point in human history, for immediate experience and the mental life of primitive peoples are on a psychological level the same. Once the *functioning* of the unconscious, the nature of its thought process, was located in his-tory, Eliot surmised that the *content* of the unconscious must then consist of the rituals and myths of that particular period in human evolution. Anthropological studies would supply such detail about primitive observances of the supernatural, and Eliot was familiar with the work of Wilhelm Mannhardt, Max Müller, Wilhelm Wundt, E. B. Tylor, Andrew Lang, J. H. King, W. Robertson Smith, J. Rendell Harris, Edwin Sidney Hartland, G. Elliot Smith, R. H. Codrington, Baldwin Spencer and F. J. Gillen, and Edgar Lee Hewett.[62] But specifically through the comparative study of fertil-ity ritual conducted by Frazer, Eliot thought that he had discovered an underlying pattern in all of these religious ceremonies and beliefs which could be considered the *structure* of the unconscious. In addition, because this pattern is evident in an evolved form in religious practice and folk customs throughout human civilization, Eliot believed that the unconscious is in fact a continuum composed of all the various aspects of consciousness and kinds of mental activity—impulses, feelings, beliefs, emotions, and ideas—that were actually experienced by man in the course of his development from a primitive to a modern. Eliot's paper in Royce's seminar on the possibility of comparative religion was based in part on Frazer's work,[63] and Eliot was familiar with *The Golden Bough* in the first edition of 1890 in two volumes, the second of 1900 in three, and the third of 1907 to 1915 in twelve.[64]

Frazer originally began *The Golden Bough* as a study of the ritualistic magic involved in the succession of priestly kings in primitive societies, but his comparative method soon had him ranging through related customs in societies all over the world and at different stages of development.[65] According to Frazer, primitive man with his rudimentary sense of the religious, associates the magician, a member of society who is particularly adept at effecting change in the world through occult powers, with the priest, who gains similar powers by functioning as an intermediary between man and the gods, and with the king, who as the leader of society relies upon such powers in order to secure its welfare. All three of these figures in many societies eventually merged into one man, a priest-king who would resort to magic in order to fulfill his responsibility for both the spiritual and material well-being of his people. Because the gods were thought to be the original possessors of magic, the priest-king was often considered to be the human incarnation of a divine being. As the king grew older and suffered physical decline, primitives thought that the divine power or force within him was in danger of being weakened or extinguished; so, the king had to be killed by a healthy and more youthful successor, at which time the divine essence would be transferred from the dying king to the slayer, now the reborn king. Later, rather than kill the original king, substitutes were sacrificed periodically in order to rejuvenate the king. At first, a son was designated because, having been conceived by the king, he too possessed a bit of divinity which would be transferred to his father upon his death. But soon any human sacrifice would do; some societies resorted to wounding rather than killing their king. Eventually the death was merely simulated at cyclical festivals in which an effigy, perceived through mystical participation to partake of the king's divinity, substituted for the king himself. Since the king was, again through mystical participation, the embodiment of society as a whole and all of its members individually, his death and subsequent rebirth meant prosperity for the tribe and salvation for each member.

These priest-kings, or man-gods, were often considered to be reincarnations of hero-gods who at one point in the society's history had themselves suffered a violent death either to be reborn in the tribe's lineage of kings or resurrected at a sacred place from which they could continue to exercise their powers over the people and the land that was once theirs. Such are Adonis, Attis, and Osiris, whose annual death and rebirth would be enacted at festivals by either burying or casting into the sea an effigy in great sorrow over the mock death, only to celebrate the resurrection of the god the next day. Although agricultural in origin, the ritualistic death and rebirth of these gods was to ensure not only the fertility of the soil and the marriage bed but also the preservation of the life of society and the world, for if there were no seasonal revival of the god, the universe would plunge into chaos and suffer extinction. Frazer often refers to certain folk customs and seasonal festivals associated with rural life of European peasants as survivals of these primitive rituals. Occasionally Frazer will also point out similarities between these various deities and the dying and resurrected God of Christianity. For instance, Christ is periodically eaten during the Eucharist in the form of bread and wine, as substitutes for body and blood, in order to partake of his spiritual purity and healing powers; so primitive effigies were often eaten in order to acquire a god's divinity. Again, Christ is symbolically sacrificed every year at Easter time in order to ensure the spiritual stability of the lives of his believers, just as the primitive gods were annually slain in effigy in order to revive their supernatural powers over the world. Clearly, The Golden Bough would suggest to Eliot the continuity of the primitive and the modern.

Initially, Eliot was more impressed with Lévy-Bruhl's analysis of primitive mentality than he was with Frazer's treatment of it in the first and second editions of The Golden Bough. No doubt enthusiastic over the resemblance between immediate experience and a world unified by mystical participation, Eliot praises Lévy-Bruhl for having emphasized an aspect of the primitive mind that had been overlooked by anthropologists before him, mentioning Frazer specifically.[66] In Royce's seminar, Eliot criticizes the "comparisons" Frazer establishes between the rituals of primitive peoples because, in seeking "similarities and identities of races very remote," he attempts to explain religious customs in terms of their purpose. But for Eliot "'purpose' is interpretation and not description." Durkheim is preferred because he seeks "efficient cause and function, no purposes," while Lévy-Bruhl comes closest to the truth, since he "affirms" that "really there is nothing to explain." According to Eliot's epistemology, then, "no causal relation, no definitions [*sic*: Costello's shorthand], no explanation seems adequate" as a method for dealing with primitive cultures; "nothing but a chronicle"[67] can get as close as possible to the reality, the actual fact, of primitive life.

With the appearance of the third edition of Frazer's work, however, Eliot perceived a marked shift in emphasis. Although the first two-volume edition of *The Golden Bough* tried to account for the Priest of Nemi, it inspired more investigations following Frazer's "comparative method," resulting in an augmented edition. By the time the work had expanded to twelve volumes, not only its size, but also its scope had changed: with each successive volume of his compilation of myth and ritual, Frazer had increasingly avoided the "attempt to explain." Frazer had come to write the "chronicle," the description, of primitive mentality that Eliot had always been seeking. Now that Eliot is able to compare such a work with his earlier enthusiasms, he is able to see how much they actually engaged in theoretical explanation. Eliot notes that Frazer's significance is not related to "brilliant theories of human behavior" as is that of certain sociologists, referring specifically to Durkheim and Lévy-Bruhl. Since *The Golden Bough* is descriptive rather than interpretative and explanatory, like their work and Freud's, it is for Eliot perhaps a more enduring achievement, because it is a "statement of fact which is not involved in the maintenance or fall of any theory of the author's."[68] Such theories depicting the nature of primitive mentality are inevitably based on a contemporary point of view and will therefore always be partially inaccurate: "to say that mind, in its beginning in child or aborigine or animal, really was as we describe it, is to commit oneself to a relative truth" because it "is a statement which overlooks the development of mind" (*KE* 22). Frazer's chronicle is free of any alien point of view such as the scientific thinking of the modern mind oriented to material phenomena, from which perspective the primitives' unified spiritual world appears 'pre-logical'; or the sexually repressed sensibility at the close of the Victorian period, which perceives all religious and artistic activity as expressions merely of inhibited erotic desires.

Yet precisely because *The Golden Bough* is neither a theory nor a "mere collection of data," it has a significance for Eliot beyond its distinction as an anthropological study that supposedly employs an epistemologically sound technique: "the absence of speculation is a conscious and deliberate scrupulousness, a positive point of view." This point of view, this "vision," makes Frazer's work superior to other thinkers' and entirely relevant to the contemporary sensibility. By refraining from imposing an alien point of view, a theoretical explanation, upon the material he was gathering, Frazer, Eliot believed, allowed those rituals and myths to organize themselves according to their *own* point of view. In this way, Frazer discovered, or rather revealed, the point of view of primitive man: "he has extended the consciousness of the human mind into as dark a backward and abysm of time as has yet been explored."[69] Because the primitive mentality, duplicating immediate experience, remains a part of our minds as our unconscious, Frazer becomes an archaeologist of the mind, and for Eliot *The Golden Bough* could be considered either as a "collection of entertaining myths, or as a revelation of that vanished mind of which our mind is a continuation."[70] Psychoanalysis, with its theoretical point of view oriented to the individual, the sexual, and the aberrant, produces only a partial and distorted view of the unconscious, which is for Eliot collective and historical; Frazer's anthropological recreation of the primitive point of view provides the necessary balance. *The Golden Bough* is just as important for the modern era as the "complementary" achievement of Freud: "throwing its light on the obscurities of the soul from a different angle."[71]

The point of view that Frazer discovered primitive man to have, according to Eliot, is the underlying pattern that organized his various stories and observances of the supernatural; the structure repeated below the divergent content of these rituals and myths of different times and places is the dying and reborn god. If the primitive mind lives on as our unconscious, then this primitive point of view becomes the structure of *our* unconscious, imperceptibly guiding our spiritual feelings and religious observances. Frazer, in fact, found that the death-rebirth pattern repeated itself in one form or another in peasant folklore of modern civilization, in Judaism, and finally in the Christian Church. Eliot indicates the religious significance of such a discovery when he compares the influence of Frazer on his generation to that of Ernest Renan on a previous one:[72] as Renan made the Christian faith an intellectually viable spiritual alternative for his nineteenth-century contemporaries by liberally interpreting the teachings and events of Jesus' life, so Frazer supplied the early twentieth century with historical evidence that the fundamental pattern governing Christianity has been shared by other religions and existed long before the founding of that religion, even as far back as man's earliest beginnings.[73] Frazer himself did not undertake his comparative study in order to give credence to Christian belief; he was, in fact, a positivist who thought that all religions, primitive, ancient, and modern, are merely superstition.[74] But this personal point of view never enters into his research: he scrupulously presents only the point of view of primitive man. For this reason, Eliot is able to integrate the conclusions about the structure of the primitive mind inevitably drawn from *The Golden Bough* into his theory of the unconscious and, in turn, is eventually able to perceive the consequences of such an integration for religious belief.

4. THE RIVAL PERSPECTIVE: PSYCHOANALYSIS

Interestingly, Eliot never did acquire his theory of the unconscious from psychoanalytic psychology,[75] instead synthesizing theories of scientific psychology, Bradley's idealism, and anthropology to derive his view of the mind. He was certainly aware of early clinical investigations of hysteria and its analysis through a theory of the unconscious as early as 1910[76] and recognized their relationship to the later Freudian school. Eliot notes that psychoanalysis had its origin in the investigations conducted at the French school for psychological disturbances at Nancy, and in the French psychiatrists Jean-Martin Charcot, Ribot, and Janet. But whereas modern French psychology had in the main concentrated "prudently" upon the "care of cases," Eliot admits in 1920 (*SE* 49) to having been acquainted as well with the "more surprising developments" to occur subsequently in Vienna.[77] Initially, Eliot glanced approvingly at those aspects of psychoanalysis that corroborated his own evolving idea of the unconscious. He recognized that Lévy-Bruhl's theory of primitive mentality shared a similarity with the latest interpretation of mythology formulated by followers of Freud.[78] Although one can only conjecture whom Eliot has in mind—Otto Rank,[79] Theodor Reik,[80] perhaps Sandor Ferenczi[81]—he would most likely be referring to Jung's significant *Wandlungen und Symbole des Libido,*[82] in which Jung relates the concept of mystical participation to his own psychological system. Freud's *Totem und Tabu,*[83] appearing a year later, was indebted, as he acknowledged, at once to Jung's book, to Frazer's work, to Andrew Lang, and to Wundt's *Elemente der Völkerpsychologie.*[84] When Eliot reviewed the English translation of Wundt's study, his criticism of it as merely descriptive anthropology and philosophy of history, and thus obsolete, derives from psychoanalysis as well as from Lévy-Bruhl and Durkheim. Eliot complained that the "influence" of the "sexual instinct" upon religion and myth was not considered; mysticism was overlooked; and despite extensive material about "religious cults," "religious feelings" were virtually ignored. Eliot concludes that "progress" in the study of primitive psychology will be "closely dependent" upon developments in individual psychology, especially psychoanalysis.[85]

That Eliot originally assumed psychoanalysis to be relevant to his own concept of the unconscious is, therefore, not surprising. Both Jung in *Psychology of the Unconscious* and Freud in *Totem and Taboo* relied in part upon the same anthropological sources as did Eliot to develop a theory of the unconscious similar to Eliot's to the extent that it also had a historical dimension.[86] Both Freud and Jung believed that myths and rituals compose the content and are thus expressions of the unconscious, and both believed that we recapitulate the experience of our primitive ancestors from childhood to maturity. But unlike Eliot, and Jung, Freud contends that myths are symbolic expressions and rituals are symptomatic behavior of mental disorder caused by an inability to adjust to sexual desire. Religious experience is, therefore, reduced to a psychological disease. Eliot did not anticipate that Freudian theory, making use of the same anthropology with which he began, would eventually transform religion into sexual aberration. Rather than a translation of religion into a function of unhealthy sexuality, Eliot was seeking an integration of sexual love and religious feeling, a union of sexual desire with religious experience similar to that achieved by Dante in *The Divine Comedy* and the *Vita Nuova* through his Beatrice. Freud's view of the unconscious proved to be unacceptable.

By contrast, Jung's theory of the unconscious appears, at first sight, to be just what Eliot would want. For Jung, myths and rituals do not express an individual's maladjustment to his sexual drives, because the fundamental psychic impulse or energy is not narrowly sexual in nature, but rather spiritual. Myths and rituals embody psychological archetypes which derive from a deeper level of the unconscious as our collective inheritance of generations of experience, and point the way to spiritual fulfillment if we understand their structure and follow their guidance. Since Jung finds the mental disorders of modern man to be spiritual rather than sexual, he is not hostile to the religions of the world, for their myths and rituals often embody those archetypes of the unconscious which direct us toward psychic health. Jung believed, in fact, that through religious experience of the Catholic church one could attain mental health. Such a psychology seems to be what Eliot was approaching; indeed, Stephen Spender,[87] Elizabeth Drew,[88] P. W. Martin,[89] and Johannes Fabricius[90] have argued that Eliot's esthetic theory contains, and his poetry illustrates, the principal tenets of Jungian psychology.

But with Jung, as with Freud, the psychological theory takes precedence over the religious: the archetypes are sanctioned for Jung by the theory, and not by religious feeling or doctrine; psychological analysis at once prompts Jung to embrace religion and Freud to condemn it. Like natural science, psychoanalytic psychology becomes for Eliot another point of view misguidedly attempting to subsume all others, whereas he sought an explanation for religious feeling which only a synthesis of all points of view, an approximation of the Absolute, could provide. Further, psychoanalysis in itself was for Eliot "a dubious and contentious branch of science."[91] Eliot had always been suspicious of such traditional psychological concepts as will and attention; surely 'ego', 'id', and 'complex', 'psychic energy', 'archetype', and 'transformation' must have seemed even further removed from reality. Perhaps recalling his own labeling of such ideas as 'half-objects', Eliot implicitly criticizes the legitimacy of psychoanalytic terminology when he contends that "a word half-understood, torn from its place in some alien or half-formed science, as of psychology, conceals from both writer and reader the meaninglessness of a statement" (*SE* 305).

Finally, although Eliot felt that the origin of his religious experience lay in a "deeper reality than that of the plane of most of our conscious living," what he sought was, not the "intellectualization" of this reality by the psychologist, but rather the "reality itself."[92] Psychoanalysis translates the unconscious from a vivid experience into lifeless abstractions, robbing it of its power and relevance to our lives. Eliot observes of the psychoanalytic fiction of May Sinclair that she elicits as much "pity and terror" as her subject, a person undergoing psychoanalytic therapy, allows; but there is no opportunity of "tapping the atmosphere of unknown terror and mystery in which our life is passed and which psychoanalysis has not yet analyzed."[93]

Rather than the half-objects of psychoanalysis, Eliot wants the reality of the unconscious itself, which he has discovered to consist of the mind of primitive man. Because Frazer presented the point of view of the primitive rather than his own, his influence, in Eliot's opinion, will probably be more lasting than that of Freud,[94] who conceived of primitive rituals and myths as expressing only his own theory of the human sensibility, or Jung, who organized all of those myths and rituals according to various archetypes which follow his own theoretical system of spiritual fulfillment. The only archetype that Eliot found repeated in the rituals and myths assembled in *The Golden Bough* was the death-rebirth pattern which pointed him, not to Jung, but toward the Christian religion. Eliot predicts that Sinclair will eventually find herself compelled to move from "psychotherapy even to the supernatural, or at least to that transfinite world with which Henry James was in such close intercourse,"[95] to what Eliot will revealingly call elsewhere "the deeper psychology"[96] of James and Hawthorne.

Eliot has developed a theory of the mind, then, in which the unconscious has a physiological basis, as indicated by scientific psychology; is continuous with the metaphysical unconscious, the immediate experience of Bradley's idealism; and is both collective and historical, as implied by the studies of primitive mentality of Durkheim and Lévy-Bruhl, and of primitive ritual by Frazer. The unconscious thus consists of a historical continuum: the deeper one probes into the mind, into the unconscious, the further back one moves in history. This spatial-temporal conception of the mind makes all past cultures of the human race a part of our own mentality, exercising a decisive, if often unnoticed, influence upon our own experience of the world: as Eliot observes, when we study

Greek, we are studying "our own mind." Modern man's "categories of thought" are predominantly the "outcome" of Greek thought, and our "categories of emotion" are primarily the outcome of Greek literature. In turn, then, "what analytic psychology attempts to do for the individual mind, the study of history—including language and literature—does for the collective mind."[97] If we can plunge down into the unconscious, back through time, and bring to the surface, into consciousness, these archaic systems of thought and modes of feeling, we can use them for our own benefit. Eliot contends that the ultimate challenge for historians is to utilize their imagination to "reconstruct" for modern man the mind of the Renaissance and the pre-Renaissance so vividly that they will no longer be "dead" for us, that is, "unconscious parts of our own mind," but rather conscious and thus usable for our "future development."[98]

In his study of mysticism, Inge noted that the idea of a collective-historical unconscious, lived out, as Eliot himself suggested in his dissertation, during the lifetime of an individual in the same order in which it had occurred during the evolution of the human race, had traditionally supplied certain mystics with a connection between mystical experience and Christianity. As Inge explains:

> It is a favorite doctrine of the mystics that man, in his individual life, recapitulates the spiritual history of the race, in much the same way in which embryologists tell us that the unborn infant recapitulates the whole process of physical evolution. It follows that the Incarnation, the central fact of human history, must have its analogue in the experience of the individual.[99]

For Eliot, preoccupied with his mystical moments and their implication for religious belief, that part of his mind which would be of most help to him was the earliest part, when the spiritual impulse dominated and religious expression first began. That portion of the unconscious which Eliot, following Frazer's lead, would try to recover and integrate into his modern sensibility was primitive experience.

IV. PRIMITIVE EXPERIENCE

I N *Knowledge and Experience,* Eliot poses this provocative question: "If knowledge of objects belongs to a world which is admittedly a construction, should we not return to the primitive experience to find reality?" (*KE* 152). Eliot came to decide that the answer must be yes, but with an appropriate qualification. If our consciousness and our experience result when the unity of Reality is disintegrated and reorganized into the world as we know it, we can never transfer immediate experience *directly* into our world: we can only sense it as undifferentiated feeling and apply these intimations of the Absolute, of Truth, to our everyday experience. Since immediate experience is continuous with primitive experience from a historical perspective, an analogous limitation arises when we wish to import primitive experience into modern life. Although the primitive mind and experience form a substratum of our unconscious, we cannot, according to Eliot, simply resort to savage behavior or mimic tribal art in order to benefit from their spiritual unity, because the evolution of mankind has made civilized mentality and modern living too different for us to be able to incorporate directly into them elements of primitive life. Only through an integration or synthesis of the primitive spirit with the modern mind can our culture at once survive and be enriched by primitive experience.

Eliot had no doubt that an understanding of the religious impulse depended upon an exploration of the unconscious, and thus primitive experience. He also thought, in turn, that civilized artistic expression involved primitive experience too; he felt that the artist is able to tap primitive sources which to other people remain unaccessible or unheeded. Inspired by the Wyndham Lewis of *Tarr,* Eliot reflects that the artist is, in general, "more *primitive,* as well as more civilized, than his contemporaries, his experience is deeper than civilization," although he uses the reality of his civilized world to express himself. In the fiction and in the painting of

Lewis, the "thought of the modern and the energy of the cave-man" are apparent.[1] In order to create art, therefore, Eliot advises that the artist should bring to consciousness those layers of his collective-historical unconscious that contain the primitive and the unifying tendency of his artistic imagination. As he observes, just as an examination of the primitive mind facilitates our com-prehension of the civilized mind, so a study of primitive art and poetry can illuminate the nature of civilized art and poetry. In-deed, such a confrontation of the modern artist or poet with the primitive could even "revivify" their current creative effort.

Eliot's doctrine of tradition and the historical sense originates, in fact, in this effort to recover the primitive, the collective-historical unconscious, for use by the modern consciousness. Eliot recommends that the poet be aware of every achievement in poetry since it was first written, "all the metamorphoses of poetry that illustrate the stratifications of history that cover savagery," in order to be able to recognize what he is accomplishing in his own verse. Because the artist is, in an "impersonal sense, the most con-scious of men," he is also "the most and the least civilized and civi-lizable"; thus he is better able to "understand" both civilized and primitive culture. But because the modern artist possesses the primitive mind as part of his unconscious and also has the benefit of the experience of additional historical ages as well as of his con-temporary moment, he will, according to Eliot, seek to integrate primitive artistic experience with his own, rather than worship the primitive as unattainable or unavailable. The artist can perceive, before anyone else, the "merits of the savage, the barbarian and the rustic," and he can sense as well in what ways the savage may be "improved upon." The artist does not regard the savage in a "ro-mantic light," nor does he believe that the savage has "any gifts of mystical insight or artistic feeling" that he himself does not have.[2]

Eliot will find, in fact, the very origin of both the religious and the artistic in the nature of primitive experience itself. What devel-oped as ritual dance out of an innate sense of rhythm later evolved into religious ceremony and secular drama. By analyzing religious experience in terms of its unconscious origins, Eliot justifies par-ticipation in institutional Christianity. Recognizing that modern ballet and the music hall reflect their primitive ancestry, he seeks a ritualistic theater and poetry as well.

1. A PHILOSOPHY OF RELIGION: HARRISON, MURRAY, CORNFORD

In order to discover the nature of primitive experience and bring it to consciousness, Eliot consulted such studies as *The Golden Bough* which actually display the inclination of the nineteenth century to employ the principle of evolution in practically all fields of learning. Eliot himself was never opposed to evolution as a mode of scientific inquiry, but only to its transformation into a metaphysical system and moral philosophy. Eliot observes with disapproval that one result of the theory of evolution and the "'time philosophy'" that developed from it is an attitude of "unconscious fatalism" that is applied to the world.[3] For instance, to presume that the past, present, and future are governed by change that is brought about by "forces which are not human," and that man simply must "*adapt* himself" to the ensuing alterations in his environment, is a fatalism inadmissible when, for Eliot, man is "*morally* responsible" for the present and the future of the human race.[4] Thus he complains that Balfour's ethical theory is a kind of "Tennysonian naturalism": between the assertion that the "best will survive" and the assertion that "what survives is best" there is little difference when actions are based upon them.[5] But certainly Eliot relied upon the principle of evolution to construct for himself that chronicle of man's development which would reveal the nature of the unconscious. Thinkers who adopted an evolutionary perspective in their work, such as Darwin, H. J. S. Maine, and Tylor, are of great utility in Eliot's estimation. He contends that if literary critics would examine the content and methodology of such books as *The Origin of Species, Ancient Law,* and *Primitive Culture,* they might discover the difference between a "history" and a "chronicle," an "interpretation" and a "fact." Once having perceived that knowledge is development rather than theory, literary critics would recognize as well that literature can be fully understood only when its "sources" are consulted, which may appear "remote, difficult, and unintelligible" to them if they cannot escape the literary expectations to which they are accustomed. Since Wundt did not realize that the "nature of the finished product . . . is essentially present in the crude forerunner,"[6] his *Elements of Folk Psychology* was criticized by Eliot in his early review because, among other shortcomings, its consideration of primitive art overlooked its "aesthetic value."[7]

Frazer's work in the evolution of primitive ritual and modern folklore was continued by Jane Harrison, Gilbert Murray, and F. M. Cornford, the Cambridge Classicists, and by C. B. Cook at Oxford, whose Classical studies applied the anthropological method of Frazer to Greek culture.[8] By tracing the origins of later Greek religion, art, and philosophy to earlier primitive rituals, these Classical scholars gave further credence to Eliot's idea, suggested to him by *The Golden Bough,* that the unconscious mind is a historical continuum. At the same time, by demonstrating that artistic expression itself evolved out of primitive religious rituals, they suggested to Eliot that the artistic as well as the religious impulse has an unconscious origin; thus art, like religion, must also be an expression of the unconscious mind, and involve primitive experience. Finally, by discovering the origin of religious ceremony and drama in primitive ritual and dance, these Classicists provided Eliot with a way to relate religious and artistic experience to his conclusion derived from scientific psychology that the unconscious mind is continuous with our physiology, and also to his belief derived from Frazer that the structure of that unconscious mind is the pattern of death and rebirth.

Harrison already seems to be suggesting a relationship between the religious impulse, primitive experience, and the unconscious as early as her *Prolegomena to the Study of Greek Religion,* whose purpose is to reveal through an examination of early Greek rituals the "substratum of religious conceptions, at once more primitive and more permanent,"[9] which underlie later Greek mythology as found, for instance, in Homer. Between her *Prolegomena* and *Themis,* Harrison consulted Bergson and Durkheim in order to help define the origin and nature of these primitive rituals and to distinguish between early Greek mystery-gods and the later Olympians. In Royce's seminar, Eliot criticized Harrison's work, along with Frazer's earlier editions of *The Golden Bough,* for involving theory and interpretation in studies that must ultimately be evolutionary chronicles, and he must certainly have been reacting adversely in part to her use of enthusiasms he had recently abandoned: "Harrison has studied evolution of ritual. But interpretation and metaphysics soon enter,"[10] specifically, the "infection of Bergsonism,"[11] as he would later observe. But Eliot overlooked the theoretical impurities to discover how relevant Harrison's work was to his own preoccupations. Perhaps Harrison may have coincidentally helped him to recognize the implications of her studies more readily by orienting her findings toward a philosophical system familiar to him, and also analogous to, if fundamentally different from, Bradley's, for whose philosophy Eliot had come to abandon Bergson's.

Harrison had always sensed that the primitive mystery-gods are essentially religious, while their evolved counterparts, the Olympians, seem products of the conscious intelligence, which reflects and analyzes. Bergson confirmed her suspicion by defining the religious, the spiritual, in opposition to the scientific, the logical. Although she recognized that "it is no part of Professor Bergson's present programme, as I understand it, to analyse and define the nature and function of religion,"[12] nevertheless, like Underhill, Harrison relies upon Bergson's metaphysics to define religion for her:

> Prof. Bergson has shown us that *durée,* true time, *is* ceaseless change, which is the very essence of life—which is in fact 'l'Évolution Créatrice,' and this is in its very essence one and indivisible. . . . It is this 'durée,' figured by the Greek as Dike, the Way, that the mystic apprehends; in the main stream and current of that life of duration, he lives and has his being.[13]

Thus, "Dionysus, with every other mystery-god, was an instinctive attempt to express what Professor Bergson calls *durée.*"[14] Incorporating Durkheim's sociological theories on religion, Harrison proceeds to postulate a course of evolution in Greek culture from primitive ritual to later mythology and then to philosophy, to which Cornford would later devote an entire book:

> The mystery-god arises out of those instincts, emotions, desires which attend and express life; but these emotions, desires, instincts, in so far as they are religious, are at the outset rather of a group than of individual consciousness. The whole history of epistemology is the history of the evolution of clear, individual, rational thought, out of the haze of collective and sometimes contradictory representations. It is a necessary and most important corollary to this doctrine, that the form taken by the divinity reflects the social structure of the group to which the divinity belongs.[15]

Harrison's application of Durkheim's impersonal, all-pervasive collective conscience to the nature of primitive ritual must have again suggested to Eliot, as had his reading in Durkheim himself, that religious experience originates in and expresses that unified whole which is the collective unconscious. As Harrison herself observes, "the religious impulse . . . is, I believe, an attempt, instinctive and unconscious, to do what Professor Bergson bids modern philosophy do consciously."[16]

Harrison provides a vivid description of how primitive feeling is unleashed during a ritual dance when the members of the tribe are gathered together in unconscious bodily movement and the rhythm of the dance unites them in a single religious expression:

> The dancers dancing together utter their conjoint desire, their delight, their terror, in steps and gestures, in cries of fear or joy or lamentation, in shrieks of war. In so uttering they inevitably emphasize and intensify it. Moreover being a collective emotion it is necessarily felt as something more than the experience of the individual, as something dominant and external. The dancers . . . sink their own personality and by the wearing of masks and disguises, by dancing to a common rhythm, above all by the common excitement, they become emotionally one, a true congregation, a collection of individuals. The emotion they feel collectively, the thing that is more than any individual emotion, they externalize, project; it is the raw material of god-head. Primitive gods are to a large extent collective enthusiasms, uttered, formulated.[17]

For Eliot, this passage must surely have been a portrayal of how primitive experience resembled the nature of the unconscious itself, how primitives in fact *lived* the unconscious. He must have noticed how the rhythms stirred by the impersonal collective unconscious could so easily be transformed into a religion. From scientific psychology Eliot knew that our physiology first senses and responds to rhythms. Thus for Eliot the physiological unconscious, continuous for him with the metaphysical and psychological unconscious, also plays a role in religious expression. Such a conclusion seems to have been first suggested to him by these and other studies of primitive experience.

Whereas Harrison discovered that early primitive rituals evolved into later Greek religion, Murray and Cornford, continuing this evolutionary study of Greek primitive experience, uncovered a relationship between these rituals and later Greek art and philosophy. In an "Excursus on the Ritual Forms Preserved in Greek Tragedy" appearing in *Themis,* Murray observes that "Tragedy is in origin a Ritual Dance."[18] In a passage characteristic of the translator of Greek poetic drama, Murray indicates that the structure of those primitive rituals still continued in modified form in the plots of later Greek tragedy:

> An outer shape dominated by tough and undying tradition, an inner life fiery with sincerity and spiritual freedom; the vessels of a very ancient religion overfilled and broken by a new wine of reasoning and rebellious humanity, and still, in their rejection, shedding abroad the old aroma, as of eternal and mysterious things: these are the fundamental paradoxes presented to us by Greek Tragedy.[19]

In *The Origin of Attic Comedy,* Cornford posited not only that later Greek comedy likewise evolved out of primitive ritual, but also that the comedy evolved out of the very same ritual as did the tragedy: "Athenian Comedy arose out of a ritual drama essentially the same in type as that from which Gilbert Murray has derived Athenian Tragedy."[20] As he elaborates:

> The supposed ritual did contain the essential germs out of which each could grow to its full form. . . . [I]ts central incidents could be given a sad or happy turn, according as emphasis were thrown on the conflict and death of the hero, or on the joyful resurrection and marriage that followed.[21]

Furthermore, this proto-ritual displayed the same structural pattern that Frazer had discovered repeatedly in primitive religious observances; as Cornford explains, "that Tragedy and Comedy should have the same divine protagonist, the dying God whose defeat is a victory, the ironical Buffoon whose folly confounds the pretence of wisdom—this is a mystery of Dionysiac religion."[22] For Eliot, that tragedy and comedy evolved from a common ritual source was not so mysterious: if the primitive mind simulates immediate experience in its tendency to perceive the world as an undifferentiated whole, then the further one goes back in history, the deeper into the unconscious, the less diversity one will encounter; the older the mind, the more unity it will perceive in the world. In an earlier book, *From Religion to Philosophy: A Study in the Origins of Western Speculation,*[23] which relied upon theories of Durkheim and Lévy-Bruhl, Cornford continued to trace the evolution of primitive ritual: Harrison had taken it up to Greek mythology, and Cornford proceeded to demonstrate that when the collective representations underlying these religious observances were sufficiently rationalized, they became the fundamental concepts of Greek philosophy.[24]

Years later, Murray would come to draw the same conclusion from these studies that Eliot had: that the evolution and continuation of primitive ritual in every facet of Athenian life, even its drama and philosophy, implied the existence of a historical unconscious:

> In plays like *Hamlet* or the *Agamemnon* or the *Electra* . . . we have . . . a strange, unanalysed vibration below the surface, an undercurrent of desires and fears and passions, long slumbering yet eternally familiar, which have for thousands of years lain near the root of our most intimate emotions and been wrought into the fabric of our most magical dreams. How far into past ages this stream may reach back, I dare not even surmise.[25]

In order to dispel the mystery that his own studies posed, Cornford became a professed Jungian. He came to maintain that "the several stages in the development of religious representations" have "corresponding systems of associations deposited, at those stages, in the racial tradition and memory of the Greeks—systems that lasted on in their minds like the superimposed layers of alluvial stratification." Thus, in this "'collective unconscious'" will be found "every phase of imagery and symbolism which the mind of the race has used in its progress to abstract conceptual thought."[26] Significantly, the Cambridge Classicists themselves came to perceive their studies as evidence of a collective-historical unconscious of one sort or another. Incorporating their findings into a more elaborate synthesis involving philosophy and scientific psychology, Eliot used these studies of primitive experience to extend his unified theory of the mind into an explanation of both religious experience and artistic expression.

Eliot's philosophy of religion and art begins, then, with the theory of the development of tragedy and comedy out of a "common form" proposed by the Cambridge Classicists. Assuming that Cornford's theory is true, as it has the corroboration of Murray, Eliot accepts that the "original dramatic impulse" is neither comic nor tragic alone, but that both qualities exist at the same time in all primitive art. He then decides that comedy and tragedy are, in turn, "late, and perhaps impermanent intellectual abstractions."[27] Eliot has already begun to integrate these Classicists' theory of the origin of Greek drama into his theory of the mind. If primitive mentality resembles immediate experience, its unity will not permit the abstractions into which the intellect dissects Reality. Such mental activity appears later in human development and is more superficial because it less resembles immediate experience itself. The origin of drama must therefore be closer to the nature of primitive mentality. The Classicists had demonstrated that "the drama was originally ritual; and ritual, consisting of a set of repeated movements, is essentially a dance,"[28] as Eliot could surmise from other anthropological studies as well. In order to find the origin of these rituals and dances, anthropologists attempted to discover the meaning of them, either by ascertaining what the ceremony meant to the primitive or by interpreting the significance of it themselves. In Royce's seminar Eliot had objected to such interpretations by outside observers because they introduced an extraneous point of view; so Eliot now observes of *The Sacred Dance: A Study in Comparative Folklore*[29] that its author, W. O. E. Oesterly, could have traced the evolution of these religious dances into drama, and that he unfortunately succumbed to the temptation of interpretation, offering "intelligible reasons" why the primitive performed these dances. As Eliot quotes Oesterly, "we suggest, then, that the origin of the sacred dance was the desire of early man to imitate what he conceived to be the characteristics of supernatural powers." Eliot notes that these primitive dancers probably "acted in a certain way and then found a reason for it."[30] By giving primacy to action first and then to reason, Eliot revives his contention, also originally made in the seminar, that, as Costello paraphrases, "the savage on a certain level interprets his ritual in a way probably not in accordance with its origin."[31]

Eliot proceeds to imply that the origin is, in fact, *prior* to interpretation either of the primitive or the anthropologist, that is, entirely prior to meaning, to reason. As Eliot argues, no interpretation of a ritual can ever account for its origin, because even the meaning that the participants may ascribe to their actions is in itself an interpretation. Furthermore, successive generations may attribute different meanings to the same basic ritual, which, in fact, may have begun "before 'meaning' meant anything at all." Eliot concludes that if the performers were suddenly persuaded that their behavior did not have the practical consequences that they had assumed, they would most likely abandon the ritual, "though with regret."[32] Eliot had advised in the seminar that, rather than explanations of primitive ritual in terms of meaning, there should be "nothing but a chronicle," as in Frazer's later editions of *The Golden Bough.* In addition, he also specified that there should be "no explanation in terms of *need.*"[33] By 'need', Eliot is referring to those reasons for which we perform certain kinds of behavior, and which give these actions meaning. Eliot sought, instead, an explanation for behavior through that aspect of the human mind which precedes the workings of the intelligence, indeed which precedes consciousness altogether, and yet which gives rise to consciousness and continually affects it. According to Eliot, Lévy-Bruhl had overlooked this determining factor in primitive mentality when he analyzed it from his own point of view as a modern man whose intellect functions in terms of logical reasoning: "he invents an elaborate 'prelogism' to account for the savage's identification of himself with his totem, where it is not certain that the savage, except so far as he had mental processes similar to his own, had any mental process at all."[34] Eliot therefore revises the evolution of civilized drama from those ritual dances, in which mystical participation may account for their content but not their origin, to conform to his concept of a preintellectual, preconscious 'desire' rather than the logical 'need':

> An unoccupied person, finding a drum, may be seized with a desire to beat it; but unless he is an imbecile he will be unable to continue beating it, and thereby satisfying a need (rather than a "desire"), without finding a reason for doing so.

For primitive man, Eliot suggests, the reason was to provoke rain, while the civilized would find a more "plausible" reason to beat the drum, which could be identified as comedy and tragedy.[35]

In order to discover the nature of this 'desire' that eventually becomes intellectualized into those abstractions, those reasons for drama itself, tragedy and comedy, Eliot returns again to the origin of drama in primitive experience, to ritual as its fundamental characteristic; he consults Aristotle for the basic components of drama: "'poetry, music, and dancing constitute in Aristotle a group by themselves, their common element being imitation by means of rhythm—rhythm which admits of being applied to words, sounds, and the movements of the body' (Butcher, p. 139)."[36] In seeking the unconscious origin of our sense of rhythm which develops from the beating of a drum into ritualistic dancing, Eliot calls upon his knowledge of scientific psychology to arrive at this crucial insight: whoever wishes to understand the "spirit" of dancing

must start by examining dance in primitive tribes, such as the
Australian ceremonies recounted by Spencer, Gillen, and Hewett;
he must consider the

> evolution of Christian and other liturgy. (For is not the High Mass—
> as performed, for instance, at the Madeleine in Paris—one of the
> highest developments of dancing?) And finally, he should track down
> the secrets of rhythm in the (still undeveloped) science of neurology.[37]

Our neurological system is that part of our physiology directly related to brain activity, and thus to thought and emotion. If the
sense of rhythm in our nervous system gives rise to dance and
then to ritual and ceremony, not only drama but also religion has a
physiological origin. In this way, Eliot unites religion and science,
the mind and the body.

The dialectic of Romanticism, opposing the spiritual and the
material, has thus been resolved in Eliot's theoretical synthesis.
The religious impulse does not have to be considered solely in
supernatural terms: it is inherent in our physiology. Because the
physiological unconscious is continuous with the psychological,
or collective-historical, unconscious, and thus with primitive
experience, the nature and the structure of that unconscious, according to Eliot, determine the nature of religious experience and
the structure of religion for civilized man. Eliot had already decided that the nature of religious experience at its most intense is a
mystical moment of unity similar to immediate experience which,
as the metaphysical unconscious, is also continuous with the
collective-historical unconscious. Now he is able to posit that the
structure of this psychological unconscious, the death-rebirth pattern that Frazer discovered to underlie all European, Mediterra-
nean, and other primitive religious myth and ritual that he had
examined, and the modern Judaeo-Christian tradition as well, in
terms of a sacrificial god or a life after death or a new life after
moral repentance, derives from the physiological unconscious.
Thus the structure of the most recent development in man's spiritual evolution, the Christian religion, is not only for Eliot the
structure of his unconscious mind, but also originates, however
remotely, in his very physical constitution. The same impulse
from the depths of his psyche and the tissues of his body that
prompted primitive man to beat his drum prompts modern man
to worship in a church or temple or mosque. For Eliot to control

and guide his mystical experiences—eruptions of or descents into the unconscious—according to the Christian religion would only be, therefore, to direct them according to the structure of their own origin.[38] Consequently, Eliot has finally formulated an intellectual justification for participating in the Christian Church.

2. A PHILOSOPHY OF ART: RITUAL, DANCE, DRAMA

Eliot's philosophy of religion becomes at the same time a philosophy of art, because both religion and art develop from the same source in primitive experience, ritual: "*all* art emulates the condition of ritual. That is what it comes from and to that it must always return for nourishment."[39] As a product of the primitive mind, ritual is the expression of a unified mentality. Living an undifferentiated wholeness similar to immediate experience, primitive man does not distinguish between the religious and the artistic; for him they are combined in a single activity. As the modern mentality develops through the disintegration of immediate experience into multiple points of view, conscious distinctions are made between the religious and the artistic, just as they are made between the self and the objects of the world, and between thought and emotion. Civilized art is thus a product of the same process that gives rise to our sense of self and other, of knowledge of a world separate from ourselves: Eliot speculates that "it is perhaps epistemology . . . that has given us the fine arts; for what was at first expression and behaviour may have developed under the complications of self-consciousness, as we become aware of ourselves as reacting aesthetically to the object" (*KE* 155).

That artistic and religious experience once were, and thus in some essential way still are, synonymous is a crucial discovery for Eliot-the-artist, who wished to create viable works of art for the modern world, as well as for Eliot-the-philosopher, who sought justification for religious experience as a modern man. Eliot contends that fine art evolved "incidentally" to the quest for talismans, magical objects. Considering the cases of the primitive Egyptian who molded a gold cowrie-shell, the Cretan who formed an octopus on his pottery, and the Indian who wore a bear's-tooth necklace, Eliot observes that they did not do so mainly for "decoration," but rather for the purpose of "invoking the assistance of life-giving amulets. At what point," he queries, "does the attempt to design and create an object for the sake of beauty become conscious? At what point in civilisation does any conscious distinction between practical or magical utility and aesthetic beauty arise?" The perceiving of such a distinction, Eliot believes, must indicate a development in man's sensibility of great significance. Eliot was therefore challenged to create art that would somehow again derive from and strive for the wholeness of primitive experience, the unity of the unconscious, the common source of religion and art: "Is it possible and justifiable for art, the creation of beautiful objects and of literature, to persist indefinitely without its primitive purposes: is it possible for the aesthetic object to be a *direct* object of attention?"[40]

The characteristic expression of the psychological and physiological unity of primitive experience is ritual. Since ritual is basically dance, Eliot explored the nature of dance in order to discover specifically those attributes of the primitive which were lacking in modern art, and which could be reintegrated into it. Because Eliot believed that the "highest forms" of dance are "the ballet and the mass,"[41] he decided that the modern ballet must possess ways of evoking the spiritual which could be adopted to other forms of art. Since the drama evolved directly out of ritual dancing, Eliot initially considered drama as that form of art most readily receptive to those lessons to be learned from the modern ballet: the contemporary ballet would, he believed, inspire the creation of a "new drama."[42] Eliot's philosophical speculations had their concrete counterpart in, and no doubt received great impetus from, the Ballets Russes of Serge Diaghilev and its star dancer and choreographer, Léonide Massine. Eliot had viewed with great delight their performances in London in 1919, 1921, and 1924.[43]

Eliot begins his esthetic inquiry into the relationship between ritual, drama, and ballet by transforming the findings of the Cambridge Classicists into a theory of his own: the "stage—not only in its remote origins, but always—is a ritual"; thus, the inability of modern drama to "satisfy the craving for ritual" is primarily responsible for its not being a "living art."[44] Ritual is able to stir the unconscious mind, and serve as an expression of it, through rhythm, which reaches the unconscious by stimulating us physiologically. For Eliot, as drama has loosened its form, it has diminished its "therapeutic value," for which audiences have begun to turn to the ballet:

The play, like a religious service, should be a stimulant to make life more tolerable and augment our ability to live; it should stimulate partly by the action of vocal rhythms on what, in our ignorance, we call the nervous system.[45]

Although the most distinctive aspect of rhythm in the drama would be verbal, rhythm is also inherent in the action of a play, both the strategic action of the plot and the physical actions of the actors. For Eliot, if rhythm cannot be found on the modern stage, either in contemporary prose or verse drama, and if it is ignored or misunderstood in recent productions of Shakespeare's plays, rhythm nevertheless makes Massine and Charlie Chaplin "great actors" and Rastelli's juggling "more cathartic" than *A Doll's House*.[46]

Such rhythm of action and acting depends upon an organizing pattern or form. On the basis of his anthropological reading, Eliot believes that such a structure derives from ritual; constructing his own dialectic of drama, he asserts that the possibilities for dramatic form can be thought to comprise a line whose endpoints are liturgy—the arrow-dance of the Todas, he suggests—and realism—Sir Arthur Pinero being his example. The form of any "genuine" drama is created by the location on the line where a "tension" between liturgy and realism occurs. Whereas in Marivaux, Congreve, Aeschylus, and *Everyman* this tension arises, Ibsen and Chekhov, however, represent the "extreme limit" beyond which drama no longer possesses esthetic structure.[47] Not only the modern theater, but all British drama since the Renaissance except for Shakespeare and Jonson, even that of their Elizabethan contemporaries of whom Eliot was so fond, strives, in his view, for realism. Eliot finds this attempt to become more and more realistic English drama's "great vice." Not surprisingly, only in the medieval morality play *Everyman* does Eliot find realistic action conforming to an underlying structure (*SE* 93).

The death-rebirth pattern that shapes the plot of Everyman's spiritual journey through the world and allegorically through his life comes from the ritual structure embodied in the religion communally professed by the society in which the play was written. Approaching drama as he does from the standpoint of ritual, Eliot decides that the form required by modern drama will be a function of convention, as ritual is an accepted pattern of behavior, a set of standard movements periodically repeated: "the realism of the ordinary stage is something to which we can no longer respond, because to us it is no longer realistic." Since the mundane world is insufficient as a dramatic medium, rather than assuming that stage action is an imitation, Eliot suggests that we "adopt a literal untruth, a thorough-going convention, a ritual."[48] Applying the idealist critique of everyday experience to drama, Eliot argues that realistic action is not 'real' in itself because it does not partake of and thus simulate the unconscious, the Reality of immediate experience. The convention necessary for modern drama must be like ritual, a deeper and more pervasive organizing of reality than dramatic conventions are customarily: although the everyday world must supply the subject matter, an "abstraction from actual life" is the essential component of a work of art (SE 93). According to Eliot, below the reality that we consciously construct out of the unity of immediate experience we must recover those feelings and structures more basic to our nature than the dramatic conventions that we devise intellectually. Then we must make the chaotic multiplicity of our world conform to these primitive patterns and express these fundamental impulses through a stylization of stage action. Rather than conventions of verse or genre that have been employed by dramatists in the past, Eliot desires "some quite new selection or structure or distortion in subject matter or technique; any form or rhythm imposed upon the world of action" (SE 93–94).

The appropriate nature of the stage convention that Eliot sought was suggested to him by Diaghilev's modern ballet, which is "more simplified, and simplifies more; and what is needed of art is a simplification of current life into something rich and strange."[49] Immediately Eliot reveals that he considers dance to be a type of ritual. The form of modern ballet, its stylization of bodily gesture and human action, like ritual, simulates immediate experience, the spiritual richness of primitive experience with its diverse points of view unified through mystical participation, and at the same time conveys the potential awe and terror, the strangeness, that would accompany such a confrontation with the unconscious, with the whole of Reality. Because only ritual expresses unconscious impulses and can in turn reach back again into the unconscious, in part through its rhythmic effect upon our nervous system, modern drama, Eliot argues, should adopt its form from the ballet.

One consequence of making modern drama conform more closely to the ballet, and to ritual, is that the acting must approach dancing more closely. Like immediate experience, ritual and dance are for Eliot impersonal. Ordinarily in realistic drama, the actor's "stage personality has to be supplied from and confounded with his real personality" (*SE* 95). But because the ballet is an artistic tradition more than three hundred years old,[50] it has developed over the centuries a "strict form"; thus in this art the form rather than the actor's personality determines the nature of his movements and the course of the action. Rather than the degree or kind of emotion projected, what makes a dancer great and not simply competent for Eliot is the "vital flame, that impersonal, and, if you like, inhuman force which transpires between each of the great dancer's movements. So it would be in a strict form of drama" (*SE* 95). Eliot had an example of the ritualistic actor of the future on the contemporary realistic stage in Ion Swinley; never expressing his personality, Swinley becomes on stage "a figure, a marionette; his acting is abstract and simplified"; the "mask-like beauty" of his facial expressions and his stylized body postures are quite different from the ordinary manner of acting. Eliot regrets, at the same time, that Swinley has not had the training in movement and gesture that only the ballet can supply. As Eliot confesses, Massine is for him the "greatest actor" to be performing in London at the time. Massine, being the "most completely unhuman, impersonal, abstract," is a representative of the drama to come, because, unlike the "conventional gesture" of the theater, intended simply to "*express*" emotion, Massine's "abstract gesture," instead, "*symbolises*" emotion.[51]

The conventional stage attempts to duplicate that reality our consciousness constructs by separating the unity of immediate experience into the various components of our world. From this multiplicity of points of view, we become aware of emotions as separate entities from the objects that accompany them and from the consciousness that experiences them. An actor on the conventional stage, therefore, seeking to imitate this reality in which emotion is considered to be a separate object isolated by itself, will try to 'express' it through his gestures which simulate the real world. Since the ballet as ritual is attempting to simulate immediate experience, on the other hand, the dancer strives to 'symbolize' the emotion, become the emotion himself. Because they partake of the unity of immediate experience which ritual derives from and portrays, the emotion and the object experiencing it, the dancer, are one. Moreover, because the ritualistic primitive mentality approximates a single finite center, a unified point of view, any alien point of view, any interpretation, will destroy this wholeness. For this reason, the realistic drama is unacceptable to Eliot as a modern art form because, in relying upon the personality of the actor, it interposes an "interpretation" between the action itself and the potential participants in the action, the audience: the actor can "interpret" or "alter" the "direct relationship" between the play and the person in the theater (*SE* 96). Only in ritual, whose form determines the action, is the work of art completed and not altered by the participation of both actors and audience in its predetermined structure and pattern.

Like personality or our sense of self, ideas are also constructed when the finite center breaks down into a number of points of view through which we become conscious of ourselves as an object in space and time, and through which we can regard other objects simultaneously from different points of view. Drama whose action is organized around a given idea in order to communicate or illustrate a philosophy, such as Shaw's, is also unacceptable as modern art for Eliot, because it effects only a superficial union between the idea that governs the action and the emotion that the action stirs, and thus reflects the fragmentary personality itself. The idea is too weakly formulated to achieve a significant unity of experience and the emotion comes only from the idea and not from experience. Action for Eliot must be determined by a structure which derives from the unconscious and not by ideas that are personal and incomplete. Eliot again consults Aristotle to help him define the ritualistic drama he wishes to establish, for the Greek drama Aristotle analyzed was closer to its primitive origins than any subsequent dramatic tradition:

> The undigested "idea" or philosophy, the idea-emotion, is to be found also in poetic dramas which are conscientious attempts to adapt a true structure, Athenian or Elizabethan, to contemporary feeling. It appears sometimes as the attempt to supply the defect of structure by an internal structure. "But most important of all is the structure of the incidents. For Tragedy is an imitation, not of men, but of an action and of life, and life consists in action, and its end is a mode of action, not a quality." (*Poetics,* vi. 9. Butcher's translation.) (*SW* 67)

Through the modern ballet of Diaghilev, then, Eliot perceived one way in which primitive experience could be reintegrated into modern art. The stylized movements of Massine within the ritualistic progress of the dance suggested that modern drama must also approach ritual by partaking of that rhythmic mode of expression characteristic of the ballet. In addition to this fine art, one other contemporary art form supplied Eliot with a concrete example of ritualistic expression toward which modern art should strive. The folk art of the music hall, with its unique kind of humor, demonstrated one other way through which the modern artist could recover the unity of primitive experience. As with the ballet, Eliot's anthropological studies provided him with a theoretical justification for what was his instant attraction to music-hall entertainment ever since he took up residence in London.[52]

Eliot perceives the music-hall comedian to be the modern incarnation of a very old stock drama character—the Fool. He devises an evolutionary origin for the Fool of Elizabethan drama based on the discovery of the Cambridge Classicists that tragedy and comedy develop out of the same ritualistic origin. Taking Shakespeare as an example, Eliot believes that the Fool in *King Lear,* for instance, derives from the tribal priest-god of primitive societies, whom not only Murray and Cornford but also Frazer had studied: Lear's Fool is a "*possessed;* a very cunning and very intuitive person; he has more than a suggestion of the shaman or medicine man." Such other Fool-like figures as the witches in *Macbeth* and Caliban, Eliot notes, indicate that the Fool is not exclusively a comic character but has a serious side as well. Considering the porter in *Macbeth* and Antony in the scene on Pompey's galley as generic Fools, Eliot observes that in these cases there is "no question of supernatural powers"; although they are comic when compared to the tragedy around them, still, each character is a "master of the situation." As drama developed, the comedy became distinct as the comic servant, and the seriousness, or tragedy, became distinct as the powerful hero. Eliot notes that the similarity between the Fool and the comic servant is implied in plays where the supernatural power is divorced from the servant; Faustus and Friar Bacon, for example, possess this power while their servants are simply comic. Although these instances do not offer a "complete Fool," Eliot observes that the "prototype" of the "true" Fool occurs in St. George and the Dragon, the Mummer's play that is the English rendition of the Perseus myth. Eliot points out that the doctor who revives St. George is usually played as a comic character.[53]

The true Fool, therefore, plays both a comic and a serious role in the action of the drama and in fact has at once a comic and tragic status. Such a character as Shakespeare's Fool in *Lear* is really a blending of the comic and the serious into a form of humor beyond the distinctions of comic and tragic. Jonson's satiric comedies have the same effect: Eliot decides that between the tragedies and comedies of either Shakespeare or Jonson there exists a "relation," indicating that both dramatists each possessed a "personal point of view which can be called neither comic nor tragic" (*SE* 141). Both approach the unity of the primitive sensibility that preceded and incorporated into itself the subsequent intellectual distinctions of comic and tragic; for Eliot, these "abstractions" must be "replaced" or "renewed" after their prolonged development over the course of several centuries of Western culture. Since "we have lost the drum,"[54] we must recover the rhythm of primitive ritual that embodied the unity of our unconscious; part of that rhythm is a synthesis of the tragic and the comic.

The tragic and the comic were unified in primitive ritual in the person of the priest-god. This religious leader and healer was also an entertainer and an artist. Eliot recounts how a field anthropologist studying a primitive tribe was fortunate enough to hear its "*Shikkamim,* or wandering bards, prophets, and medicine-men, recite or chant, to the music of the *pippin* or one-stringed gourd, the traditional poetry of love, warfare, and theology."[55] Eliot views the modern artist as a descendent of these priest-poets, participating in the same kind of unity of sensibility that was the primitive's through the serious humor of satire, the civilized synthesis of the comic and tragic. Tellingly, Eliot refers to Wyndham Lewis as a "magician" in his review of *Tarr* just as he is about to observe that the artist is more primitive as well as more civilized than his contemporaries. Like the ritualistic ballet dancer, Lewis is "deliberate, frigid," "inhuman."[56] Lewis is for Eliot only the most recent representative of a long tradition of British satire. In *Tarr* there is, according to Eliot, an aspect of British humor that is "serious and savage," to which Baudelaire was attracted. Lewis shares this quality with Hogarth, Rowlandson, and Cruikshank, Eliot observes, because, as a painter, his imagination most often functions visually. His humor resembles that of Dickens as well, who also had a visual imagination when he was being "humorous and not consciously droll."[57] Eliot continues to define the tradition by noting elsewhere that Lewis's humor is close to that of Dickens in an admirable way because it is not too far from that of Ben Jonson.[58]

According to Eliot, Jonson's comedy of humors originates in a liberation of unconscious impulses. Jonson constructs his characters by giving a seemingly human form to a primitive instinct emerging from below the level of his consciousness. In order to construct these symbols of unconscious feelings, Jonson employed a kind of simplification in his satires similar to that intrinsic to the ballet as an art form. By depriving his characters of numerous individual traits whose conflicting variety would have endowed them with a realistic personality, a character for Jonson *becomes* the humor for which he is named, and is synonymous with it. Because the character symbolizes rather than expresses the given emotion, he approximates the unity of immediate experience that is primitive mentality. Since these characters embody impulses of Jonson's unconscious, the resulting drama is a portrayal of the unconscious itself, of primitive experience within the civilized world. When Jonson developed a new dramatic genre with *Every Man in His Humour,* Eliot observes, Jonson was just "recognizing unconsciously" the artistic form that would most readily accommodate his "instincts." His characters are "simplified" by a reducing of "detail" and a retaining of only those qualities appropriate to the "relief of an emotional impulse" from which the character never varies as he confronts a given setting. Eliot advises that this "stripping is essential to the art, to which is also essential a flat distortion in the drawing. . . . It is a great caricature, which is beautiful; and a great humour, which is serious" (*SE* 138).

Eliot finds the same subliminal qualities of Jonson's and Lewis's art in those caricaturists who comprise the visual counterpart of this tradition of British humor. Impressed by the primitive "ferocity" of their distorted images, Eliot observes that he always considered Lewis's "design at its greatest when it approached the border of satire and caricature." Eliot remembers that for Baudelaire English caricature is characterized by "*féroce,*" "*spleen,*" and "*violence.*"[59] This liberation of the unconscious in British satire also lives on in the serious humor of the music hall, whose primitive qualities civilized drama, like Shakespeare and Jonson, once had, and modern drama again requires. Eliot wonders why the "directness, frankness, and ferocious humour which survive" in the music-hall comedians is "extinct," and "so odious to the British public, in precisely those forms of art in which they are most needed, and in which, in fact, they used to flourish."[60]

Eliot views the contemporary music hall, like Diaghilev's modern ballet, as ritual, in terms of the extravagant, fantastical, and thus savage, quality of its humor, and the participation required of the audience during the comedy routines and musical numbers. The most famous performers of the original music hall are of Lancashire origin, and Eliot observes that "Lancashire wit is mordant, ferocious, and personal; the Lancashire music-hall is excessively *intime;* success depends upon the relation established by a comedian of strong personality with an audience quick to respond with approval or contempt."[61] In this ritual of satiric comedy, jokes that depend upon "exaggeration" become the medium of communication and establish a kind of social, or tribal, unity. Through the exchange of words and laughter, comedian-priest and audience-worshippers participate in a litany of humor. Eliot suggests that the resulting ritual resembles some of the more exuberant and licentious primitive rites and celebrations: most music-hall comedians are "a kind of grotesque; their acts are an orgy of parody of the human race" (*SE* 406). Sometimes the audience participates with "jeering or hostile comment" (*SE* 405) as well as laughter to interrupt the ceremony, and the comedian-magician must rely upon her superior cleverness to work a spell of silence: the "fierce talent" of Nellie Wallace "holds the most boisterous music-hall in complete subjection";[62] "I have seen her, hardly pausing in her act, make some quick retort that silenced her tormentors for the rest of the evening" (*SE* 405).

The comedy of the revue, which evolved out of the music hall and was in the process of replacing it, is in quality perhaps a more successful integration of the primitive and the modern than its predecessor. Reminiscent of a modern ballet dancer such as Massine, Ethel Levey is the "most aloof and impersonal of personalities; indifferent, rather than contemptuous, towards the audience; her appearance and movement are of an extremely modern type of beauty. Hers is not a broad farce, but a fascinating inhuman grotesquerie." Eliot notes that her humor is characteristically bizarre, a "*bizarrerie* more mature, perhaps more cosmopolitan," than that of the music-hall comedian. But Eliot nevertheless finds the revue to be inferior to the music hall because that element of audience involvement, crucial to ritual itself, is lacking: Levey "plays for herself rather than for the audience."[63]

For this reason, Marie Lloyd was Eliot's favorite comedian. As the priest-artist, she represented the spiritual values of her community, the collective representations that made it a cohesive social structure. Through her comedy routines she conducted a ritual that renewed these shared values in the minds of its members; each individual again recognized that he belonged to a larger social group, and thus was reassured of his place in the felt whole that is the collective conscience. Recalling this function of the priest-artist in primitive religious ceremony, Eliot terms Lloyd's superiority as a performer a "moral superiority," for she was distinguished by "her understanding of the people and sympathy with them, and the people's recognition of the fact that she embodied the virtues which they genuinely most respected in private life." She had the "capacity for expressing the soul of the people" and the "dignity of their own lives" (SE 406–7).

This participatory aspect of the music-hall comedy, both a sympathetic sharing of common beliefs and values, and an actual involvement in the action of the routine itself, makes the music-hall comic sketch a ritual. Such ritualistic participation is for Eliot an essential quality of art, especially drama: "the working man who went to the music-hall and saw Marie Lloyd and joined in the chorus was himself performing part of the act; he was engaged in that collaboration of the audience with the artist which is necessary in all art and most obviously in dramatic art" (SE 407). Only a live performance, and only one like a comedy routine in which the comedian solicits audience involvement, can approach ritual. Eliot was particularly hostile to such forms of entertainment of modern civilization as silent movies because the audience was entirely excluded from direct contact with the action; even a live stage would be better: the working man will now attend the "cinema, where his mind is lulled by continuous senseless music and continuous action too rapid for the brain to act upon, and will receive, without giving, in . . . listless apathy." Eliot once again consults anthropology for proof that this absence of ritual in modern life, perpetuated by the gradual replacement of theaters with movie houses, opposes basic human nature as defined by the primitive. Eliot notes that, in Essays on the Depopulation of Melanesia, W. H. R. Rivers had concluded from his research that the native population is decreasing because the "'civilization' forced upon them has deprived them of all interest in life. They are dying from pure boredom" (SE 407).

3. THE POETIC DRAMA AND THE DRAMATIC POEM

If art is essentially ritual, as Eliot has learned from his examination of primitive experience, then the principal way to make modern art express its unconscious origins is to make it more ritualistic: by investing it with a structure recalling the death-rebirth pattern of primitive rites and ancient drama, with a rhythmic stylization similar to the modern ballet, and with a savage, serious humor and social awareness like the music hall. Since drama evolved out of primitive religious ritual, Eliot was continually preoccupied throughout his life with reinvigorating the modern dramatic form, especially by reinstituting poetry as a dramatic medium. Grover Smith[64] and D. E. Jones[65] have demonstrated how ancient rituals and myths provide the structure for Eliot's own plays; Carol Smith,[66] finding the Cambridge Classicists to be a governing influence on Eliot's dramatic craft, has devoted a study of his drama to its various levels of ritual, including overt ritualistic stage action and underlying Greek and Christian ritual patterns.

Eliot's first dramatic experiment, *Sweeney Agonistes: Fragments of an Aristophanic Melodrama* (1924–26), derives its structure directly from the prototypical ancient dramatic ritual that Cornford had defined: Eliot, in fact, wrote Hallie Flanagan in 1933 that before she performed the play at Vassar she should read *The Origins of Attic Comedy.* Convinced that the music hall was one of the few surviving rituals in modern life, Eliot imported for his drama the colloquial vernacular and low-life figures characteristic of its comedy, and the jazzlike rhythms of its repartee and music. Considering the modern ballet to be another contemporary ritual, Eliot wished to duplicate its 'inhuman' symbolizing of emotion and stylization of action in an effort to recover the primitive rhythm inherent in ritual. Since the drum was lost, he would revive it in a modern form: he advises Flanagan that the actors should wear masks and that their elocution should have little expression; the entire production should be accompanied by soft drum beats that highlight the accented syllables of the verse, which, during the chorus, should mimic a jackhammer.[67]

Eliot's next involvement with the drama was not until 1934, when he wrote the choruses for *The Rock,* a religious pageant intended to raise money for the construction of churches. Signifi-

cantly, Eliot referred to *The Rock* as a "*revue*," and the characters
again wore masks when performing. Still maintaining the music
hall as his criterion of modern dramatic ritual even in this overtly
religious production, Eliot said that his sole theatrical purpose was
to demonstrate that the Chorus has a place in modern drama.[68]
Eliot perceived the Chorus as the one viable convention of Greek
ritualistic drama through which he could either achieve or simulate the kind of audience participation he had witnessed at the music hall. If the audience could not speak in unison the words with
chorus members, they could nevertheless identify with the Chorus
as a group of ordinary people like themselves, for the Chorus did
not participate in the dramatic action proper and usually voiced
the sentiments of the common man as observer; the Chorus, perhaps at one time the audience itself, now at least symbolized it and
gave its feelings a role in the drama.

The ritualistic sacrifice underlying the black humor of *Sweeney
Agonistes* overtly assumes its religious significance in Eliot's first
mature dramatic work, *Murder in the Cathedral* (1935). In this play
Eliot again incorporates into the plot action elements of Greek dramatic ritual as Thomas prepares himself to die. Through this ritual
structure, Eliot suggests that a martyr of the Church reenacts on a
different level the sacrifice of the dying and reborn god, Jesus for
Christianity, in order to save his people. Employing what he
learned from his experience with *The Rock,* Eliot uses the Chorus
to represent the audience and draw us into the drama by portraying the reactions and responses of admiration, fear, and bewilderment which we would supposedly have to the action if given the
chance to speak. In this play Eliot involves the audience as actively
and intimately as is possible on the modern stage by having the
Knights directly address the audience after the murder to solicit
our sympathy. Our moral values are evoked, however complexly
and deviously, as the comedy of Marie Lloyd engaged those of her
audience.

In *The Family Reunion* (1939), the religious aspect of ritual
becomes covert again, as Eliot patterns the plot of a modern
drawing-room melodrama after an ancient Greek drama that derives its structure from the primitive dramatic ritual defined
by Cornford: the *Oresteia* of Aeschylus. As the hero of *Murder in
the Cathedral* was analogous to, but a level below, the dying-
resurrected god, so the hero of *The Family Reunion* is analogous to,
but a step below, the religious martyr: a sinner seeking moral re-

demption, a sufferer wishing to be spiritually reborn. The Chorus remains but is now composed of the characters on the stage, who are all ordinary people. The Christian rituals and sacraments of the previous play become stylized ritualistic speech and movements, like, for instance, the end of the play when the characters revolve around a birthday cake chanting.

Eliot's later plays become more realistic, and less poetic, but still retain a structure based upon a Greek drama of ritualistic origin. *The Cocktail Party* (1949), for instance, refers to *Alcestis* of Euripides, in which is portrayed a death and a subsequent rebirth through divine agency. Ritual is now portrayed, not through stylized behavior, but just through a given social custom that suggests a religious ceremony; thus, the cocktail party functions in the play as a Eucharistic celebration. The psychiatrist Harcourt-Reilly has a role in the action of the play similar to the primitive medicine man, the doctor of Cornford's ritual comedy, bringing about the spiritual rebirth of the principal characters.

Eliot's experiments in modern drama, as he himself was to admit late in life, were not entirely successful as works of art.[69] Eliot's enthusiasm for the drama actually appears to be an offshoot of a more compelling and pervasive effort to revive an art form closer to the true nature of his creativity, poetry. Significantly, Eliot's first mature poems had a dramatic character. The dramatic element of this early poetry surely helped him to appreciate the esthetic possibilities of ritual and myth which he soon encountered through his studies in anthropology. These primitive forms of expression, inherently dramatic themselves, would be readily accommodated by the kind of verse he was writing and could, in turn, strengthen and enrich its dramatic quality. Eliot perceived at once the ritualistic, or rhythmic, elements of the theater that ally it with poetry but was never comfortable creatively with those inevitably mimetic and realistic aspects—the play as a copy of life and, in turn, as a live physical production—which make it drama. Both realism and reality encumbered his artistic expression, despite his later recognition of their necessity (*SE* 162, for instance).

Although Eliot applauded the ability of such dramatic forms as the ballet to communicate to us physiologically through our sense of rhythm and thus reach the unconscious, he wanted at the same time to integrate the modern mind as he found it, to unify both the senses and the intellect in a single esthetic effort to reach below the level of consciousness. The artist is, after all, both primitive *and* civilized. Eliot will acknowledge that "the egregious merit of Chaplin is that he has escaped in his own way from the realism of the cinema and invented a *rhythm*,"[70] that, likewise, the juggling of Rastelli "appeals to our sense of beauty of form" and the modern ballet to "the senses,"[71] that is, to the sense of rhythm in our nervous system. But at the same time he recognizes that the resulting esthetic experience is strictly visual, and can only engage the mind to a limited degree. For this reason, Eliot criticizes the contemporary avant-garde theater of Russia and Germany for allowing visual "spectacle" to obscure dramatic structure. Although the abstract stage sets and stylized groupings of actors may be emotionally stimulating and even have symbolic implications, these productions, in his opinion, do not engage the intelligence. Eliot's criticism of silent movies reveals at once the source of his discontent and inadvertently the true nature of his creativity: because the cinema functions "without words," it is a "potent agent against the intellect."[72] For Eliot, words have logical meanings and at the same time a rhythmic dimension which stirs us physiologically; consequently, only in poetry can the mind and the body be fully integrated. Thus Eliot contends that the verbal component of ancient drama supplied the rhythm that could carry the mind back to the unconscious: when Aristotle specified that the proper result of tragedy is catharsis, he had witnessed "dramatic performance only in rhythmic form," and thus did not have the opportunity to consider "how far the catharsis could be effected by the moral or intellectual significance of the play *without* its verse form and proper declamation."[73] Indicative of his reliance upon poetry and its verbal rhythms as an artistic medium, Eliot cannot conceive of a contemporary theater apart from the poetic: the dramatic form of the future must be a poetic drama that consists of "new verse forms."[74]

Understandably, then, every esthetic innovation that Eliot wishes to introduce through a modern poetic drama could also be achieved as well in poetry alone. As Eliot was later to observe, "poetry begins, I dare say, with a savage beating a drum in a jungle" (*UPUC* 155). Eliot's new kind of drama is, of course, based upon the ritualistic Classical drama, in which the components of "thought, word, and scene, of visual and aural rhythm, form a unity."[75] Eliot initially accomplished this same unity of expression deriving from primitive experience, not in his poetic drama, but in his first long poem, *The Waste Land,* because poetry always was for Eliot inherently dramatic, and yet, being poetry, permitted a rhythmic stylization of life unencumbered by the realities that the stage cannot avoid or must inevitably acknowledge. Pondering the fact that Browning composed "dull plays" and yet invented the dramatic monologue, Eliot surmised years before his first dramatic effort that when the poetic drama has "wholly disappeared," as currently it is a "lost art," then the "natural evolution" for writers would be to follow Browning's lead, "to distil the dramatic essences" and "infuse them into some other liquor."[76]

The kind of verse that helped Eliot find his mature poetic voice was itself dramatic in nature: the "form" of his first poems of 1908 and 1909 was "directly drawn" from Laforgue and late Elizabethan drama.[77] After avidly digesting the powerful speeches of Elizabethan and Jacobean poetic drama, Eliot would certainly have felt that poetry expresses the most intense emotion only within a dramatic situation consisting of a persona whose identity is separate from the author's, and who addresses other characters and an audience according to particular circumstances dictated by plot action. This notion that poetry is inherently dramatic stayed with Eliot throughout his life. In "The Three Voices of Poetry" (1953), he explains that the first voice, of the lyric, expressing the poet's deepest personal feelings (PP 107), is never separate from the second voice, with which a poet addresses an audience, even if they are merely overhearing him (PP 108). The addition of character in the form of a persona or mask, and of a sense of situation from the third voice, of drama (PP 111), actually creates what Eliot calls the fourth voice of Browning's dramatic monologues (PP 103). Eliot has difficulty distinguishing this dramatic monologue from a speech of a play precisely because he resists the mimetic tendency of drama which differentiates it as an art form from poetry. Thus Eliot treats the language of verse drama as a subsidiary of poetry when in fact it is a different mode of discourse or artistic communication, despite its resemblances to poetry; its context and goal are ultimately mimesis, not authorial meditation or self-expression. At the same time, Eliot views the lyric, the first voice, in dramatic terms, as always a form of addressing: "the voice of the poet talking *to* himself, or *to* nobody" (PP 96; my emphasis). He seldom recognizes the true lyric voice, the poet simply *talking*, which he comes to term "'meditative verse'" (PP 106); yet it appears periodically in all of his poetry, and most frequently in *Four Quartets*.

Eliot's early monologues are, in fact, a peculiar blend of the lyric and the dramatic that makes them 'internal' monologues, as distinct from Browning's more typical dramatic monologues and some Metaphysical lyrics, which overtly acknowledge a definite external situation and a specific if silent interlocutor.[78]

By the time Eliot writes *The Waste Land,* he has come to perceive the individual and society as inextricably related. The self-inflicted indictment of himself in the early monologues and the succeeding condemnation of others in the quatrain satires are united in the self-implication inherent in *The Waste Land.* Such an identification of himself with the plight of society can be attributed in part to the nature of the ritual that Eliot incorporates into that poem. Perhaps the most important technical innovation to arise out of Eliot's sense of poetry as drama is the derivation of a structure for the longer poem from ritual patterns. Since poetry is for Eliot dramatic by nature, and since drama is fundamentally ritual, as studies of primitive experience had indicated, Eliot wrote three long poems which essentially *are* rituals. Eliot the poet performs through poetry the same rite that the ritualistic structure would dictate a religious celebrant to perform. The first poetic ritual is *The Waste Land,* in which Eliot patterns the poetic action after a composite of ancient fertility rituals; *Ash Wednesday* and *Four Quartets* also display ritual structures.[79]

But just as Eliot evolved a philosophy of religion as well as a philosophy of art out of his examination of primitive experience, so his use of ritual in the practice of art has certain implications for the practice of religion. Eliot has not only solved the esthetic problem of form in a long poem when the preoccupation of the post-Romantic twentieth century with organic form renders such extraneous structures as metric regularity, stanzas, and cantos inadequate. He has also solved the problem of participation in an established religion when the pervasive post-Naturalistic skepticism of the twentieth century makes literal belief difficult, if not impossible. Since religious experience is essentially ritualistic, reaching the unconscious in part physiologically through rhythm, and through primitive patterns of experience underlying the dogma and Scripture of modern religion today, would not religion consist of our engaging these rituals and myths at an unconscious level, rather than just consciously and intellectually? Out of his reading of anthropological studies of primitive experience, combined with his other interests in philosophy and psychology, Eliot will recognize and develop one more crucial esthetic innovation, the 'mythic method', and, in turn, evolve a uniquely modern mode of religious participation, 'mythic consciousness', both of which integrate the primitive and the civilized through the perspective of myth.

V. MYTHIC CONSCIOUSNESS

ELIOT perceived myth, like ritual, to be an essential aspect of primitive experience.[1] In his view, after the sense of rhythm inherent in the nervous system led to the savage's drum beat, when the resulting tribal dance evolved into a ritual, various stories were devised to accompany the ceremony and explain why it was performed. Although ritual is thus more fundamental, myth is nevertheless an integral expression of primitive mentality also, because for thinking beings reasons inevitably become necessary to justify behavior. Since the mind is physiological, the same unconscious process that instigated the rhythm that led to rituals must in some way be responsible as well for the myths that evolve from them. But myths in themselves constitute richer, more comprehensive reasons for action than the subsequent philosophical or scientific explanations characteristic of modern civilization. As the most rudimentary expression of the human intellect, myths combine the simplest of logical thinking with the emotional and the spiritual. Only later when various myths began to be perceived apart from their religious function, sometimes losing it entirely, would this original unity disperse into separate rational and esthetic components. As Cornford demonstrated, for instance, the eventual development of Greek philosophy and science from mythic origins was accompanied by a more detached viewpoint and cavalier treatment of the original stories,[2] and Harrison even suspected Homer's rendition of ancient lore to be "essentially literary rather than religious, sceptical and moribund already in its very perfection."[3]

The creation of and reliance upon myth as an explanation must then be practically as primitive an exercise of the mind as ritual experience itself. Like rituals, the various myths of primitive civilizations assume their appropriate place in the historical unconscious and become a part of the collective mind of modern man. Although all myths are essentially religious in origin, serving to explain the nature of reality through recourse to the supernatural, not all of them display the death-rebirth pattern as distinctly as the myths and rituals Frazer had examined. As Durkheim and Lévy-Bruhl had found, myths as the collective representations of a primitive society originate as religious justifications for the existence of that society and reflect the life of the tribe as well. Often embodied in myths, therefore, are a variety of social customs, religious practices, and behavioral attitudes. Some myths in their evolved form may ostensibly seem remote from religious concerns, but having once been integral to religious experience, they retain the religious dimension of the rituals which they once accompanied: that rhythmic, cathartic ability to stir the unconscious and satisfy the religious impulse.

Eliot decides that myths, as an inherent part of unconscious experience, must partake of its unifying tendency. He proceeds to define an artistic technique, the mythic method, that is based upon this organizing function of the unconscious mind. The mythic method's deliberate fusion of myth and contemporary experience into a work of art suggests to Eliot how the skeptical, self-conscious modern mind operates, and, in turn, how the obstacle of literal belief in a dogma can be overcome through a new kind of religious experience, mythic consciousness.

1. A THEORY OF MYTH

Being well-read in anthropology, Eliot is particularly aware that the nature of a society will affect the nature of its religion, and that any myth will thus have simultaneously a religious and a social function. From an anthropological perspective, assessing British society as a racial whole, Eliot observes that "humour is distinctively English";[4] the principal cultural product of the English sensibility for Eliot is the evolution of a 'serious humor' in literature and the other arts. The mythic accompaniment of the ritual of Jonson's satiric comedy and its contemporary development, the comedy routine of the music-hall comedian, Eliot perceives to be the "romantic Englishman," that recurring character of British art and culture who embodies the national spirit: comic, gregarious, fun-loving, good-natured, hard-drinking. As Eliot traces his evolution, Sir Tunbelly Clumsy, Sir Giles Overreach, Squire Western, and Sir Sampson Legend are "different contributions by distinguished mythmakers to the chief myth which the Englishman has built about himself." Such a lineage proliferates because a myth, like a ritual, possesses an underlying structure that remains constant through successive embodiments; the structure may be a pattern of action, or a certain tendency of behavior, a specific combination of character traits: "the myth that a man makes has transformations according as he sees himself as hero or villain, as young or old, but it is essentially the same myth." Although Tom Jones may not be the same character, Eliot oberves that he is still the embodiment of the same myth as is Squire Western. Midshipman Easy is a representative as well, while Falstaff is "elevated above" the myth, greater than a "national character." Tennyson's "broad-shouldered genial Englishman" is related to Tunbelly Clumsy, while such contemporaries as G. K. Chesterton, if and when he drinks beer, and J. C. Squire, if and when he plays cricket, also participate in the myth.[5]

But Eliot fears that this mythic tradition, especially in its more respectable and official form, is moribund: even "in that great but decadent humourist, Dickens, and in some of his contemporaries it is on the way to the imbecilities of *Punch*."[6] Assessing its contemporary form, Eliot regrets that the "English myth" is at present "pitiably diminished." The "modern" John Bull, a cartoon character in *Punch* like Britannia, is merely a "degenerate descendent," a blend of Podsnap and Bottomley. Consequently, John Bull is neither the cultural "force" that he used to be, nor a significant influence in politics. As Eliot perceived the theater to be the inevitable vehicle for the enactment of a modern ritual, since drama is essentially ritual, so he again finds the stage to be the appropriate perpetuator of the national myth, for myth and ritual are inextricably related. However, although the theater may be the "best platform" for the myth, it "affords in our time singularly little relief." As the contemporary stage was too realistic to serve as a ritual, so the modern drama functions on a too exclusively intellectual level to supply a myth: a character of the "serious stage," Eliot contends, is either a commonplace, unexceptional human being, and thus boring, or is "confected of abstract qualities, as loyalty, greed and so on, to which we are supposed to respond with proper abstract emotions." The response of the audience must be solicited at a deeper, more unified level.

In the context of this criticism of the modern stage, Eliot presents his theory of the nature of myth and how it functions. Myths, for Eliot, actually resemble the unconscious mind, since they are patterns that turn the chaos of our world into a unity similar to immediate experience. As he believes, reality comes to each one of us individually in the form of this finite center, having its own particular way of perceiving the world and of organizing everyday experience. Before the intellect has dissected and analyzed it, this unconscious feeling enjoys a unity according to which emotions are not objectified as isolated abstract entities, but rather form an indistinguishable whole with the object that accompanies them. A myth consists of this point of view, this unconscious structure of our experience as expressed through the various components of our world. Always having a remote sense of immediate experience, man throughout his evolution has taken these intimations, these impulses of the unconscious and, using his imagination, has incorporated the particular point of view he sensed into his experience of reality. The result is a myth: "the myth is not composed of abstract qualities; it is a point of view, transmuted to importance; it is made by the transformation of the actual by imaginative genius." Because myths express unconscious impulses, desires, and fears that influence us from below the placid surface of everyday living, their structure or point of view must be clothed in reality in order for us to be moved emotionally as well as intellectually by them. Yet they necessarily exaggerate that fabric of the everyday world because, being unconscious, they gain in power through the unity of immediate experience that makes intellect and will work *with* emotion rather than *against* it, as in conscious reality when intellect and will are able to temper emotion, being at that point separate and opposed faculties.

Myths for Eliot, then, give us a glimpse into our unconscious, a sense of Reality as immediate experience. Through the cathartic purgation that myths offer, they make possible civilization itself, which depends upon a harmonious cooperation or working together of faculties at present irrevocably separated by consciousness. As Eliot observes, the ordinary person wishes to "see himself on the stage, more admirable, more forceful, more villainous, more comical, more despicable—and much more else—than he actually is." From the standpoint of religion, man needs to experience periodically the spiritual unity of the unconscious in terms of his own world in order to be reassured that such fulfillment is possible; his vigor for life is restored as he renews his effort to achieve this wholeness. Similarly, from the standpoint of civilization, man needs to witness the more primitive and anarchic impulses of his nature concretely, for then he vicariously experiences desires that could not be satisfied in a civilized world, thereby attenuating their power over him. Thus, when Eliot observes that "the myth is imagination and it is also criticism, and the two are one," he is acknowledging that the point of view inherent in a myth at once imaginatively organizes our everyday experience in a certain way and, as a consequence, 'criticizes' the real world by demonstrating either how far it strays from a given ideal, or how near it comes to a given disaster. Structure becomes criticism, and myth the accumulated wisdom of generations of human experience: the seventeenth-century theater is a "criticism of humanity far more serious than its conscious moral judgments. *Volpone* does not merely show that wickedness is punished; it criticises humanity by intensifying wickedness."

Eliot once more finds the music hall to be the only modern artistic source of primitive experience, as he again surmises the effect of drama on the unconscious from Aristotle rather than Freud. The moral and psychological fulfillment that a secular myth can furnish appears to reside in this contemporary folk art: English comedians such as Little Tich, George Robey, Nellie Wallace, and Marie Lloyd

> unconsciously . . . provide fragments of a possible English myth. They effect the Comic Purgation. The romantic Englishman, feeling in himself the possibility of being as funny as these people, is purged of unsatisfied desire, transcends himself, and unconsciously lives the myth, seeing life in the light of imagination.

Likewise, in terms of a myth for the entire human race, "Charles Chaplin is not English, or American, but a universal figure, feeding the idealism of hungry millions in Czechoslovakia and Peru." But in order that the myth be *completely* effective for modern man in transforming his consciousness and organizing his mind, Eliot specifies two necessary conditions which will have a bearing as well on his own personal participation in myth. To begin with, myth must be engaged unconsciously: we must not be aware that we are participating in an imaginative artifice which is taking us deep into our unconscious to our most basic desires and fears: "only unconsciously, however, is the Englishman willing to accept his own ideal." Eliot suggests that if the audience suddenly became "aware" that the "fun" of such a comedian as Little Tich transcended humor, they would be unable to "appreciate" the "compliment" and tolerate the criticism, and if the comedian were conscious of the seriousness of his role, he would probably not be able to "perform" his comic routine. Such would also be the case, Eliot conjectures, with the actors and audience at a performance of one of Jonson's comedies. We must, in essence, literally believe in the myth, entirely engross ourselves in its performance such that we identify with it as a living extension of ourselves, a part of our lives, and not be aware of it as the expression of a primitive structure, an impulse of our unconscious. At the same time, however, we must not mistake the literal content of the myth, the reality in which the structure is embodied, for a literal truth or meaning that directly dictates an appropriate course of action. Eliot stipulates that he is not implying that a person is inspired to imitate the fantastic behavior of Volpone or some other scoundrel of seventeenth-century drama as children are tempted to mimic the exploits of a movie villain. The myth is simply "degraded" by the youngster who assaults, robs, or in some other way attempts to act it out in real life. Neither a seventeenth-century nor a modern audience can be transformed by the myth into heroes of epic proportion. "The myth is based upon reality, but does not alter it."[7] What is Real in a myth is not the contemporary experiential form that it assumes at any given point in history, but the permanent, underlying structure or point of view. Further, this point of view, originating in the unity of the unconscious, can have no direct practical application to our everyday world of multiplicity, consciously divided and objectified, other than the profound relief afforded by such infrequent glimpses of the unified Reality.

2. AN ARTISTIC TECHNIQUE

Once having discovered that the comedy of the music hall functions to keep alive the secular mythology of a living culture, Eliot began to investigate how dead mythologies of past cultures might be recovered for use by living cultures. Although myths from foreign cultures of the past could not serve as the unconscious identity of another people, when incorporated in their art forms they could nevertheless supplement the ability of the national mythology to provide spiritual fulfillment. Since the structure or point of view of all myths originates in the unity of the unconscious, the mythology of a past culture will supply additional orders of experience, other possibilities for unifying the mind, different criticisms of life. In his well-known statement on *Ulysses,* Eliot identifies the 'mythical method' as the technique through which primitive and ancient myths can be reclaimed for modern art and thus for the modern world. He credits Yeats with its discovery, Joyce with its fruition, and anthropology with its foundation:

> In using myth, in manipulating a continuous parallel between con-temporaneity and antiquity, Mr. Joyce is pursuing a method which others must pursue after him. . . . It is simply a way of controlling, of ordering, of giving a shape and a significance to the immense pan-orama of futility and anarchy which is contemporary history. It is a method already adumbrated by Mr. Yeats, and of the need for which I believe Mr. Yeats to have been the first contemporary to be conscious. It is a method for which the horoscope is auspicious. Psychology (such as it is, and whether our reaction be comic or serious), eth-nology, and *The Golden Bough* have concurred to make possible what was impossible even a few years ago. Instead of the narrative method, we may now use the mythical method. It is, I seriously believe, a step toward making the modern world possible for art, toward . . . order and form.[8]

The crucial aspect of the mythic method, therefore, is the si-multaneity of the past and the present achieved by presenting the structure of the ancient myth through the content of modern civi-lization. Such a simultaneous existence of historical periods, a conflation of time-orders, is a characteristic of the Absolute, and of immediate experience, which is continuous with the unconscious mind. Because ancient mythic structures and primitive ritual pat-terns actually comprise a portion of our collective-historical un-conscious, the mythic method assumes that our experience must be in some fundamental way similar to the experiences of our primitive and ancient ancestors. Contrary to the Romantic view of past cultures, primitive or classical, which elevates those ways of life above ours, the modern mythic method recognizes a profound kinship among all civilizations, regardless of historical period: "we realize better how different—not how much more Olympian— were the conditions of the Greek civilization from ours; and at the same time . . . how the Greek dealt with analogous problems" (*SE* 50). We rummage past civilizations, digging further back into our unconscious, for myth and ritual that will, once resurrected and expressed in contemporary terms, explain, order, and unify our experience for us. Because in the twentieth century ethics has been "eclipsed" by psychology, Eliot observes that the modern era "objects" to the heroic and the sublime. Yet through the mythic method, we can recover structures of meaning past civilizations once enjoyed: "the heroic and sublime, banished as reality, we take back as myth: Mr. Bloom is Ulysses."[9]

As the presence of this simultaneity makes *Ulysses* for Eliot "the most important expression the age has found,"[10] so its absence in the ballet Diaghilev provided for Stravinsky's *Sacre du Printemps* makes that performance for Eliot problematic. As Eliot explains, music that is supposed to form an aesthetic whole with "action" must be provided with a dramatic structure that has undergone a "process of development" similar to the music itself. In the performance that Eliot attended, the "spirit" of the music might have been "modern," but that of the ballet was "primitive ceremony." Thus, the vegetation rite reenacted by the ballet stayed a "pageant of primitive culture," mildly entertaining only to those familiar with *The Golden Bough*. "In art there should be interpenetration and metamorphosis." Such interpenetration of past and present, resulting in their metamorphosis into a new form of art, occurs in *Ulysses*. In Joyce's book, the reader follows both Bloom walking through early twentieth-century Dublin *and* Ulysses voyaging home to Ithaca at the same time, not one *or* the other, not antiquity to the exclusion of the modern, or vice versa. With the dancing that accompanied Stravinsky's music, however, for Eliot "the effect was like *Ulysses* with illustrations by the best contemporary illustrator": illustrations of Bloom would exclude Ulysses and antiquity; of Ulysses, would exclude Bloom and modernity; by a contemporary renderer, in contemporary style, would eliminate the ancient sensibility expressed in the myth; by an ancient, in ancient style, would eliminate the relevance of the myth to the modern mind. In the ballet, the choreography merely reproduced the myth in its primitive form, while Stravinsky expressed the underlying feeling of the myth in the materials of contemporary life. There was the "sense of the present" only in Stravinsky's music, which appeared to "transform the rhythm of the steppes" into such "barbaric cries of modern life" as, for instance, the automobile horn, the subway, and machinery, and to convert these "despairing noises into music."[11]

Eliot perceived that the esthetic program of the mythic method, to preserve primitive modes of thought and feeling for the modern world by adopting the structures of ancient myths in contemporary art, was particularly appropriate to that form evolving directly out of primitive ritual, the poetic drama. Because the twentieth-century mind lacks the unity of consciousness that would encourage the creation of universal dramatic forms, conventions, themes, and a basic sensibility common to all members of a given society, "a preparedness, a habit on the part of the public, to respond to particular stimuli" (SW 64), the poetic dramatist must "supply his own framework, his own myth."[12] Such patterns of dramatic character and action, and of intellectual and emotional response, could be achieved by restoring to the stage those myths found in our unconscious mind. But the mythic structure must be portrayed within modern life in order for the drama to unify rather than merely entertain the civilized mind, in turn unifying modern society as a whole. The requirement of simultaneity must be satisfied even in the texture of the verse itself: as Eliot advises, both blank verse and the heroic couplet are inadequate, and obsolete; rather, "new verse forms" are required, because the "conditions of modern life (think how large a part is now played in our sensory life by the internal combustion engine!) have altered our perception of rhythms."[13] When Eliot came to write poetic drama, he experimented with various forms of dramatic simultaneity, using the modern drawing room, and even jazz rhythms for the verse in *Sweeney Agonistes,* to develop plot action derived from primitive rituals and ancient myths.

But Eliot first used the mythic method to write poems, the quatrain satires. Often conflating several myths in a single poem, Eliot finds ancient prototypes for contemporary characters and situations. Satiric comment does not ultimately evolve from an ironic contrast between a heroic past and a debased present, but from the moral deficiencies inherent in the given dramatic structure, whether the person or action depicting the structure be modern or classical. Figures from antiquity more often display complicity rather than contrast. As with ritual structure, the mythic method finds its first complete expression for Eliot in *The Waste Land,* in which primitive, ancient, and modern mythologies are synthesized to form a statement about himself and the modern world.

3. A FRAME OF MIND

If the mythic method could recover dead myths of past cultures for use by the modern world, it also suggested a way to renew the religious tradition of Western civilization that had itself ceased to be a living faith for modern man. The mythic method made possible for Eliot a kind of participation in Christianity in spite of the skepticism of nineteenth-century naturalism and the more pervasive skepticism of the early twentieth century which had discredited religious belief. Just as the structures of ancient myths and primitive rituals could serve as patterns of action and emotional response for poetry and drama, so the refinement of sensibility and organization of experience provided by the myths and rituals of modern religion can function as an ordering of daily living and a philosophy of life. The mythic method cannot, however, restore the Christian religion to its former level of literal belief during the Middle Ages when it was, like the romantic Englishman of today, a living mythology, possessed unconsciously. As Eliot notes, the mythic method does permit contemporary art forms to be enriched by incorporating into them aspects of primitive rites now alien to the modern world. Eliot feels that the ballet could "*borrow*," for instance, gestures of the hand from the priests of the island of Bali. Although the mythic method suggests that such ritual forms can pattern modern life as well as modern art, the belief that originally accompanied these myths and ceremonies cannot be restored along with them. Eliot cautions that "*founding*" the ballet of the future on a "dead" ritual is not really possible. To reenact the Sword Dance, for example, would simply be to introduce another sport into British life; it would merely be physical exercise to the participants. "For you cannot *revive* a ritual without reviving a faith. You can continue a ritual after the faith is dead—that is not a conscious, 'pretty' piece of archaeology—but you cannot *revive* it."[14]

The nature of the mythic method, in fact, inherently *prevents* the possibility of literal belief, of faith, in the myths and rituals that it reclaims. The simultaneity of past and present which must occur in the mythic method when the structure of an ancient myth is incorporated into contemporary experience results in the holding of two points of view, past and present, simultaneously. Yet, to believe literally in a myth, to live it as an absolute truth about our world and entertain no other possibilities, is to hold only a single point of view and not be aware of any other. Once we become conscious of a second point of view which conflicts with the first, we have already passed to a third point of view from which we perceive and are able to compare the other two points of view. The first point of view can no longer be considered true, and neither can the second: faith in either is impossible, and we can believe in the third point of view only so long as we are not conscious of holding it. As Eliot explains the problem of truth and error, a difficulty occurs when one point of view is claimed to be superior to another. This claim can only be made from the standpoint of a third point of view that "somehow contains" the first two. When we become aware that we are holding a third point of view, then we have actually arrived at a fourth that now contains the first three. Thus, only when we can "support" a particular point of view, which "involves not recognizing it as such," have we overcome the "contradiction" between truth and error (*KE* 121). Truth becomes for Eliot, therefore, the third point of view, or self-consciousness; in turn, the third point of view that unites the mythic pattern and contemporary life, a past faith and a modern skepticism that finds it no longer true, is 'mythic consciousness': a *conscious* living of a myth no longer a faith. Only a myth still felt to be valid, such as the romantic Englishman, could be *unconsciously* lived, as Eliot noted, for instance, in the music hall.

The self-consciousness that is inherent in the mythic method and produces mythic consciousness also plays a fundamental role in Eliot's analysis of half-objects and works of fiction, which he believes to function like myths. Mythic consciousness utilizes myths as if they were half-objects which, as ideas about reality rather than perceived objects of reality itself, originate through our perception of two points of view "at once" and "pursuing neither" (*KE* 159–60). With the mythic method, both a mythic structure and the modern world are apprehended simultaneously, neither point of view taking precedence over the other. In this way, both myths and half-objects ultimately escape intellectual consideration, whether they are real or unreal, true or false. They are not a part of the experiential physical world which can be scientifically analyzed, and yet at the same time they bear a relation to it such that they are not completely nonreferential and thus exclusively imaginary. Moreover, as the living of a myth consists of viewing reality in light of the imagination, so myth itself resembles other products of the imagination, such as fiction, in which reality is also imaginatively structured. As a myth contains a structure or criticism of life clothed in the material of reality, and yet at the same time can be believed literally as an actual truth of, or event in, reality, so the characters and situations of a novel can be considered as "*meanings*," that is, as a "criticism" of the real world from the writer's point of view, or as "real," historically and ontologically.

But like myth, this dual aspect of fiction makes it also a special kind of half-object, existing between the actual world of experience and the entirely imaginary or nonreferential as "'mere idea'" (*KE* 123); that is, a fiction lacks sufficient and proper relations to qualify as a real object, but has enough relations to connect it with the real world. Thus, objects of fiction, like those of myth, occupy two points of view simultaneously: they possess a "reality in their own space and time, and a different reality in our space and time" (*KE* 162–63). As Eliot summarizes, a myth or fiction is a "complex which comprehends two points of view—a real object with few relations and an intended object which consists of relations." As mythic consciousness is the third point of view which unites the mythic structure with the real world, so the reader or author supplies the third point of view through which a work of fiction is compared to reality and a criticism of life perceived: the imaginary object "exists as such only from a third point of view" (*KE* 125).

In Eliot's analyses of half-objects, works of fiction, and myths, then, the self-conscious perspective, the third point of view mediating between idea or structure and objects, synthesizes the dialectic between meaning and the world, between truth and reality. Eliot's fascination with Laforgue's ironic self-critical monologues, and the self-awareness he displays through the masks of his own early poetry, suggest a natural self-consciousness that found expression at the same time in his philosophical speculations. Eliot even regarded his own personal identity as a function of self-consciousness. Through Bradley's idealism Eliot came to recognize the self or soul, the personal order that our mind makes out of the multiplicity and disunity that is our world, not as a merely static single point of view, but as a process of definition. Various opposed and isolated points of view of reality are transcended and then considered simultaneously through a superior point of view. As a function of this amalgamating and continually changing point of view, the self resembles a deliberate construction, like fiction, a spatial and temporal organization of reality in which both experience and an informing meaning are, as with half-objects, joined together and simultaneously perceived by an additional point of view.[15]

For Eliot, our experience comes to us first as a single finite center which then disintegrates into various points of view that comprise our world. The self attempts to unite these fragments of reality once again by joining together, for instance, two points of view under a third point of view (KE 147–48). The third point of view that holds together the two inferior points of view, physical reality and idea, for example, Eliot actually considers to be the self. This function of the self as a conjoining perspective makes it analogous to mythic consciousness, the superior point of view that unites the structure of a myth with the contemporary world: one point of view recognizing another becomes a third "centre of feeling," at this point, however, no longer actually a center of feeling, but "more properly a self, a 'construction based on, and itself transcending immediate experience'" (KE 149). The self, therefore, like mystic consciousness, is really self-consciousness, for only self-consciousness can consider simultaneously two different points of view, and only self-consciousness can in turn transcend both idea and reality, myth and the world, the individual and the other.

Not only did Eliot's self-conscious temperament lead him to believe that both the self and mythic consciousness are themselves only various forms of self-awareness, it also led him to claim that self-consciousness plays a role in modern artistic creation as well. He contends that those people who are able to observe their emotions as "passive spectators" feel more deeply than do others (KE 23). To conceive of poetry as inherently dramatic is to consider oneself when one writes poetry from two points of view at once, as a spectator and as an experiencing consciousness. The soliloquy in Elizabethan drama, as well as the dramatic monologue of Browning and Laforgue, exemplified this self-consciousness to Eliot. Noting "those situations where a character in the play *sees himself* in a dramatic light," Eliot finds that "in many of those situations in actual life which we enjoy consciously and keenly, we are at times aware of ourselves in this way, and these moments are of very great usefulness to dramatic verse" (SW 81, 83). Eliot sees this modern artistic self-consciousness beginning to emerge in the seventeenth century through the influence of Seneca, Machiavelli, and Montaigne. The self-dramatizing hero of Shakespearian tragedy, most notably Hamlet, comes to mind. This attitude appears to Eliot to begin a new "stage" in man's development (SE 119). Eliot finds this self-awareness even in a passage from one of Donne's sermons in which, he explains, the writer seems to be an "Eye" that views himself functioning as a human being from a distance.[16]

Such self-consciousness Eliot perceived as a condition, rather than a blessing, of the modern world with which one had to cope, both in art and in life. While making possible fervent joy, self-awareness can also cause poignant suffering, not only in literary works, but also in ordinary lives. Prolonged but unperceived or ignored affliction is thus a constant theme in Eliot's poetry depicting contemporary Boston or London, and he observes, somewhat ungenerously, at the height of his own grief from his marriage, that the majority of people are too unaware of their own misery to feel very miserable.[17] Moreover, this self-consciousness, as its Renaissance philosophical sources would indicate, is inherently skeptical and prevents literal belief of any kind in anything. Only in the twentieth century did modern man finally realize that this skepticism denied him a belief in science as well as in religion. A self-consciousness that constantly transcends any given point of view by recognizing another opposing point of view from the vantage point of a third could not possibly permit the unconscious possessing of any single idea as truth, as reality. Such self-consciousness is a symptom of disunity, for only in a fragmented world of various conflicting points of view, having an awareness of all points of view and thus unable to adopt just one of them as truth, must we retreat to an aloof self-reflection as the only way of uniting any two or more of them. In such a world, art is possible for Eliot only through the mythic method, and religious belief only through mythic consciousness.

4. A MODE OF BELIEF

By means of the mythic method, Eliot transforms the very self-consciousness that caused the fragmented modern world into a solution for the resulting problems of truth and belief. Integrating the concept of mythic consciousness into the philosophy of religion which he had developed out of Idealism and anthropology, Eliot formulates a theory of religious participation which overcomes the skepticism of the modern mind. Through Bradley's philosophy, Eliot had developed an intellectual justification for religious experience, perceiving mystical moments to be a sensing of immediate experience, which is, in turn, an intimation of the unified nature of the Absolute, identified by the studies of mysticism he read to be the Divine. Anthropologists and Classicists helped him to devise the idea of a collective-historical unconscious which, being continuous with immediate experience as well as our physiology, and consisting of primitive experience, indicated that specific myths and rituals are integral to religious expression. Now Eliot's mysticism could be related to a religious tradition which could give it definition and guidance. The mythic method, by demonstrating how dead myths could be recovered for use by the modern artist, also implied that the mythology of the Judaeo-Christian religion, no longer believed in literally, could nevertheless still serve the religious needs of modern man. The rituals of the Church embody structures that originated with the beginnings of primitive man, when the rhythms of his nervous system transformed themselves into dance, then religious ceremony and myth, and drama. By living mythic consciousness, self-consciously participating in these rituals, modern man can once again find a satisfactory expression for his religious impulse.

Although mythic consciousness automatically precludes literal belief, since it is based upon a self-awareness that is inherently skeptical, it nonetheless permits a participation in the myths and rituals of orthodox religion. Such participation is ultimately the most important aspect of religious experience. Literal belief in a religion depends primarily upon a conscious, intellectual and emotional engaging of the merely superficial content of its mythology. This transient shell only reflects the fragmented, contemporary reality of any given point in time in the constant evolution of a religion. Participation in a religion's myths and rituals, on the other hand, engages the unconscious, where both the intellect and the emotions are unified through the permanent inner structure that lies below the outer covering of a myth. This unified state more closely approximates the unity of the Divine as the Absolute. Contemporary religious myths and rituals inherit their structures from primitive experience, when they evolved through primitive man from the rhythms inherent in the nervous system. These structures now stir us unconsciously at once because our unconscious remains continuous with our physiology, and because these structures have themselves become a part of the unconscious, since primitive mentality survives in the civilized mind. Thus a religion naturally will, and necessarily must, affect us unconsciously when we participate in it.

Even as early as Royce's seminar, participation in a ritual, that is, behavior, was for Eliot the one certain fact, the only reality, in religious experience. Eliot argues, "What is the status of a fact which includes a belief or meaning? . . . What is he [primitive man] sincere about? *Behavior is the chief fact you have.*"[18] Reasons, conscious beliefs and meanings given to an unconscious impulse, could only misrepresent it; literal belief, the intellectual acceptance of the surface story of a myth, can only hinder religious experience, making it exclusively conscious, simply rational and emotional. Eliot repeatedly praised Baudelaire for what he perceived to be an instinctual knowledge of the structures underlying the Christian religion, as evidenced in Baudelaire's unconscious tendency to express a fundamentally Christian view of life in his poetry. Eliot quotes Charles DuBos approvingly on the nature of Baudelaire's religious experience, characterized by a recourse "d'un Dieu qui plutôt qu'objet de foi est receptacle de prières— j'irai jusqu'a dire d'un Dieu qu'on puisse prier sans croire en lui" (*EAM* 75). To pray to a god in whom one does not believe is just an extreme form of participation in a religion without literal belief.

Thus, for Eliot, literal belief in the content of a religion is ultimately irrelevant to religious experience. Because skepticism determined the nature of mythic consciousness, it is overcome by being incorporated into religious participation from the beginning. If the content of a religious mythology cannot be considered intellectually without causing doubts, the underlying structures of the myths and rituals do provide a religious truth which, if still impervious to any direct scientific proof, nevertheless offers a kind of certainty because it appears to originate with human life itself, evolving out of our physical nature, and forming a part of our unconscious minds.

Although literal belief in the content of a religious mythology is contrary to living mythic consciousness, this substance of the real world that clothes the structure of the myth is nevertheless integral to religious experience. Only when the structure is expressed through the fables, ceremonies, and symbols of a religion can it reach the unconscious once again. In religious myth and ritual, the surface story, action, or icon, consisting of aspects of the world of our everyday experience and yet organized by the underlying unconscious structure, relates this religious structure to the conscious sensory reality in which the worshipper lives. The rhythms inherent in the language, plot, and movement of the Scripture and service stimulate the nervous system. The unconscious is stirred, in turn, at once by the submerged structure, and by the content of the ceremony which, having evolved from primitive rites, still remotely resembles them. All facets of mental experience, the intellectual, emotional, unconscious, and physiological, are thus integrated in a single movement that brings unity and order into our world when myth and ritual direct the flow of the mind. We both feel and become conscious of the essential mystery of our being, because we are entering the recesses of our mind and reviving primitive experiences of terror, humility, and awe that arose from man's first encounter with existence, as we participate in the rhythms of the modern ritual that derive from ancient myths and primitive dance.[19]

Eliot's religious experience began with vague and disorienting mystical states of overwhelming intensity, and a subsequent desire to understand rationally what these moments were. He wished to overcome his pervasive skepticism about orthodox religion, so that he might integrate his mysticism with a religious tradition that could guide and develop it, and make it relevant to his daily life. Bradley's philosophy provided Eliot with a metaphysical explanation for his mystical moments, considering them as intimations of immediate experience, and of the God of orthodox Christianity, defining him as the Absolute. But the Absolute is an intellectual abstraction, and immediate experience is a frightening state of totality, foreign to the world in which we live, where ideas, emotions, objects, and our self lose their separate identity. The philosophical system governing these concepts may serve to justify religious experience and the existence of the Divine, but being a conscious and rational approach, it cannot contribute to the nature of religious experience, which consists of an unconscious unity of intellect and emotion. Only the myths, rituals, and symbols of a religion can give definition to mystical experience; thus Eliot acknowledges that it is not our "feelings" alone but the "pattern" into which we shape them that is the "centre of value."[20] If the structure of the myth provides a pattern for the religious impulse, the content allows us to experience these ineffable states in terms of our own concrete reality: "the mystical experience is supposed to be valuable because it is a pleasant state of unique intensity. But the true mystic is not satisfied merely by feeling, he must pretend at least that he *sees*" (*SW* 170). Dogma translates religious feeling into something that the intellect can understand, myth and ritual into something to which the emotions can respond, and the senses perceive.

The last period in history that attempted to 'see' reality in terms of a myth was for Eliot the Middle Ages. In keeping with his conception of religious experience as mythic consciousness, Eliot perceives this age of faith as utilizing the mythic method rather than embracing literal belief. By viewing all of reality and experience in terms of Judaeo-Christian mythology and its Greco-Roman embellishments, Dante, according to Eliot, employed the mythic method not only in his poetry, but also in his life, resorting to myth in order to stimulate the unconscious and evoke mystical experience at will. Eliot explains that Dante's imagination was visual, not, however, in the same way that an artist's imagination is visual, but in that Dante, as a medieval man, possessed the "psychological habit" of seeing visions. Modern man only has dreams, which come "from below," whereas having visions was a "more significant, interesting, and disciplined kind of dreaming" (SE 204). This intentional provocation of religious visions Eliot considers to be a prototype of his own mythic consciousness, by which one willfully, consciously, sees reality in terms of myth. He distinguishes between "*high dream*," the conscious use of myth to excite deliberately the religious impulse and induce a mystical moment, and "*low dream*," the involuntary emergence of what Eliot conceived to be the entirely personal, individual unconscious mind that occurs while we sleep (SE 223). Eliot considered the allegorical method of Dante to be, in turn, a literary technique comparable to the mythic method, seeing reality in the light of religion and producing a 'high dream': allegory is "really a mental habit, which when raised to the point of genius can make a great poet as well as a great mystic or saint" (SE 204).

To live mythic consciousness, then, is to organize consciously reality and one's daily experience according to the patterns of meaning embodied in a given mythology, for Eliot Christianity. Such a psychological state in which two points of view are maintained simultaneously, the value system of the historical myth on the one hand, and the skepticism of the modern world on the other which no longer considers the myth to be literally true, resembles the mystic participation of primitive man. As Lévy-Bruhl and Eliot interpreted primitive mentality, the Bororo saw himself as a parrot and a man "at the same time"; he did not 'adopt' the parrot as a "heraldic emblem," simply as a symbol of identity, nor did he feel a mere "kinship or participation in qualities" that he admired or found expressive of his own being or situation in life, the primary motive for the use of mythology in poetry since the Renaissance.[21] But Eliot's mythic consciousness remains fundamentally different from primitive mentality because the myth is embraced self-consciously: Eliot is aware that he is living a myth in which he cannot literally believe, whereas primitive man lives the mythic system under which he is both a parrot and a man unaware that any other truth exists. The devout believer of the Middle Ages resembles primitive man to the extent that he too unconsciously lives a myth, acknowledging no other valid system of truth, and is therefore a literal believer. Through his version of mythic consciousness, Eliot has discovered a new kind of belief, a mode of belief appropriate to the modern world.[22]

Eliot himself thought that the nature of belief itself changes throughout human evolution, as demonstrated not only by the history of Christian dogma, but also by the history of religious poetry. Although Dante, Crashaw, and Christina Rossetti all professed a belief in certain doctrines framed in basically the same language, and although their beliefs were equally "strong," still their beliefs are, Eliot admits, "as different from each other as they are from myself."[23] The truths inherent in the Judaeo-Christian religion, the underlying structure of its dogmas and mythology, remain constant throughout history, but the way in which these truths are held, the quality of the belief in them, will differ with each phase of the human mind. Conscious, intellectual modifications of Christianity, which attempt to reshape the religion into something literally believable by either altering or replacing its intrinsic unconscious structure with the contemporary philosophical and scientific theories of a given period, will only pervert the religion into an anachronism irrelevant to succeeding generations when the Zeitgeist again changes. Eliot considered Arnold's substitution of poetry for religion, and of an ethical sense for a supernatural deity, to be conscious modifications to Christianity that Arnold performed when he capitulated to Victorian naturalism and morality. Both Schleiermacher's mysticism and Alfred Loisy's Modernism at the turn of the century were also for Eliot conscious attempts to transform Christianity into Romantic spirituality, the former pantheistic and the latter Naturalist in tendency, but both personal, and lacking definition. If a religion is to retain its unconscious structure, it must be allowed to evolve unconsciously: the interpretation of its dogma and mythology will alter according to the age, but because such changes of understanding occur unawares, they are caused by unconscious feeling from which the structure of a religion originates and in which it is preserved throughout human history. Even if the mythic content again alters its form and the Christian religion evolves into some other religious mythology, just as Christianity itself evolved out of primitive rituals, the structure will continue to survive in its new guise, still making belief through mythic consciousness possible. In relation to the question of poetry and belief, Eliot observes that poetry can never really be "separated from something which I should call belief"; yet,

> it will not inevitably be orthodox Christian belief, although . . . Christianity will probably continue to modify itself, as in the past, into something that can be believed in (I do not mean *conscious* modifications like modernism . . .). . . . [I]n doubt we are living parasitically . . . on the minds of the men . . . of the past who have believed something.[24]

Eliot is thus fully aware that his belief in Christianity is not the literal faith of past centuries, and openly acknowledges that, although he still considers himself a believer, his belief as a modern man is inferior to that of a medieval man. The same modern point of view that results in the inferior belief of mythic consciousness also perceives that the nature of belief itself is in continual evolution. Through Bradley's idealism Eliot had substantiated a pervasive skepticism which was not, however, nihilistic: there definitely are truths valid for our world, but we can never know what they are (*KE* 164). From our limited point of view at any given period of history, we can only arrive at an interpretation of Reality and of our world, at conjectures rather than truths. We are for Eliot by nature condemned to being critics, exercising that "refined and subtilized common sense which is Critical Taste" to arrive at qualified rather than literal truths: "the true critic is a scrupulous avoider of formulae; he refrains from statements which pretend to be literally true; he finds fact nowhere and approximation always. His truths are truths of experience rather than of calculation." We are therefore committed to a constant process of interpreting our world, and reinterpreting our former interpretations as time passes and we enter another age in human development with a different point of view. Our consciousness occupies the synthesizing third point of view in a dialectic that opposes the previous point of view now held to be obsolete, the myth of Christianity for instance, with the new point of view, in this case skepticism. The truths most comfortable to such a mind are truths with which we can live rather than prove rationally; thus one *lives* a belief through mythic consciousness rather than attempts to possess it exclusively with the intellect, for any truth in this world, however tentative, is ephemeral:

> Even these lived truths are partial and fragmentary, for the finest tact after all can give us only an interpretation, and every interpretation, . . . has to be taken up and reinterpreted by every thinking mind and by every civilization. . . . [B]oth God and Mammon are interpretations of the world and have to be reinterpreted. (*KE* 164)

The nature of religious belief, therefore, is destined to change, because our point of view toward the structures inherent in religion alters over time. Eliot resorts to mythic consciousness as a third point of view that will allow for constant reinterpretation of both Christianity and skepticism. Otherwise, if he accepted skepticism as literal truth, then Christianity would appear invalid, thus excluding religious experience from life. If he accepted Christianity as literal truth, on the other hand, then skepticism would appear nonsensical, thus excluding the modern world from consciousness. Criticism becomes for Eliot, in fact, another variety of mythic consciousness, a perennial self-consciousness from which perspective all intellectual and artistic endeavor is judged. As a work of fiction contains an author's criticism of life and a limited reality in which this idea is clothed, with the reader providing the third point of view that determines how well the author's meaning explains reality itself, so the critic provides the third point of view for any work of art, comparing it to the reality out of which it is made and to which it refers. By contrast, psychology, as a single point of view perceiving the work of art, will yield, according to Eliot, only a limited self-referential explanation of the work, doctrinaire rather than interpretive (*KE* 75–76). The critical point of view even judges the validity and usefulness of metaphysical systems, comparing the point of view of the philosopher to the reality that we all share:

> To the builder of the system, the identity binding together the appearance and the reality is evident; . . . to a critic, the process is perhaps only the process of the builder's thought. From the critic's standpoint the metaphysician's world may be real only as the child's bogey is real.

The one thinks of reality in terms of his system; the other thinks of the system in terms of the indefinite social reality. (*KE* 167–68)

Eliot's myth, then, was Christianity, and the nature of his belief was mythic consciousness. Through philosophy, anthropology, scientific psychology, and studies in mysticism, Eliot had finally arrived at a philosophy of religion and a theory of religious participation that explained his mystical moments and justified their guidance under the most recent mythic expression of man's religious impulse, the contemporary incarnation of the death-rebirth structure inherited from the primitive rituals out of which it evolved. Eliot was baptised into the Church of England on 29 June 1927.[25] Although he did not literally believe in the dogmas and mythology of the Christian religion, or in the miraculous claims of its rituals, he nevertheless did believe in the structures underlying the content of Scripture and liturgy. Because these concepts and ideals had survived the perennial changes of religious myth and ritual in which they were expressed throughout the course of history, they were for Eliot permanent and unalterable truths about human nature and the universe. Because they evolved from rhythms in our physiology and comprise the structure of our unconscious, they represent our most genuine knowledge of the nature of our existence, a direct impression of the nature of Reality. Belief for Eliot begins, therefore, with a conviction that the religious impulse is the fundamental experience of man in the world and a basic characteristic of human nature. Religious feeling provides certainty through the mythic structures it engenders. As a participant in the Church, Eliot will often speak of these basic structures in the metaphors of the mythology through which he has chosen to embrace them: while explaining that the "Christian scheme" appeared to him to be the only one which preserved "values" that he had to "maintain or perish," he specified such beliefs as "holy living and holy dying," "sanctity, chastity, humility, austerity."[26] But Eliot constantly translates these mythic metaphors, as well as the various fables and images of Christianity, into the structures they symbolize and represent. He experiences Christianity as a reader understands allegory: as coherent in itself but always meaning something else. Eliot, after all, considered Dante's allegorical technique to be a kind of mythic method; but for a literal believer like Dante, Christian mythology was the meaning behind the allegory of life, whereas for Eliot a permanent religious structure lies behind the allegory of Christianity.

Eliot does not conceive of the Christian doctrine of an afterlife, for instance, in its literal meaning of a supernatural reward as depicted by the mythic imagery of the Bible. Eliot explains that to "believe" in the transcendent is not to expect that after death we will "continue to exist in the best-possible substitute" for an earthly life that has been fairly comfortable, or that we will be "compensated" in a future life for our suffering in this one; rather, it is to believe that the "supernatural is the greatest reality here and now."[27] For Eliot's hypothetical literal believer, Heaven is a specific, concrete place, a transcendent, metaphysical locale. The myth, literally understood and unconsciously experienced, brings the permanent religious structure into his life. As he works his way to Heaven through good works, he engages in a number of timeless emotional states and moral categories. Living the myth only on its literal level, he is unaware that the underlying structure is actually organizing his everyday world. He may interpret the myth like the medieval scholastics, for instance, whose biblical exegesis sought such other senses of Scripture as the 'allegorical' (doctrinal or devotional), 'moral', and 'analogical' (describing the future life). But such interpretations do not replace literal belief in the content of the myth: they merely supplement it with other meanings which themselves arise from accepting the myth on its literal level. By contrast, in order for Christianity to apply to his everyday experience, Eliot must seek the structural significance of the dogma of a future life at the same time that he participates in the literal content of the myth. Just as he views Heaven from the perspective of mythic consciousness, so he views Hell; as he reads it, Dante's *Inferno* teaches us that Hell is not a "place but a *state;* that man is damned or blessed in the creatures of his imagination as well as men who have actually lived; . . . and that the resurrection of the body has perhaps a deeper meaning than we understand" (*SE* 211–2).

The content of the myth helps both the literal believer and Eliot to appreciate the structure by portraying it in terms of sensory experience and behavioral imperatives, the concrete reality and the necessity for action characteristic of our everyday world. Streets paved with gold communicate the beauty and happiness of Heaven, and fire the torment of Hell; an afterlife as reward conveys the value of living a moral life. But once the content of the myth makes the structure vivid for Eliot, mythic consciousness then permits the religious concept to acquire an additional relevance for his life. By not believing literally in the myth, Eliot is able to liberate the underlying structure and provide additional surface content for it, specifically by using it to organize and interpret his own experience of the world. This process of finding additional applications for a myth in contemporary experience is, after all, the basis of the mythic method and simply continues the perpetual reincarnation of a mythic structure as it assumes different appearances throughout history. Hell becomes for Eliot a state of mind rather than a place, a sense of existential nihilism or moral guilt which robs life of joy and worth. Not only might the damned souls of men who have actually lived undergo a period of expiation, but a living man's very state of mind may for Eliot require a salvation that must be achieved as soon as possible in order for life to continue.

Eliot perceives the other important dogmas, myths, and rituals of Christianity through mythic consciousness as well, finding the underlying structures that have meaning for his life. The idea of God as a supernatural being with paternal concern for the human race makes the mystery of our existence, the unknown that surrounds not only our daily lives but the universe with which we are familiar, at once comprehensible, approachable, and less fearful for the literal believer. Eliot himself feels that, just as there are certainly truths for the universe, although we cannot determine what they are, so there is indeed a supernatural, the Absolute, which is by nature unknowable. Thus Eliot's God exists but is ultimately inscrutable, and the structure that he perceives through the Christian God is the concept of the 'wholly other': that there does indeed exist something that lies beyond the universe, beyond our sensory experience, and although it is intuitively immanent, we can never know precisely what it is.[28] The beginning of the world in the Judaeo-Christian tradition, the Garden of Eden, is for Eliot not the geographical location of a significant event in human history, the Original Sin, but rather the mythic expression of the idea that human nature is not entirely good, but contains both good and bad, and thus requires guidance to nurture the good and discourage the bad. Not only may some of man's impulses be harmful to others, but his moral judgment may at times be fallible and his insight into human feelings and motives limited: he may do things that he will later regret, such as, for Eliot, entering into an ill-fated marriage. The central event of the Christian religion, the Crucifixion and Resurrection of Jesus, continues the death-rebirth structure of man's earliest primitive rituals. The saving of mankind by a God incarnate who takes upon himself all of the sins of the world and suffers the retribution for them symbolizes for Eliot the perpetual possibility of spiritual self-renewal of which one can always avail oneself in life. If one were humble enough to sacrifice one's personal will for a selfless generosity toward other people and the world at large, one's own private hell of suffering would be relieved and one's life would begin afresh. The coming of such relief to one's life is analogous to the Incarnation of the supernatural in the world. To Eliot, a believer of mythic consciousness, these structures were Christianity, and in his poetry the Christian religion is actually only one, if certainly the predominant one, of many myths to which he resorted to express these fundamental ideas about the world.

VI. A SURREALIST POETIC

A S Eliot's concept of the unconscious formed the basis for his philosophy of religion and philosophy of art, so the unconscious again is fundamental to his theory of poetry. Eliot insists repeatedly that both the impetus for a poem begins in the *poet's* unconscious and the process of communication of a poem ultimately ends in the *reader's* unconscious: poetry "may make us from time to time a little more aware of the deeper, unnamed feelings which form the substratum of our being, to which we rarely penetrate" (*UPUC* 155). Eliot's preoccupation with the functioning of the unconscious as the source of artistic experience leads him to define the esthetic according to those qualities peculiar to the images and feelings residing in that subliminal region of the mind: "the craving for the fantastic, for the strange, is legitimate and perpetual; everyone with a sense of beauty has it."[1]

Eliot's criterion for art resembles that of those other explorers of the unconscious, the Surrealists. Their terms for artistic success—that art should "provide the emotive shock in man which really makes his life meaningful,"[2] that is, induce a "precious terror," a "shudder"[3]—are also his. Eliot observes that both *Ulysses* and *Tarr* are "terrifying." For him the ability to terrify is not only the criterion for judging a new work of art, but it is also the basis for the continuing merit of an older one: *Othello* and *King Lear* should still be "frightful."[4] By the same token, Eliot speaks of the "element of surprise so essential to poetry" (*SE* 267). That Eliot could find 'terror' and 'surprise' in such diverse and eccentrically chosen literary products as the stream of consciousness of Joyce and the satire of Lewis, the Jacobean tragedies of Shakespeare, the conceited verse of the Metaphysicals and the heroic couplets of Dryden suggests the exercising of a personal taste which seeks those qualities in any given work of art that most appeal to it, rather than any systematic generalization on the nature of literature. By choosing terror to the exclusion of pity, and specifying its origin in the 'fantastic' and 'strange', Eliot updates Aristotle's observations on Greek tragedy for the twentieth century with the help of modern psychology and philosophy.

The Surrealists developed their artistic theory from similar sources. As a medical student specializing in neurology and mental disorders just before World War I, André Breton, the preeminent Surrealist theoretician, was educated in the same French tradition of scientific psychology beginning with Charcot, whose investigations of hysteria anticipated psychoanalysis that Eliot had encountered in the Paris of 1910. Although Breton relied principally upon Freud in his attempts to analyze the patients under his care while an assistant physician in the neurological division of the hospital at Nantes during the war and later at the psychiatric center in Saint-Dizier, his attempts at automatic writing with Philippe Soupault, published in 1919 as *Les Champs magnétiques,* were inspired as much by Janet, with whom Eliot was more sympathetic. Breton and the Surrealists even found in Hegel the same philosophical justification for the metamorphosis of physical properties and relationships that the surreal image effects in order to infuse matter with mind, the objective with the subjective, that Eliot had found in the Idealist tradition.[5]

As the similar heritage of their thought would suggest, Eliot was formulating his poetic at about the same time that Breton was devising his esthetic theory, although the Surrealists did not declare their existence as a group and publish their first manifesto until 1924.[6] Eliot was never influenced by the Surrealist Movement proper. He never sought any connection with Breton's official group in Paris, nor with the circle that formed in London during the mid-1930s that affiliated itself with them. He did not sponsor any Surrealist writing in *The Criterion,* although he did publish a number of reviews and articles on Surrealist theory and practice that were usually serious and informative, displaying a range of judgment.[7] Eliot is not, therefore, a Surrealist: he never subscribed to the Surrealist way of life in its ethical and political dimensions. The esthetic of Surrealism does represent, however, a particular kind or mode of artistic theory to which Eliot's poetic thought belongs. Thus Eliot's poetic is not specifically Surrealist, but it is *generically* surrealist, beyond the point of merely sharing certain resemblances, such as those observed by Paul C. Ray.[8] Fathoming the unconscious in order to bring to consciousness and into the world a Superreality is more than just analogous to descending into the unconscious in order to gain a sense of immediate experience, and thereby of the Absolute. Both Eliot and the Surrealists believed that the unconscious is the source of an ultimate Reality, and both therefore were seeking unconscious experience in their art. Because Eliot and Breton postulated that the unconscious functions dialectically, they both specified that art must fuse dislocated experience into startling images.

The extent to which Eliot's poetry resembles Surrealist art, then, depends upon the extent to which Eliot's and the Surrealists' theory of the unconscious and its role in artistic creation coincide. Surrealist poetry varies from Breton's exercises in free association and Robert Desnos's disjunctive meditations to Louis Aragon's enigmatic narratives and monologues and Paul Eluard's measured, hypnotic lyrics. Eliot's dreamlike internal monologues and disjointed dramatic lyrics certainly fall within this range. Eliot's verse approaches Surrealist poetry in its local texture, uniting disparate objects and experiences through metaphor. But the resemblance between Eliot's poetic language and Surrealist painting is more striking. Eliot practiced a visual discipline in his image formation that is inherent to that medium. The characteristic of Eliot's verse least like Surrealist poetry is the overall structure he employed in his longer poems. Eliot's investigation of the historical dimension of the unconscious supplied him with a comprehensive structure for *The Waste Land,* for instance, which would not interest the Surrealists, who did not emphasize this aspect of the unconscious. Further, Eliot's insistence that some conscious control be exerted over unconscious material in the creative process accommodated such a structure, while the Surrealists' emphasis on the unconscious, automatic aspects of creation would not allow for so definite a pattern.

As with other aspects of his thought, Eliot's poetic is at once a synthesis and an extension of ideas from philosophy, scientific psychology, and theoretical anthropology. Yet a number of attempts have been made to relate the various concepts of Eliot's literary theory to Bradley's idealism alone.[9] Consequently, the philosophical dimension of Eliot's literary theory, even in terms of Bradley, has not been presented in its full complexity. To relate a given term to immediate experience, but not to the collective-historical unconscious, for instance, limits the meaning of the original philosophical identification. When Eliot's literary theory is explained according to his complete philosophical system, and the true meaning of such terms as tradition, the impersonal, objective correlative, and wit is discovered, the surrealist aspects of his poetic become apparent.

1. RHYTHM: GOURMONT

One French critic in particular appears to have provided Eliot with the impetus to apply ideas from contemporary philosophy, scientific psychology, and anthropology to literature. Eliot was to observe of his first literary essays: "at that time I was much stimulated and much helped by the critical writings of Remy de Gourmont" (SW viii). Eliot might very well have first encountered Gourmont's writings during his year in France as a visiting student, for his retrospective account of the Paris of 1910 mentions Gourmont. Certain ideas on literature and physiology in Eliot's dissertation concur with those of the French critic in a general way, but they could have been developed independent of Gourmont as well, given Eliot's reading in neurological studies and Idealism. Only with those early literary essays beginning in 1919 does direct evidence of influence appear. Of Gourmont's voluminous writings we know for certain that Eliot read Le Problème du style (1902) and Lettres à l'Amazone (1914), which he quotes (SW 1, 8; SE 192, 193), and the essay on Laforgue of Promenades littéraires I (1904), phrases of which he echoes. Eliot's remark years later that his earliest essays were written "when I was somewhat under the influence of Ezra Pound's enthusiasm for Remy de Gourmont" (UPUC 10) suggests that Pound probably intensified whatever interest Eliot may have had in Gourmont before that time. Eliot's move to London from Oxford in mid-1915 after his marriage, when he began meeting with Pound on a regular basis, just precedes Gourmont's death, which elicited Pound's two eulogistic essays later that year.[10] Eliot's observation in 1923 that Gourmont was a "real master of fact," and in disciplines other than literature, a "master illusionist of fact" (SE 21) was probably prompted by Pound's recent translation of Physique de l'amour (1903), which even Pound did not consider to be science, but as his title indicates, The Natural Philosophy of Love.[11] But certainly this book still continued to remind Eliot of a certain view of physiology that he also shared in his own way, as the title of the concluding chapter implies: "Tyranny of the Nervous System."

Gourmont began as a propagandist for Symbolist poetry and

then modified his Symbolist polemic with a naturalism selectively culled from Taine and his own studies in scientific psychology. To this last phase of Gourmont both Pound and Eliot were attracted.[12] No doubt Eliot found Gourmont's ideas on literature readily applicable to his own system of thought because they all derived from the central role Gourmont gave to physiology in mental phenomena. Eliot tellingly praises Gourmont as "an amateur, though an excessively able amateur, in physiology" (SW 13–14), and Gourmont often mentions Ribot in his writings, whose work in neurology Eliot had also studied. Because Gourmont postulates that reality and the self are entirely material, feeling and thought are for him strictly physiological processes. Mental activity, according to Gourmont, consists of a cycle in which sensations of the world are transformed first into images (mots-images), primarily visual; these images then become ideas (mots-idées); and finally, ideas become emotions (mots-sentiments). Ideas evolve directly out of sensory impressions, therefore, and language is inherently metaphoric, being the verbal translation of physical movement in the world. As a consequence, for ideas and language to be of any value, they must remain as close to sensory experience as possible, at that point where words as images of the world begin to suggest ideas. Our mental life thus becomes a constant revitalizing of concepts and words through the continual imbibing of sensations from the world.

Since this process of image transmutation and language formation is entirely physiological, a writer's style for Gourmont is determined by his physiology: his style will be concrete, or abstract, or sentimental, depending upon what point in this neurological cycle his brain is structured to function. His writing will also depend upon what sensations he received on a given day, which activate only those ideas and words that correspond to them. At the same time, new sensory impressions are being collected and stored in what Gourmont calls the 'visual memory', ready to be either refreshed by related sensations or called up by the author's imagination to form new combinations. Gourmont stated, in reference to Laforgue, that the tendency of a civilized, modern, and mature mind is for skepticism to dissociate the intelligence from the sensibility, an idea which Eliot strictly interpreted, according to Gourmont's theory of mental activity, as a separation of thought and feeling, of object and emotion.

Despite the various echoes of Gourmont's phrases and ideas

that appear in Eliot's early essays, Gourmont served more as a catalyst for applying certain ideas Eliot had come to hold to literary theory than as the exclusive source of those ideas: the influence was primarily inspirational and corroborative. Eliot assimilated Gourmont into his own elaborate synthesis of Idealism, anthropology, and scientific psychology, so that Gourmont at once reinforced Eliot's philosophical system and, in turn, was interpreted according to it. As Glenn Burne points out, Gourmont's cyclical theory of mental activity is a strictly linear process: sensations become idea and then emotion; the reverse is not possible, as it is for Eliot.[13] What Eliot does, in fact, is to view Gourmont's theory from an Idealist's dialectical perspective in terms of Bradley's doctrine of immediate experience, in which object, emotion, and thought are united as feeling, out of which they evolve as isolated phenomena only to be combined once again in the wholeness of the Absolute. Encouraged by Hegel's dialectical conception of historical process, Eliot will project this theory of the mind onto the entire course of English literature since the Renaissance, using it to define the esthetic quality of a given period's poetry and to justify through this historical evolution the kind of verse he felt appropriate to the modern world.

Other concepts of Gourmont that resembled Eliot's just enough to be of use to him ultimately derive from signficantly different intellectual prejudices. In "La Création subconsciente" of *La Culture des idées* (1900), Gourmont states explicitly what he implies in the essays that we can be certain Eliot read, and what Eliot would have at any rate understood from them: that the unconscious mind is physiological, and affects every aspect of our lives through physical processes. For Eliot, the unconscious certainly has a physiological dimension, but it is also psychological and metaphysical as well. Gourmont's exclusively materialist definition of the unconscious indicates his partial allegiance to Naturalism. Further, Gourmont's subjectivist interpretation of the physiological unconscious reveals a continuing affinity with Symbolism. For Gourmont, each person's physiological constitution is fundamentally different, resulting in unique works of art expressing peculiarly personal visions of the world. For Eliot, on the other hand, the physiological unconscious is also immediate experience, in which all points of view are united in a totality similar to the Absolute. Works of art produced by a physiology continuous with this collective-historical unconscious would express a composite world that we all can recognize, for it is a world that we all share.[14] In *L'Idéalisme* (1893), reprinted in *Le Chemin de Velours* (1902), "Dernière conséquence de l'idéalisme" of *La Culture des idées,* and "Les Racines de l'idéalisme" of *Promenades philosophiques* (1904), again none of which we can be certain Eliot read, Gourmont defends philosophical idealism. Although he states in the latter that idealism and materialism are compatible and opposed to spiritualism, a position to which Eliot will subscribe in the form given to it by Bradley and Bernard Bosanquet (*KE* 153, 164), Gourmont's idealism is really again the subjectivism of Symbolist poetic rather than Eliot's unifying philosophy. Gourmont's world consists of a myriad of private and ultimately irreconcilable visions because his idealism stops with the solipsism of the experiential world and does not proceed to acknowledge an all-encompassing Absolute and its counterpart, immediate experience.

Passages from Gourmont that Eliot did quote or paraphrase are read outside of the larger context of Gourmont's thought. Consequently, statements that appear to Eliot to reinforce his own views often have contrary implications overall. When Gourmont draws a distinction between the emotion in a work of art and that of the man in his daily living, he refers to the emotion joined with its image in the unconscious physiological process out of which art grows, as opposed to the emotion of conscious thought abstracted from sensation in our practical thinking. He certainly does not mean the impersonal feeling of Eliot, for physiology for Gourmont is always personal and subjective, as must be the art it produces. If Gourmont insists that a man in writing of himself writes his time, he is merely stating that art must be composed of the sensations that affect a given physiology; what that unique physiology does to those sensations can only be personal, not the "universal and impersonal" (*SE* 117) work of art that Eliot specifies when he alludes to this idea of Gourmont's.[15] Gourmont is in the end a historical relativist: as periods of history change, available sensations change accordingly, making art dependent at once upon the uniqueness of a historical age and of a given sensibility. For Eliot, we discover what is permanent in human nature by what remains immune to social evolution and unchanged throughout history, and what remains unchanged is embedded in the physiology of our unconscious.

Eliot may very well have been unaware of these essential differences, or perhaps he chose to ignore them when confronted with

an idea so readily applicable to his own thought as that of Gourmont's that style is a product of the entire physiological state of a
given writer. Certainly this notion corresponds to Eliot's view of
the unconscious which, being continuous with immediate experience, is a unified state of thought and emotion. As Eliot says in
reference to John Davies, "his appeal is, indeed, to what Hallam
calls the heart, though we no longer employ that single organ as
the vehicle of all poetic feeling" (PP 153). If for most Victorians
poetry simply expressed emotion, coming from the heart, for
Eliot, subscribing to Gourmont's belief that poetry evolves from
physiology, poetry expresses the entire human being: "'look into
our hearts and write' . . . is not looking deep enough. . . . One
must look into the cerebral cortex, the nervous system, and the
digestive tracts" (SE 250). Since for Eliot the psychological and the
physiological unconscious are continuous, that element of a poem
that reveals the essence of a writer is the rhythm implicit in a
writer's neurological system which governs every aspect of poetic
composition. Eliot explains that rhythm is not a verse form, nor
can it be described through scansion; it is, rather, a "highly personal matter" and "very uncommon." It is the "scheme of organization of thought, feeling, and vocabulary, the way in which
everything comes together." [16]

As myth and ritual evolve out of rhythms inherent in man's
physiology, so the structure and content of a poem derive from a
writer's nervous system. Rhythm thus comprehends for Eliot
every feature of a writer's style, which can, in turn, reveal the
quality of a poet's mind: "a style, a rhythm, to be significant, must
embody a significant mind, must be produced by the necessity of a
new form for a new content." [17] For this reason, style and technique become for Eliot the fundamental aspects of poetic communication: a careful inspection of a writer's "method and form" is
the most reliable procedure for ascertaining his "'human value'" [18]
because "every vital development in language is a development of
feeling as well" (SE 185). Eliot's continual praise of Bradley's style
(SE 395, for instance) and his delight late in life in finding that his
early prose style resembles Bradley's (KE 10–11) are not obstinate
evasions either of Bradley's philosophical merit or of Eliot's own
debt to him but are actually an acknowledgment of them. As Eliot
observes of Russell, he is a philosopher who has "invented a new
point of view; and a new point of view is style." [19] Bradley's style
evinces a point of view, a mind, that approaches the unity of the

Absolute which forms the basis of his philosophy, for Eliot the unity of the unconscious: Bradley's is the "finest philosophic style in our language, in which acute intellect and passionate feeling preserve a classic balance." [20]

Perhaps the most significant consequence of Eliot's idea that physiology plays a central role in the creative process is that a poet's sense of rhythm permits him to delve into the collective-historical unconscious and recover the primitive experience that resides there for modern man:

> What I call the 'auditory imagination' is the feeling for syllable and rhythm, penetrating far below the conscious levels of thought and feeling, invigorating every word; sinking to the most primitive and forgotten, returning to the origin and bringing something back, seeking the beginning and the end, . . . fus[ing] the old and obliterated and the trite, the current, and the new and surprising, the most ancient and the most civilised mentality. (*UPUC* 118–19)

Thus the auditory imagination can recover primitive rituals and ancient myths that might provide structures for modern poems and can liberate the primal feelings and experiences that engendered ritual and myth in order to enrich the contemporary emotion and idea that finds expression in modern art. But if the psychological unconscious is truly collective and historical, the entire tradition of the world's literature must also be found there, and therefore it must, in addition, enter into literary creation in some more direct manner.

2. TRADITION AND THE HISTORICAL SENSE

If Gourmont suggested to Eliot what role the physiological unconscious might play in the creative process, other philosophers and social critics whom Eliot read each provided ideas that, when taken together, indicated to Eliot how the collective-historical psychological unconscious is integral to the writing of poetry as well. Gourmont's visual memory, that repository of visual images which is continually being refreshed by new sensations and periodically rummaged for poetric material, is actually the individual unconscious defined as personal memory. Although Gourmont probably derived the idea from his reading in scientific psychology, his visual memory resembles Bergson's 'memory', the personal unconscious which evolves from his concept of the timeless duration.

According to Bergson, any perception that we experience in the present is really composed of past sensations brought to consciousness from the memory by processes of association that depend upon similarity and contiguity. We never actually perceive the present, therefore, but only the past as it progresses into the future.

Although Eliot probably encountered this idea of past sensations composing present perceptions first in Bergson, he comes to interpret the idea, as Lewis Freed points out,[21] in terms of Bradley's idealism. Bradley also has a version of the theory of past defining present, but he claims to have developed his notion of time from Hegel rather than Bergson.[22] If Appearance, the world as we experience it, is an intellectual construct, and if Reality, as immediate experience, reconciles and thus eliminates all linear time schemes in its unity, then past and future must be ideas formulated in the present. The present moment thus consists in part of its own ideas of past and future: "the present of ideal construction, the present of meaning and not simply of psychical or physical process, is really a span which includes my present ideas of past and future" (*KE* 55). In stressing that the present consciousness formulates our conception of the past and future, Eliot follows closely Bradley's axiom that any point of view necessarily determines our sense of the world. When Eliot analyzes the soul in terms of time, his emphasis on the past seems Bergsonian, but he has again located the idea within Bradley's system. If the soul is only another Appearance based on a linear time scheme, that is, the history of events that occur to it, "the whole world of its experience at any moment," then the soul is also an idea consisting of its past: "the soul is its whole past so far as that past enters into the present, and it is the past as implied in the present" (*KE* 79). Eliot immediately quotes Bradley for support: "but at any one time . . . the soul is the present *datum* of psychical fact, plus its actual past and its conditional future."

Eliot proceeds to apply this account by Bergson and Bradley of the functioning of the individual unconscious to the collective-historical unconscious and perceives that the racial memory combines with the personal memory to determine the present moment of consciousness. Such a synthesis was perhaps inevitable for Eliot, since he considers both Bergson's *durée* and Bradley's Absolute or immediate experience to be aspects of the unconscious, and both contain, despite their differences, all of history in a timeless unity. What served to relate the racial history of the unconscious directly to the act of creating literature in Eliot's mind were those modern classicists of his early years who insisted that literature is a historical enterprise, that literary works always constitute part of a tradition which automatically determines to a certain extent the nature of new works and serves as a criterion against which they would be judged.

Babbitt's precept at Harvard that standards for literature and life should be derived from a classical tradition of art, in opposition to an egocentric, subjectivist romanticism, was immediately reinforced by Charles Maurras, whose *L'Avenir de l'intelligence* (1905) Eliot first read during his student year in France.[23] Maurras conceived of tradition in more narrow, exclusivist, and self-enclosed terms than Eliot ever would, asserting that the literature of a given people constitutes an inheritance peculiar to them which serves to distinguish them from other peoples. But simply the idea of a tradition to which any work of art stood in relation appealed to Eliot, as well as Maurras's again much narrower medievalist, antiromantic, and clerical bias. Eliot found in both Maurras and Julien Benda an assessment of modern romantic art and a definition of classical art that helped secure his dialectic of thought and emotion, and of object and feeling, a basis in history. Eliot was familiar during his year in France with the journal for which Benda wrote, and was quoting Benda's *Belphégor: essai sur l'esthétique de la présente société française* (1918) by 1920 (*SW* 44–46). Benda's emphasis on intelligence over emotion, his prescription for the concrete rather than the indistinct in art, and his indictment that contemporary society desires emotional stimulus rather than thought from art Eliot tempers for his own use and incorporates into his dialectic of reason and emotion.

Eliot's ideas of 'tradition' and the 'historical sense', then, are a synthesis of these various sources along with his conception of the psychological unconscious derived from anthropological studies. Literary tradition for Eliot is actually synonymous with the collective-historical unconscious: as a cumulative and timeless repository of human experience, it is "a mind which changes," but "this change is a development which abandons nothing *en route,* which does not superannuate either Shakespeare, or Homer, or the rock drawing of the Magdalenian draughtsmen" (*SE* 6). Because the psychological unconscious is continuous with the metaphysical unconscious, Eliot perceives tradition in terms of immediate experience, or the unified, all-embracing Absolute: the idea of poetry as a "living whole of all the poetry that has ever been written" (SE 7). Eliot's view of tradition in terms of Idealist philosophy approaches Royce's Community of Interpretation, that universal human mind which acts as ultimate arbiter, evolving throughout the course of history: not the mind of a single era, with its particular styles and preconceptions peculiar to itself, but rather a "greater, finer, more positive, more comprehensive mind than the mind of any period."[24] From Royce's metaphysical Community Eliot moves easily to a conception of tradition as Durkheim's sociological collective conscience: "a common inheritance and a common cause unite artists consciously or unconsciously: it must be admitted that the union is mostly unconscious. Between the true artists of any time there is, I believe, an unconscious community" (SE 13). As the psychological and the metaphysical are continuous with the physiological unconscious, so Eliot perceives tradition even in physiological terms as authors who are not affiliated with a particular period of time, but who are "related so as to be in the light of eternity contemporaneous, from a certain point of view cells in one body."[25]

The historical sense that a writer should exercise, in turn, consists of an awareness of tradition, and for this reason is also described by Eliot in terms of Bergson's duration, "a perception not only of the pastness of the past, but of its presence"; the writer with a historical sense is considered by Eliot to be in touch with immediate experience, having a "feeling" that the "whole" of the literature of the Western world, including the "whole" of the literature of his own nation, has a "simultaneous existence and composes a simultaneous order" (SE 4). The historical sense brings to the present moment of consciousness the literature of the past in the same way that Eliot believed that the collective-historical unconscious could be brought to consciousness for the use of modern man: "the conscious present is an awareness of the past" (SE 6). When we write with a sense of literary history, "we have not borrowed, we have been awakened, and we become bearers of a tradition"[26] as the unconscious is brought to the light of consciousness.

Like the mythic method and mythic consciousness, the historical sense enables a writer to see the simultaneous existence of the past and the present, "a sense of the timeless and of the temporal together." In this way only the relevance of the past to the present is perceived and we continue to live in an enlightened present rather than living in the past: in order to view Jonson as our "contemporary," we do not need the ability to transport ourselves to Jacobean London, but rather the ability to locate Jonson in twentieth-century London (*SE* 128). As one self-consciously uses a myth to organize modern experience, so one consciously uses tradition to interpret the modern world; an unconscious use of tradition would only result in imitation, as an unconscious use of myth consists of literal belief. Because it employs so many styles in the history of the English language, and because words are often used such that they recall their own history, Joyce's *Ulysses* is again, as with the mythic method, Eliot's paradigm of modern literature: Joyce does not merely possess "tradition" but also the "consciousness" of it, because the "essential" aspect of possessing tradition consists of putting the "whole weight of the history of the language behind his word."[27] Thus, *Ulysses* not only "realises untried possibilities" in the English language, but also "revivifies the whole of its past."[28] Likewise, Eliot admired Pound's esthetic program, in which an awareness of all the important innovations in the history of poetry is gained through study and imitation, thus making them a part of his own sensibility and technical resources. Eliot justifies Pound's method using that characteristic of duration that he has come to associate with immediate experience: "as the present is no more than the present existence, the present significance of the entire past, . . . when the entire past is acquired, the constituents fall into place and the past is revealed."[29]

3. PERSONALITY AND THE IMPERSONAL

Eliot's idea of 'impersonality' in artistic creation also derives from the collective-historical unconscious. Personality is for Eliot only a superficial psychological experience analogous to our sense of self, really just a conscious intellectual construct. Eliot confidently speaks of the "universal sameness" of people despite "superficial variations," of the "uniformity of human nature,"[30] because for him the essential part of our mind is the unconscious. Being by nature collective and historical, the unconscious ensures that people all over the world have had throughout history similar desires and experiences. When Eliot asserts that great poetry "expresses in perfect language, some permanent human impulse," he implies that such poetry somehow embodies the feelings of this communal and comprehensive region of our mind. Eliot describes the impersonality of poetry, in fact, with terms he had used to characterize the unconscious: the "struggle" of the great poet is "to transmute his personal and private agonies with something rich and strange, something universal and impersonal" (*SE* 117). That "something outside of the artist to which he owes his allegiance, a devotion to which he must surrender and sacrifice himself" (*SE* 13), is tradition as found in the collective-historical unconscious. The creative process begins in individual experience and acquires universal significance by being enriched with the content of the unconscious: "personal emotion, personal experience, is extended and completed in something impersonal—not in the sense of something divorced from personal experience and passion." The artist gains "something greater than himself" when his personality is "extended and transformed by the poet's superior organisation,"[31] which comes from the subliminal mind.

If the creative process remains entirely subjective, however, when, for instance, the poet cannot unite his personal experience with the collective-historical unconscious, or then satisfactorily bring it into consciousness, Eliot belives that a *Hamlet* is produced, "full of some stuff that the writer could not drag to light, contemplate, or manipulate into art" (*SE* 124). Conceiving the unconscious to be continuous with the physiological, Eliot concludes that such subjective, uncommunicative, or incomplete works of art are the product of a psycho-physical malfunction: a work of art is "personal if you like, but a work of imagination is never simply personal. So far as we consider it as *only* personal—i.e., significant only to the author—we explain it not as imagination but as the product of pathological conditions," as "morbid physiological activity" (*KE* 76). For Freud and his followers, *Hamlet* is rich in psychoanalytic material, indeed a paradigmatic case of the Oedipus complex;[32] for Eliot, who believes individual psychology reduces to physiology rather than the half-objects of psychiatric terminology, *Hamlet* betrays "the intense feeling, ecstatic or terrible, without an object or exceeding its object, . . . doubtless a subject of study for pathologists" (*SE* 126). Such information on a writer's "heredity and nerves," in turn, is useful only "for the purpose of knowing to what extent that writer's individuality distorts or detracts from the objective truth which he perceives" (*EAM* 67).

When Eliot explains that the poet does not possess a "'personality' to express, but a particular medium, . . . in which impressions and experiences combine in peculiar and unexpected ways" (*SE* 9), "a more finely perfected medium in which special, or very varied, feelings are at liberty to enter into new combinations" (*SE* 7), he is implying that the poetic faculty itself really consists of the psychological unconscious. Because Eliot believes the psychological unconscious to be continuous with the metaphysical unconscious, immediate experience, they both function for him in a similar manner, constantly striving to unify once again the isolated components—emotions, thoughts, objects, selves—of our experiential world of Appearance. The collective-historical unconscious thus creates poetry by uniting the content accumulated in the individual unconscious or private memory according to its own perennial impulses or feelings: the poet's "mind is in fact a receptacle for seizing and storing up numberless feelings, phrases, images which remain until all particles which can unite to form a new compound are present together" (*SE* 8). It is, therefore, not "the intensity of the emotions, the components, but the intensity of the artistic process, the pressure, so to speak, under which the fusion takes place, that counts" (*SE* 8) in creating a poem, because a poem is composed, not of individual experiences by themselves, but of such emotions and events compelled into a unity that approaches immediate experience. The greater the unity achieved, the deeper into the unconscious a poet, and in turn his poem, delve, and thus the closer to immediate experience they come. As Eliot explains, the "intensity" of an author's "imagery" depends upon its "saturation . . . with feelings too obscure for the authors even to know quite what they were" (*UPUC* 147–48). What was once personal experience and isolated memory is transformed by the unconscious into something impersonal and unfamiliar, expressing an unconscious tendency rather than a private emotion: "an author's imagery . . . comes from the whole of his sensitive life since early childhood. . . . [S]uch memories may have symbolic value, but of what we cannot tell, for they have come to represent the depths of feeling into which we cannot peer" (*UPUC* 148).

Eliot thus comes to define the "poetic sensibility" as the "sensitiveness necessary to record and bring to convergence" on a given experience "a multitude of floating but universal feelings" (*SE* 318). When the poet allows these feelings of his unconscious to combine with an ordinary emotion, "having an affinity to this emotion by no means superficially evident," he produces an "art emotion," one of those "feelings which are not in actual emotions at all" (*SE* 10) because he has expressed an unconscious feeling, entirely different from the emotions of which he is conscious in daily life. Such "emotions of art," partaking of the "austerity" and "frigidity" that results from the unfamiliar unity of immediate experience, Eliot characteristically finds "terrifying."[33] Poetry becomes an "escape from emotion," an "escape from personality" (*SE* 10), therefore, because it no longer expresses our fragmented world of consciousness, of self and other, but rather the collective unconscious: "the emotion of art is impersonal." And Eliot is able to argue that the poet cannot "reach" this "impersonality" without living "in the present moment of the past" (*SE* 11), indeed is able to imply that history and the impersonal are synonymous, as he does in "Tradition and the Individual Talent" (1919), only because the unconscious for him is historical, the repository of primitive experiences which embody permanent and universal impulses that persist over the course of time.

Given Eliot's theory that great art strives for the impersonal, his critical assertion that Massinger's "defect is a defect of personality" (*SE* 195), more precisely, a "deficiency" (*SE* 192) of personality, seems at first contradictory. But as Eliot elaborates, we are reminded that for him, if the impersonal consists of immediate experience as well as the collective-historical unconscious, it must then be continuous with the metaphysical unconscious also, and thus consists of a point of view. Eliot explains that the comedies of Marlowe and Jonson are a "view of life," that is, they are, as all "great" literature, the "transformation of a personality into a personal work of art." Massinger, on the other hand, is not merely a "smaller personality: his personality hardly exists. He did not, out of his own personality, build a world of art," as did Shakespeare, Marlowe, and Jonson (*SE* 192). A point of view in Eliot's philosophical system is the finite center, that unity out of which our spatio-temporal world of daily experience evolves. A finite center, as the unconscious immediate experience, is not, strictly speaking, synonymous with our sense of self, personality, or soul, which are conscious intellectual constructions, assessments of our experience made in relation to time and space. As Eliot warns, we must not "confuse the soul which is a whole world . . . with the soul which can be described by its way of acting upon an environment. . . . The concept of centre, of soul, and of self and personality must be kept distinct." The finite center is, however, *continuous* with the soul or personality: "the soul only differs from the finite center in being considered as something not identical with its states" (*KE* 205). For this reason, the more comprehensive and unifying a personality is, the closer it approximates a finite center:

> The soul itself may be considered in a loose sense as a finite centre. The more of a personality it is, the more harmonious and self-contained, the more definitely it is said to possess a 'point of view,' a point of view towards the social world. Wherever, in short, there is a unity of consciousness, this unity may be spoken of as a finite centre. (*KE* 148)

Thus, the way to impersonality and immediate experience is, paradoxically, through personality, but a personality so extended and so unified that it ceases to be a personality in the ordinary sense at all. Neither eccentric nor exclusivist, this kind of "personality," with its breadth and coherence, moves beyond the merely subjective to the universality and unity of the impersonal unconscious, of the finite center.

If an author creates a work of art out of a personality that functions as a finite center, then his work of art must somehow reveal his point of view, in the metaphysical sense of the term. Reality as a union of all possible finite centers, as the Absolute, functions as a limit. In itself unattainable, Reality serves as a "background which is merely felt" (*KE* 20, 163), out of which a soul selects a portion organized according to its own distinctive point of view which becomes its world of experience. Hence, an "event taken as happening to that particular soul . . . from the point of view of that soul . . . qualifies external reality" (*KE* 77). Likewise, "what is in the mind of the avaricious or generous man is not avarice or generosity, but a real world qualified in a certain way" (*KE* 79). If a point of view, by 'qualifying' Reality, creates *our* world, then a work of art, by organizing an artistic universe according to an author's point of view, also qualifies Reality, and thus consists of its own *world*. As Eliot observes of Ivanhoe, "the story itself, as a story, qualifies reality" (*KE* 37).

When Eliot repeatedly insists in his literary criticism that works of art express, indeed consist of, an author's 'point of view', he is actually referring to this metaphysical theory. For example, Eliot asserts that certain poets, including Shakespeare, Dante, and Villon, and certain novelists, including Conrad, offer, not "ideas" or "concepts," but rather "points of view," or "'worlds,'" which are "incorrectly called 'philosophies.'" Tellingly, Eliot describes a point of view as "one man's experience of life."[34] A point of view is not an idea or a philosophy precisely because it is immediate experience, in which object, emotion, and thought are reconciled in a unified whole, in a world. The more purely artistic a work of art, that is, the more it presents Reality as we initially experience it, creating its own world to the exclusion of theoretical interludes and intellectual analyses, the more it will approach a point of view. Eliot praises James's novels for "maintaining a point of view, a viewpoint untouched by the parasite idea." Otherwise, "instead of thinking with our feelings . . . we corrupt our feelings with ideas," that is, we defy the unity of immediate experience, of feeling, producing "the emotional idea, evading sensation and thought."[35] Again, Eliot notes of Jonson's criticism that he posited "in abstract theory what is in reality a personal point of view" which, however, "escapes the formulae" and is thus best experienced in his plays, "makes them worth reading," in fact, because in them "he created his own world" (SE 136).

That a work of art presents reality from the author's point of view, and thus qualifies reality, leads Eliot to speak of a work of art as a 'criticism of life'. For instance, Hawthorne's fiction is "truly a criticism—true because a fidelity of the artist and not a mere conviction of the man," just as the fiction of James is a "criticism of the America of his times."[36] Such criticism is not an exclusively rational exercise, however, as the phrase might indicate: James was a "critic who preyed not upon ideas, but on living beings."[37] Such works of art are criticisms of life because they present life, its objects and emotions as well as its thoughts, together from a particular point of view, just as a finite center brings us our world, Reality 'criticized' in a certain way. Eliot censures both Paul Elmer More (SW 43) and Matthew Arnold (UPUC 111) for the predominantly intellectual reference that they give to the term. Lacking Eliot's philosophical system which locates the origin of our world in the unified feeling of immediate experience, these critics neglect the role that the unconscious mind plays in artistic creation. Immediately after Eliot explains how the auditory imagination makes available primitive experience to the poet, he observes that "Arnold's notion of 'life,' in his account of poetry, does not perhaps go deep enough" (UPUC 119); and Eliot quotes More as wanting to make literature "more consciously a criticism of life." To eschew such conscious constructions as ideas and personality in a work of art, seeking rather the unified and the impersonal, is Eliot's esthetic goal. As Eliot observed of the Lawrence up to *Aaron's Rod,* the novelist had not, up to that time, "surrendered himself to his work. He still theorizes at times when he should merely see. His theory has not yet reached the point at which it is no longer a theory." Still, in certain scenes, Lawrence simply presents a point of view, recreating immediate experience by descending into the awesome and unfamiliar world of the unconscious, achieving the "terrifying disinterestedness of the true creator." [38]

4. CONSCIOUS AND UNCONSCIOUS CREATION

For Eliot, then, the creative process occurs in the unconscious: feelings mix with emotions, thoughts, and events and fuse them into a unity resembling immediate experience in a "concentration which does not happen consciously or of deliberation," and there can only be "a passive attending upon the event." But this unconscious process does not automatically result in a work of art; it simply provides the necessary creative materials: "there is a great deal, in the writing of poetry, which must be conscious and deliberate. In fact, the bad poet is usually unconscious where he ought to be conscious, and conscious where he ought to be unconscious" (*SE* 10). The former error results in a poem that is formless and inconsistent, thus ineffectual in stirring the reader, and the latter in an artificial poem containing no genuine feeling. The unconscious mind provides material for the structure or form of a poem, and for its imagery or content. But various parts of the structure or certain aspects of the imagery may often be at odds with the general esthetic direction that the unconscious material suggests as a whole. Or this material itself may entirely lack an esthetic program, which must be supplied by the poet's conscious mind. Thus, "probably, indeed, the larger part of the labour of an author in composing his work is critical labour" (*SE* 18).

The artistic consciousness for Eliot is actually a third point of view similar to mythic consciousness. As mythic consciousness mediates between the mythic structure embedded in the unconscious and the modern world and its skepticism, believing in neither one but synthesizing the two by viewing them simultaneously from a superior point of view, so artistic consciousness mediates between the feelings, images, and structures coming from the unconscious and the actual world of conscious experience, combining them into an esthetic whole from the artist's superior point of view. As Eliot points out, the artistic consciousness is always occupying never a single point of view but two points of view at once, a frame of mind made possible only by a third point of view: "the author may shift from a creative to a critical point of view, and back at any moment" (*KE* 124).

> He may be conscious of the continual *va-et-vient* of ideas in the process of realization; the intended reality shifts and changes as he deserts one outcome for another; and he may be conscious furthermore of the effort to express felt emotions and abstract ideas by 'clothing them in flesh and blood.' So that I do not believe that the author in process of composition is ever, in practice, occupied with a single point of view; or that in practice any moment ever exists when one point of view is in exclusive possession. (*KE* 125)

Eliot discusses the respective roles of the unconscious mind and the conscious, rational intellect in relation to Shakespeare and Jonson. C. K. Stead's pioneering remarks on this aspect of Eliot's poetic theory, based on his reading of "Ben Jonson" (1919), are in certain respects misleading, despite his perceptive observation that Eliot holds different meanings for 'emotion' and 'feeling'.[39] Stead claims that Eliot distinguishes between a poetry of "design," in which the form is devised by the intellect, the resulting poem making a rational appeal to the reader's conscious mind, and a poetry of "detail" as well as design, in which the imagery filling out the design emanates from the unconscious, the poem consequently affecting the reader unconsciously. Because Eliot asserts that Shakespeare's is a poetry of detail and design, while Jonson's is simply of design, Stead argues that Eliot is implying that Shakespeare's poetry is written with the use of the unconscious, while Jonson's is a purely conscious creation.

But when Eliot observes that with Jonson's poetry "unconscious does not respond to unconscious; no swarms of inarticulate feelings are aroused," that the "immediate appeal is to the mind," he is referring to "the lazy reader's fatuity" (*SE* 128), a superficial perusal of the play. Eliot believes, in fact, that *both* 'detail' *and* 'design' originate in a writer's unconscious; once brought into the conscious mind of the creator, he then passes judgment on their esthetic utility from his superior third point of view. Both design and detail, therefore, are subjected to rational scrutiny, control, and alteration. Although with Shakespeare an image may erupt from his unconscious, in such a raw state "it is not *used:* the poem has not been written." When the image is being incorporated into an esthetic whole, both feeling and reason are consulted: "the right imagery, saturated while it lay in the depths of Shakespeare's memory, will rise like Anadyomene from the sea. In Shakespeare's poetry this reborn image or word will have its rational use and justification" (*UPUC* 146–47).

The design of a literary work, on the other hand, is not merely a conscious imposition on unconscious material; the structure also originates in the unconscious, and is, in fact, intimately related to the imagery that accompanies it when they erupt into consciousness. The form of the resulting work of art integrally reflects the feeling expressed in the content: "to create a form is not merely to invent a shape, a rhyme or rhythm. It is also the realization of the whole appropriate content of this rhyme or rhythm. The sonnet of Shakespeare is not merely such and such a pattern, but a precise way of thinking and feeling" (*SW* 63). Because a work of art originates in the unconscious and an artist strives to approximate immediate experience, the work of art will approach the finite center from which it evolves and will, therefore, constitute its own world with its own appropriate unconscious structure. As Eliot observes of *Ulysses,* although "the strange, the surprising," is crucial to a work of art, it also must "create a new world, and a new world must have a new structure." Joyce is successful in his novel because he commands a "very great constructive ability"; this "structure" is, in fact, responsible for the work's great significance.[40] Eliot notes that, like Joyce in *Ulysses,* Jonson in his plays also "created his own world" and expressed a "point of view"; there is "a kind of power animating" his characters that "comes from below the intellect" (*SE* 136). Just as the structure of Joyce's novel derives from ancient myth and thus from the collective-historical unconscious, so Jonson's satire, like the modern music hall, recovers the primitive experience embedded in that subliminal mind.[41]

Contrary to Stead's assessment, then, Eliot appears to conclude that the difference between Jonson and Shakespeare is not that the plays of the former are a conscious and rational product while those of the latter are unconscious but that Shakespeare's plays originate at some level *deeper* in the unconscious than do Jonson's. The distinction between their characters is not that Shakespeare's spring from the feelings or imagination and Jonson's from the intellect or invention; they have equally an emotional source; but that Shakespeare's represent a more complex tissue of feelings and desires, as well as a more supple, a more susceptible temperament. (*SE* 137)

Because Shakespeare is able to delve deeper into the unconscious when he writes a play, he comes closer to achieving a finite center than does Jonson; his point of view is more comprehensive, because the closer one gets to immediate experience, the broader the world compelled into a unity that one discovers. Consequently, Shakespeare's words "have often a network of tentacular roots reaching down to the deepest terrors and desires" (*SE* 135), and "the world" his characters "live in is a larger one." Falstaff, for instance,

> was perhaps the *satisfaction* of more, and of more complicated feelings; and perhaps he was, as the great tragic characters must have been, the offspring of deeper, less apprehensible feelings. . . . It is obvious that the spring of the difference is not the difference between feeling and thought, or superior insight, or superior perception, on the part of Shakespeare, but his susceptibility to a greater range of emotion, and of emotion deeper and more obscure. (*SE* 137)

According to Eliot's esthetic theory, a poet seizes upon the unconscious material that periodically erupts into consciousness and fashions out of it a poem whose structure and content were already inherent in these subliminal feelings. A poem so composed will, in turn, be capable of reaching down into the reader's unconscious to stir primal feelings latent in his mind. Because the unconscious is collective and historical, the structures that most often evolve into poems resemble ancient myth and primitive ritual. Since the unconscious for Eliot contains those universal impulses that persist in human experience throughout history, it is impersonal, common to all men and peculiar to no single personality. Stead's assertion that Eliot's "escape from 'personality' . . . is not an escape from the self but an escape *further into* the self,"[42] therefore, is inaccurate, because the unconscious is not the heart of the self for Eliot but exactly the opposite: the deeper one plunges into the mind, the further away from personality and egocentricity one travels and the closer to universal experience one gets.

Stead's contention that Eliot is a romantic, then, is true only in

the most general sense. Eliot is romantic to the extent that all artists after the beginning of the nineteenth century are romantic:
they all seek truth inside their own minds in terms of some essentially nonrational experience apart from a prior and exclusive allegiance to intellectual inquiry and social institutions outside of
themselves. For the Romantics, the truth they found in their own
minds was primarily emotional and personal, such that rational
truths like scientific theories or communal authorities like social
institutions were perceived as invalid. The Victorians, on the other
hand, maintained a divided allegiance between emotional, private
experience and such rational and public sources of truth as biology and moral duty, restlessly struggling for some kind of reconciliation. By contrast, Eliot plunges into his own mind only to find
immediate experience or feeling, a fusion of the emotional and
the rational, and the collective-historical unconscious, containing the structures inherent in such public, social institutions as the
Church. Eliot cannot, therefore, be Romantic in Stead's more restricted sense of depending upon his individual self or unique personality as a private source of truth in the world. On the contrary,
Eliot paradoxically discovered the impersonal, the communal, and
the objective in his unconscious mind. Eliot chose to call his theory of the mind 'classical', in opposition to 'romantic', but he is
really occupying that third point of view, of which one cannot be
aware, that subsumes these other two points of view. Clearly he has
both romantic and classical aspects, but they are blended together
in a new synthesis, making it impossible to label him either Romantic or Classical.

Perhaps writers of the early twentieth century will come to be
called Modern, not in the sense of being contemporary writers,
but in the sense of having begun another phase of human sensibility. Yeats, Joyce, Conrad, Lawrence, and Pound all postulate
some form of mental experience that is a synthesis of the emotional and rational, and subscribe to some kind of collective-
historical unconscious that permits the primitive and ancient to
live on in the present. Certainly Eliot does not recognize such sincerity defined by the Romantic maxim Be true to 'one's self',
which urges one to write poetry by coloring the world one describes with one's own subjective feelings: "we are not to believe
that sincerity in poetry is the same as, or is due to, sincerity about
the facts of the poet's life,"[43] because the poet is "responsible to a
much more difficult consciousness and honesty," namely, to "ex-

pressing his genuine whole of tangled feelings."[44] That 'whole' is
the poet's unconscious mind, and it is for Eliot collective and
impersonal.

5. THE OBJECTIVE CORRELATIVE:
BRADLEY, GOURMONT, RUSSELL

Because Eliot thought that literary creation originated in the unconscious, his theory of the 'objective correlative', of the artistic
process as the expressing of ideas and emotions through objects,
inevitably evolves out of the nature of immediate experience itself,
that unity of object, emotion, and thought. Gourmont's theory
that language formation and usage depend intrinsically upon images obtained from experience, and thus upon objects, helped
Eliot to apply Bradley's idealism directly to the writing of poetry.
But Eliot's notion of the objective correlative is broader than the
conceptual framework provided by these two sources alone. The
concept seems to have acquired an extended philosophical dimension from Eliot's acquaintance with Logical Atomism and its successor, Logical Positivism—both movements of the early twentieth
century—and then to have assumed a significant place in his
analysis of intellectual history.

Along with his education in German Idealism and its Anglo-
American successor, then represented by Bradley and Royce, part
of Eliot's training as a philosophy student was conducted by the
New Realists at Harvard, who had certain affinities with the logical
atomism of Bertrand Russell and Ludwig Wittgenstein. In turn,
the analytical program of Logical Atomism, without its metaphysics, was adopted to a large extent by the Logical Positivists, the
Vienna Circle that formed during the early 1920s. Despite Eliot's
subsequent criticism of Logical Positivism as inadequate to serve
as a *complete* philosophy, which should offer "wisdom and insight,"[45] he would always implicitly endorse its logically rigorous
analytical technique as a prelude to such a philosophy, that is, as a
philosophical method. The New Realists at Harvard had their
counterpart in England in the form of a movement centering
around G. E. Moore, Russell, and Alfred North Whitehead.[46] Eliot
took a course in symbolic logic in the spring of 1914 from Russell,
who was then a visiting professor at Harvard;[47] J. O. Urmson cites
this same year as the beginning of Logical Atomism.[48] Eliot and

Russell were later to share each other's company frequently from the time when Eliot took up residence in England.

Because Eliot committed himself to Bradley's philosophy, he was opposed to most of the metaphysical and epistemological positions of the New Realists, who were intent on refuting Idealism. He was sympathetic, however, to certain of those doctrines of Neo-Realism that were eventually to comprise Logical Atomism proper and that did not conflict with his Idealism. These doctrines were proposed by Russell initially in those books and essays by him that Eliot mentions in his dissertation [49] and were influenced by Wittgenstein when he was Russell's pupil at Cambridge just before Eliot encountered Russell at Harvard.[50] The purpose of philosophical analysis, according to Logical Atomism, is to discover the simplest, most elementary components of our world. These atomic facts are assumed to have the same logical structure as those basic logical functions into which Russell and Whitehead had analyzed all the more complex mathematical operations in *Principia Mathematica* (1910–13). The intention, then, is to construct atomic propositions that obey the logic of the *Principia* and therefore accurately portray the external world, since the implication is that the everyday world and a logically perfect language, in their simplest forms, have the same structure.

As a student in Russell's classroom at Harvard and a reader of *Principia Mathematica*,[51] Eliot learned that natural language is inherently logical through its grammatical structure, and that the laws of a more rigorous logic than that already operative in grammar can be incorporated into the structure of ordinary language. The *Principia* itself encouraged this expectation, because it offered a general symbolism for fundamental logical relationships that could be made specific with particular words of natural language, and thus with things from the everyday world. In effect, this study encouraged Eliot to expect logical rigor in the use of language and thus provided in part the impetus for his demands of precision and clarity in both thought and poetry: the study of grammar should precede the study of logic, Eliot advised later in life, for then students would be able to recognize "how much the work of logicians has done to make of English a language in which it is possible to think clearly and exactly on any subject." *Principia Mathematica* are "perhaps a greater contribution to our language than they are to mathematics."[52] Eliot would always affirm this relationship between thought and language that Logical Atomism encouraged: "language can only be maintained if it is the vehicle for thinking"; therefore, if people "cannot think clearly, they cannot write well."[53]

If, according to Logical Atomism, language is reducible to logically simple statements depicting the elementary phenomena of our world, then, Russell argued, language is used accurately only when it is 'denoting' sensory experiences, that is, only when it is presenting ('naming') objects ('things') and their characteristics ('characters') or relationships with each other ('relations') that we are currently experiencing or have actually experienced in the past (with which we are directly 'acquainted'). Accounts of objects and events of which we have no perceptual experience ('descriptions') consist of only secondhand knowledge and thus cannot be atomic in nature but require further 'reductive' analysis. Moreover, Russell argued that a logically perfect language must observe a one-to-one correspondence between each word and the thing, or character, or relation that it depicts. Thus, an atomic proposition would have only as many words as components of the corresponding empirical fact. Likewise, Wittgenstein would also assert in his *Tractatus Logico-Philosophicus* (1922) that every word must correspond to a particular object or event in the world in order to have any meaning at all. This criterion of direct correspondence between language and sensory experience the Logical Positivists were to develop into their 'principle of verification' for the meaningfulness of any statement, and ultimately into their precept that only propositions of science are verifiable.[54]

Such a notion that language in its fundamental state only names objects and events rather than expresses ideas or emotions, and that such words and phrases represent perceptual sensations and images we directly experience, is similar to Gourmont's theory, no doubt obtained from scientific psychology, that words themselves originate as direct verbal translations of sense perceptions, most often of physical movements. Both Gourmont's view and that of Logical Atomism, in fact, must have coincided in Eliot's mind. Considering that Eliot praises Russell's "On Denoting" (1905) as "clear and beautifully formed thought" (*SE* 66) in an essay written at the height of his interest in Gourmont, we are not surprised to find that Eliot's own version of this idea recalls Russell, and Wittgenstein through Russell, as much as Gourmont. Finding Swinburne's verse inadequate "because the object has ceased to exist, because the meaning is merely the hallucination of meaning," Eliot contends that "language in a healthy state presents the object, is so close to the object that the two are identified" (*SE* 285).

Eliot's critique of nineteenth-century philosophy leads directly to his literary theory of the objective correlative. In his analysis of the Hegelian tradition, Eliot utilizes the idea of a relationship between logic and language as found in Logical Atomism and Positivism, and the idea that words correspond directly to physical objects, obtained from Russell and Wittgenstein, and reinforced by Gourmont's contention that language is created out of sensory experience. Eliot incorporates these theories, as expected, into his larger philosophical system derived from Bradley, making particular use of Bradley's conception that in Appearance emotions become separated from the objects that accompanied them and acquire the status of objects themselves in their abstract form. Eliot believes that, fundamentally, German Idealism was an attempt by a school of thought to supply a philosophical substitute for orthodox religion whose creditability had been questioned by the scientific positivism of the nineteenth century, and whose conceptual basis had been weakened by the imaginative interpretations of dogma by liberal theologians. Eliot contends that the Hegelians and those thinkers whom he considers the legacy of that tradition, including Bergson and Eucken, misused language in order to make philosophical terminology serve both a theological and a liturgical function.

Incorporating definitions from Gourmont into the context of logical positivism, Eliot distinguishes between two kinds of mind, one that uses 'concrete' and 'abstract' language correctly, and one that is merely "verbal" and thus "unscientific." Eliot makes a further distinction between two kinds of abstract language, each characteristic of the two types of mind. Abstractions used by the first kind of mind, *properly,* "may have . . . a meaning which cannot be grasped by appeal to any of the senses" and "may require a deliberate suppression of analogies of visual or muscular experience" but nevertheless have a specific and exact meaning, as with the "trained scientist." Abstractions used by the second kind of mind, *incorrectly,* have no definite meaning at all and thus cannot be used as objects of thought, but only for emotional stimulation; they are mere words.

Historically, Eliot argues that if we "accept certain remarks of Pascal and Mr. Bertrand Russell about mathematics, we believe that the mathematician deals with objects . . . which directly affect his sensibility."[55] By the same token, "during a good part of history the philosopher endeavoured to deal with objects which he believed to be of the same exactness as the mathematician's" (*SW* 9). But in a philosophy which is attempting to do more than philosophize, which tries to supply emotional stimulus through language that lacks a definite referent in the real world, "in an unbalanced or uncultured philosophy words have a way of changing their meaning—as sometimes with Hegel" (*SE* 404). Language without empirical reference would be immune to the censure of science that orthodox religious language could not escape. In order to formulate philosophical concepts that could be endowed with theological overtones, Hegel resorted to "dealing with his emotions as if they were definite objects which had aroused those emotions." Such an attempt to substitute emotions conceived of as objects for real objects of sense perception defies our experience of the world and therefore despoils language: Hegel's "followers have as a rule taken for granted that words have definite meanings, overlooking the tendency of words to become indefinite emotions" (*SW* 9).

Eliot considers the precise use of words in the philosophical analysis of the world to be fundamentally related to the precise use of words and images in the portrayal or expressing of experience in poetry: "we talk as if thought was precise and emotion was vague. In reality there is precise emotion and there is vague emotion. To express precise emotion requires as great intellectual power as to express precise thought" (*SE* 115). Both accurate thinking and effective poetry depend upon language that refers to particular objects or sensory experience. Philosophy and poetry that are 'verbal', that use words that have no concrete referent, can be neither clear nor precise because they are out of touch with the real world. They treat emotions as objects in themselves and rely upon the use of such abstractions for the excitation of *indefinite* emotion rather than for the expression of *precise* emotion stirred by a particular sensory experience: "as a mixture of thought and of vision provides more stimulus, by suggesting both, both clear thinking and clear statement of particular objects must disappear" (*SW* 67). Eliot contends that a philosophy displaying precise thought and a poetry expressing precise emotion involve the same mental activity because he believes, in fact, that such poetry can give the impression of presenting a logical idea explaining the world: "all great poetry gives the illusion of a view of life. When we enter into the world of Homer, or Sophocles, or Virgil, or Dante, or Shakespeare, we incline to believe that we are apprehending something that can be expressed intellectually; for every precise emotion tends towards intellectual formulation" (SE 115).

A poet's "world" is his point of view, or finite center, which displays the kind of precision, that unity of sensory experience, logic, and emotion, that Eliot is seeking in philosophy and poetry. As immediate experience, the finite center is that unity of feeling in which subject and object, emotion and idea, are as yet indistinguishable and thus inseparable, as in a great work of art. As Eliot explains our initial impression of a painting, for instance, "we stand before a beautiful painting, and if we are sufficiently carried away, our feeling is a whole which is not, in a sense, *our* feeling, since the painting, which is an object independent of us, is quite as truly a constituent of our consciousness or our soul" (KE 20), that is, "in feeling the subject and object are one" (KE 21). But in our subsequent experience, this "whole of feeling" tends to "expand into object, and subject with feelings about the object" (KE 20), giving us consciousness and our world of Appearance. The mind proceeds to analyze immediate experience into emotion as an object in itself rather than as part of the original object experienced, and into logical ideas, or 'relations', attributed to the object as distinct and separate from, and therefore capable of being related to, other objects composing the finite center or world. Such a complete dissociation of a finite center, like the similar dissolution of the world of an art object, or the author's point of view, would yield a philosophy of life, an idea or system of relations, divorced from the objects expressing it and the emotion accompanying it. To separate a work of art into its constituent parts is for Eliot to reduce it to the world of Appearance. In turn, to create a work of art one must again unify the objects, emotions, and ideas of our world of experience according to the author's point of view, duplicating the unified feeling of his finite center in the art object.

Eliot's theory of the objective correlative, then, evolves out of his philosophical methodology prescribing the precise use of language: words must depict a concrete object or perceptual experience and should not become objects themselves, like the abstract concepts labeling emotions that have been isolated from the objects or events engendering them. The fragmentation of experience that causes such misuses of language is a consequence of ordinary

consciousness itself. In order to remedy this fragmentation, therefore, the poet must try to simulate unconscious immediate experience by once again unifying emotions with the objects that
originally accompanied them into our world, that is, with objects
that tend to induce the given emotion in his mind:

> The only way of expressing emotion in the form of art is by finding
> an "objective correlative"; in other words, a set of objects, a situation,
> a chain of events which shall be the formula of that *particular* emo-
> tion; such that when the external facts, which must terminate in
> sensory experience, are given, the emotion is immediately evoked.
> (*SE* 125)

The same theory is stated philosophically in Eliot's dissertation:

> Pure feeling is an abstraction, and in reality is always partially objec-
> tive: the emotion is really part of the object, and is ultimately just as
> objective. Hence when the object, or complex of objects, is recalled,
> the pleasure is recalled in the same way, and is naturally recalled on
> the object side rather than on the subject side. (*KE* 80)

If the artistic method of the objective correlative enables a poet
to write a poem approaching the condition of immediate experience, then the poem itself, as objective correlative, will consist of
the poet's point of view as well: "permanent literature is always a
presentation: either a presentation of thought, or a presentation of
feeling by a statement of events in human action or objects in the
external world; . . . this precise statement of life . . . is at the same
time a point of view, a world" (*SW* 64–65, 68). The finite center is
continuous with the psychological unconscious, which as a consequence functions like immediate experience, uniting the objects,
emotions, and ideas of our world. The writer who presents his
point of view as the objective correlative, therefore, writes his unconscious mind. Because this psychological unconscious is also
continuous with the physiological unconscious, Eliot attributes
the persistent separation of objects and emotions in a poet's work
to some reluctance or inability of the poet to consult or reach unconscious experience through his physiology, causing him to
dwell in the fragmented world of consciousness and resort to mere
verbalism instead of objective correlatives. Observing, for instance, that Massinger's "feeling for language had outstripped his
feeling for things; that his eye and his vocabulary were not in cooperation" (*SE* 185), Eliot concludes that Massinger "dwelt not

with emotions so much as with the social abstractions of emotions. . . . He was not guided by direct communication through the nerves" (SE 190).

6. UNITY OF SENSIBILITY

Through his theory of the objective correlative, then, Eliot stipulates that the esthetic act involves the artist seeking the unconscious mind and then simulating in his work of art the nature of immediate experience that he found there. But immediate experience does not simply consist of the union of objects with emotions and ideas: it is also the unity of logic and emotion. Because ideas and emotions become separate from each other only when a finite center disintegrates into our world, they are inherently related, and, as Eliot observes, "there is no greater mistake than to think that feeling and thought are exclusive—that those beings which think most and best are not also those capable of the most feeling" (KE 18). For this reason, when a poet simulates immediate experience through an objective correlative, his poem will effect a fusion of logic and emotion. Art, therefore, does not merely express emotion: "in really great imaginative work the connections are felt to be bound by as logical necessity as any connections to be found anywhere" (KE 75). Because it is "impossible . . . to draw any line between thinking and feeling," Eliot concludes that one cannot claim that "'feeling,' in a work of art, is any less an intellectual product that is 'thought.'"[56]

A poet displays a 'unity of sensibility', then, when he can reach beyond the superficial conscious distinctions of thought and emotion into the unconscious where they are fused together with objects, and in expressing this finite center, present a unified world in his poetry. Eliot indicates that such poetry depends upon the objective correlative when he states that poets of a unified sensibility "feel their thought as immediately as the odour of a rose" (SE 247), ending the sentence with his own sample image. Such poets work to express thought through sensory experience, imbuing thought with an emotional dimension by means of the appeal to the emotions the imagery will naturally make. In this kind of poem ideas are never stated directly, nor are they merely decorated with tropes, but are embodied in the movement of the imagery, in the world the poem delineates. Eliot's "Preludes" immediately comes to mind: a sequence of concrete images depicts

an entire world which, when we consciously analyze our unconscious response to it, we find at once that it suggests *ideas* or
themes of isolation, boredom, indifference, and social and eco-
nomic oppression, and stirs conflicting *emotions* of horror and fascination, pity and repulsion.

When Eliot attempts to express the essentially philosophical
idea of the unity of sensibility in a literary context, he will speak
in the paradoxes that result when the fragments of our world are
forcibly joined together: object, thought, and emotion metamorphose into each other, often exchanging roles. For instance,
poetry of a unified sensibility displays "a direct sensuous apprehension of thought, or a recreation of thought into feeling" (*SE*
246); it demonstrates the quality of "transmuting ideas into sensations, of transforming an object into a state of mind" (*SE* 249);
poets of unified sensibility "had a quality of sensuous thought, or
of thinking through the senses, or of the senses thinking" (*SW* 23).
But Eliot will also resort to philosophical terminology to describe
the unity of sensibility, just as he imports 'point of view' to explain
that writers create worlds rather than ideas. Eliot characterizes
Lewis's "purely intellectual curiosity in the senses," for example, as
a "perception of the world of immediate experience with its own
scale of values."[57]

Eliot is usually most explicit about the philosophical founda-
tions of his concept of unity of sensibility when speaking of Donne
and the Metaphysicals, the last poets in his opinion to display such
a unity. When Eliot observes that Metaphysical poetry "moves
between abstract thought and concrete feeling," that it "shows
thought and feeling as different aspects of one reality," and that
"this borderland where an emotion turns into a thought and a
thought turns into an emotion" can be considered Donne's "special
province," we recognize at once that he is describing immediate
experience where thought and emotion are one. In turn, when
Eliot explains that Donne, like Baudelaire, is a "master of surprises: . . . every new mood is prepared by and implicit in the
preceding mood—the mind has unity and order,"[58] we also realize
that such a unity that immediate experience achieves of our ordinary world results in the unfamiliar and startling combinations of
objects and feelings that we have come to associate with the content of the unconscious.[59]

7. WIT, METAPHYSICAL AND SURREAL

Eliot's notorious idea of the 'dissociation of sensibility' is his theory of the unity of sensibility projected onto the movement of history. Since the seventeenth century, he argues, poets have been unable to unite their thoughts and emotions through their expression in sensory images. Their poetry, therefore, simply mirrors the dissociated world of conscious experience. Eliot adopts the term 'wit' to signify that quality of mind and verse displayed in Metaphysical poetry that results from a unified sensibility. Like the objective correlative, wit for Eliot has philosophical as well as literary dimensions, both of which lead him beyond seventeenth-century verse to a definition of the surreal in poetry. When Eliot observes that Marvell's wit consists of his giving an ordinary emotion of daily experience "a connexion with that inexhaustible and terrible nebula of emotion which surrounds all our exact and practical passions and mingles with them" (*SE* 259), Eliot indicates that Marvell has reached what he defines in this way as the unconscious, for he is echoing Bradley's very definition of immediate experience that he quoted in his dissertation: "a sort of confusion, and a nebula which would grow distinct on closer scrutiny" (*KE* 19).[60]

Eliot can, therefore, agree only in part with Samuel Johnson's definition of the Metaphysicals. Eliot has no quarrel with the assessment that "'the most heterogeneous ideas are yoked by violence together'" (*SE* 243), because any unity that could approach immediate experience would be almost indiscriminately pervasive, joining objects and ideas quite distinct and isolated in our everyday experience with an apparently willful distortion of our world. Thus Eliot observes that, although Johnson notes that "'their attempts were always analytic,' he would not agree that, after their dissociation, they put the material together again in a new unity" (*SE* 245), the unity of the unconscious. Eliot prefers to apply Coleridge's definition of the Imagination to Metaphysical verse because, no doubt inspired by Coleridge's own acquaintance with early German Idealism (Kant, Fichte, Schelling), it coincidentally approaches at first a description of the Absolute: "'the balance or reconcilement of opposite or discordant qualities: of sameness with difference; of the general with the concrete; the idea with the image; the individual with the representative . . .'" (*SE* 257).

Eliot's description of wit as skeptical detachment and self-consciousness relates it, in fact, to the artist's unifying point of view, the third perspective that fuses reality, its objects and events, with ideas, emotions, and unconscious impulses, forming a work of art. Only from such a third point of view can a criticism of life be made and a unified view of the world as a whole be formed. Eliot stipulates that wit involves a "hold on human values," a "firm grasp of human experience" (SE 256), a "constant inspection and criticism of experience" (SE 262). Because mythic consciousness depends upon such a third point of view, permitting the modern world to be perceived in terms of a religious structure, Eliot observes that wit "leads toward, and is only completed by, the religious comprehension" (SE 256).

Because such a point of view is really the author's finite center, Eliot inevitably relates wit to the unconscious mind as well. Wit effects an "alliance of levity and seriousness" (SE 255), a kind of 'serious humor', the very quality of unconscious experience that Eliot discovered in British satire from Jonson to Lewis and the music-hall comedians. As the unconscious is collective and historical, so Eliot finds that wit "belongs to an educated mind, rich in generations of experience" (SE 262).

Perhaps most revealing of the scope and nature of Eliot's concept of wit is his remark that it "involves, probably, a recognition, implicit in the expression of every experience, of other kinds of experience which are possible" (SE 262). Such a definition goes beyond a description of immediate experience to suggest an esthetic program. With its emphasis on the simultaneity of different organizations, both perceptual and expressive, of experience, this definition certainly describes the process whereby mythic consciousness perceives mythic and ritualistic patterns in modern life. But it also suggests the simultaneous association of objects and experiences otherwise remote from and discordant with one another. This tendency to assimilate is responsible for the metamorphosis of objects and the juxtaposition of otherwise isolated events that form the basis of surrealist art.

Eliot perceives wit to be an intrinsic property of the poetical figure most characteristic of Metaphysical verse, the conceit. Ever since Eliot's essays discussing the relevance of seventeenth-century poetry to the modern sensibility, critics have been attempting to rescue Donne and his contemporaries from their kidnapping by the twentieth century and restore them to their proper literary context. Following Merritt Y. Hughes,[61] critics have researched various historical sources that might account for Metaphysical wit and the conceit. Joseph A. Mazzeo finds a "poetic of correspondence," expounded by Italian baroque theoreticians, responsible;[62] Ramist rhetoric-logic is accountable, according to Rosamond Tuve;[63] Donald L. Guss believes Donne to be a continuation of the "extravagant Petrarchan mode" as opposed to "humanistic Petrarchism."[64] But Eliot never claims that he is offering a comprehensive theory that is the poetic behind Metaphysical verse, nor that Donne could ever be *mistaken* for a modern.

More recently, critics have examined Metaphysical poetry itself more closely in order to distinguish it from the poetry of its twentieth-century admirers. Josephine Miles emphasizes the logical-argumentative structure of the individual Metaphysical poem.[65] Stephen Orgel, adopting a similar view of the rhetorical and persuasive cast of the verse, notes that, contrary to early twentieth-century opinion and poetic, the emblems used in Metaphysical conceits were considered to be verbal, not visual, elements, that the comparisons they make were recognized as intellectually ingenious rather than surprising, and that elaboration was the esthetic aim, rather than the compression valued by modern poets.[66] If we disregard the uses to which Eliot's followers put his ideas and examine his own statements carefully, we notice that he at once acknowledges those qualities of the conceit that make it a peculiarly seventeenth-century figure, and also those qualities that make it relevant to modern poetry. He subsequently isolates these latter qualities and analyzes their relevance to the contemporary sensibility in characteristically modern terms. Significantly, that aspect of Metaphysical verse which critics claim Eliot applauds, but which is peculiar only to seventeenth-century verse and hardly ever found in the twentieth century, is ultimately only tangential to the quality that really attracts Eliot to this poetry.

Eliot distinguishes between two qualities of Metaphysical verse: "the far-fetched association of the dissimilar, or the overelaboration of one metaphor or simile."[67] The latter quality Eliot regards as the conceit proper. This logical elaboration of a poetic figure is the one most often attributed to Metaphysical poetry and to Eliot's penchant for it, and it is precisely this quality that least interested him. Well aware of the rhetorical basis of the conceit, Eliot observes that Donne's conceits develop according to a "method of dialectic,"[68] and that the strophes of Marvell's "To His Coy Mistress" bear "something like a syllogistic relation to each other"

(*SE* 254): the third verse paragraph resembles the "conclusion of a syllogism of which the other two are the premisses."[69] Eliot's principal example of this "elaboration (contrasted with the condensation) of a figure of speech to the farthest stage to which ingenuity can carry it" actually is the most famous of all Metaphysical images, Donne's "comparison of two lovers to a pair of compasses" (*SE* 242) in "A Valediction: Forbidding Mourning." The appeal of these conceits is for Eliot primarily rational, as he speaks of "the intellectual pleasure in this ingenuity."[70]

That quality of juxtaposing the ordinarily dissimilar through a condensation of the poetic figure and poetic language, on the other hand, is that aspect of Metaphysical poetry most admired by Eliot: "but elsewhere we find, instead of the mere explication of the content of a comparison, a development by rapid association of thought which requires considerable agility on the part of the reader," producing in Donne's "A Valediction: Of Weeping," for example, "connexions which are not implicit in the first figure, but are forced upon it by the poet." Such a quality is also "secured by brief words and sudden contrasts: 'A bracelet of bright hair about the bone,' where the most powerful effect is produced by the sudden contrast of associations of 'bright hair' and of 'bone.'" This "telescoping of images and multiplied associations" (*SE* 242–43) that fascinates Eliot in Metaphysical verse approaches the technique of Surrealist poetry. The only other poetry that Eliot found to deliver a comparable effect was that of the Symbolists (*SE* 248–49), whom the Surrealists also claimed as their predecessors.

But neither the Metaphysicals nor the Symbolists actually achieve the same surrealistic shock characteristic of Eliot's own verse, as he himself recognized. After making the revealing assertion that all of the Metaphysical poets are "more or less fantastical," and that there is "no reason why a poet should not be as fantastical as possible," Eliot adds the stipulation that the kind of "fantasticality" employed must be appropriate for a given historical era. The "fantastic" that is the "proper expression" of the modern age will not be found in any other. The "conceits" that modern poets compose cannot resemble Marvell's; instead, they "will spring, equally genuine, from a different level of feeling."[71] Thus, when Eliot moves beyond the logical elaboration of the conceit to confront the fantastic quality of seventeenth-century verse, he will describe it not according to seventeenth-century poetic theory, in terms of rhetoric or emblem, but according to his own sense as a twentieth-century man of where it originates, in terms of modern poetic theory. For Eliot, the fantastic comes, not from the ingenuity of the intellect, but from the unconscious. The reader, in turn, is not merely rationally teased or emotionally stirred, but further, is unconsciously disturbed. In Henry King's "The Exequy," in which the poet expresses his desire to see his dead wife through the comparison with a journey, Eliot notes that in the last lines, "And slow howere my marches be, / I shall at last sit down by *Thee*," "there is that effect of terror" (*SE* 244).

8. METAPHOR

Eliot gives fullest expression to his surrealist poetic, then, while distinguishing the various qualities of Metaphysical verse and the effects they have upon him. What makes Eliot's poetic theory fundamentally surrealist is the dominant place it gives to metaphoric perception, and the radical, self-conscious kind of metaphor it recommends to satisfy this emphasis. For Eliot the basic operation of the mind is metaphoric, creating not merely poetry but language itself. Acknowledging Gourmont's *Problèm du style* as his source, Eliot observes that the history of language demonstrates that "all thought and all language is based ultimately upon a few simple physical movements. Metaphor is not something applied externally for the adornment of style, it is the life of style, of language," thus proving "how completely we are dependent upon metaphor for even the abstractest thinking." Because metaphor translates physical movements into language, it makes us aware of the physiological origin of language, and of thought: the "healthy" metaphor "makes available some of that physical source of energy upon which the life of the language depends," as, for example, "'in her strong toil of grace,'" from *Antony and Cleopatra*.[72]

To put the mind in touch with the physiological, as Eliot believes metaphor to do, is also to reach back into the collective-historical unconscious, reviving primitive experience. Such a mental act as Lévy-Bruhl's mystical participation, for instance, is really metaphoric perception. Morris Cohen explains that metaphor is, in fact, the primal cognitive process, an unconscious recognition of similarity preceding any logical justification:

> The prevailing view since Aristotle's *Rhetoric* regards metaphor as an analogy from which the words of comparison, *like* or *as*, etc., are omitted. This presupposes that the recognition of the literal truth pre-

cedes the metaphor which is always a conscious transference of the properties of one thing to another. But history shows that metaphors are generally older than expressed analogies. If intelligence grows from the vague and confused to the more definite by a process of discrimination, . . . metaphors may thus be viewed as expressing the vague and confused but primal perception of identity which subsequent processes of discrimination transform into a clear assertion of an identity or a common element (or relation) which the two different things possess.[73]

The investigations conducted by Freudian psychoanalysts into the unconscious coincide both with Lévy-Bruhl's description of primitive thinking as metaphoric and Cohen's view that such thinking precedes all conscious, rational thought. As Otto Fenichel observes:

If persons are tired, asleep, intoxicated or psychotic, they think in another and more primitive way; and even in healthy, good thinkers who are wide-awake, every single thought runs through initial phases that have more similarity with dream thinking than with logic. . . . [Preconscious thinking] is less fitted for objective judgment as to what is going to happen because it is relatively unorganized, tolerates and condenses contradictions; . . . similarities are not distinguished from identities.[74]

Not surprisingly, then, metaphor for Eliot becomes the fundamental esthetic act. To use metaphor is to simulate the unity of immediate experience which the mental life of primitive man approached and which now forms the substratum of our own mind as part of the unconscious. Metaphor unites objects and events otherwise unrelated in our world of experience through feeling, that unconscious fusion of thought and emotion. Simile, on the other hand, as it was customarily used in poetry before the early twentieth century, takes us further from primitive experience by either logically modifying such primal perceptions of identity and wholeness or seeking relationships on primarily rational grounds. Like or as traditionally indicated that the author had already calculated in what ways the objects or events involved in the figure are alike and different and was inviting the reader to do the same. The conceit proper removes us even further from the unconscious, since it is formed by the intellect further elaborating a given simile. As Eliot advises, conceits are not metaphors, but rather "disguised similes."[75] Eliot admires Metaphysical verse, however, not when it is being ingenious, but when it is most like the surreal: when the rapid association of images results in their interpenetration and forms a blurred whole in the reader's mind, or when two images of contrasting associations are suddenly joined together. Eliot appreciates a passage from Marvell's "The Nymph and the Fawn," above all, for the swift and shocking metamorphosis it achieves through metaphor:

Clorinda. Near this, a fountain's liquid bell
           Tinkles within the concave shell.

Damon.   Might a soul bathe there and be clean,
           Or slake its drought?

As Eliot comments, we take delight in the "suddenness of the transference from material to spiritual water,"[76] "where we find that a metaphor has suddenly rapt us to the image of spiritual purgation. There is here the element of *surprise*" (*SE* 259).

If we examine those passages in Eliot's poetry where he employs motifs or images similar to those lines of King and Donne that he most admires with the intention of creating a comparable effect of surprise, we notice immediately how much further Eliot has gone than his Metaphysical predecessors to unite disparate experience (*SE* 247). The passage in Eliot's poetry corresponding to the last lines of King's "The Exequy" is the closing lines of "Prufrock":

We have lingered in the chambers of the sea
By sea girls wreathed with seaweed red and brown
Till human voices wake us, and we drown. (129–31)

In King's poem, the juxtaposition is that between life and death. The living traveler, have reached his time, sits down into death, into his grave. Although we are shocked that an action in life suddenly becomes that of a dead man, the course of our world of experience, of nature, is not violated. By contrast, in Eliot's image the act of living is presented as dwelling under water, rather than on land in the air of a drawing room; we die, consequently, at the moment that the actual living world breaks into this imaginary life at the bottom of the sea. The natural course of events is disturbed initially because a man is said to live underwater, and later when he is said to die at the moment that he is awakened from his revery to a real-life situation. Two juxtapositions defying physical reality are thus created: one in which life is being submerged, ordinarily causing death, and the other in which death is the air of a drawing room, usually sustaining life. We expect the living to die and can anticipate the moment when life passes into death, but nothing in our experience of the world suggests that waking is drowning.

A similar distinction can also be drawn between Eliot's favorite line from Donne's "The Relique" and his own response to it in "Whispers of Immortality":

> breastless creatures under ground
> Leaned backward with a lipless grin.

> Daffodil bulbs instead of balls
> Stared from the sockets of the eyes! (3–6)

The macabre humor of portraying skeletons as living beings is, to be sure, a perennial literary device depicting a common fantasy of the human race. But within this traditional graveyard convention, Eliot presents juxtapositions of images and objects that contradict our sense of reality: one cannot smile without lips, and daffodil bulbs do not function like eyes and stare. In Donne's line, on the other hand, the contrast between bright hair and bone recalls, like King's, the opposition of life and death. We are shocked at first by the presence of what we ordinarily associate with life in a place reserved for the dead. But in the context of the grave-digging scene in which the line occurs, the natural laws of our world are not violated by finding hair to survive the decay of flesh. Metaphysical poetry shocks us with the presence of life in death, and death in life, and by dealing with emotional experiences in terms of esoteric philosophical theories about reality, but it does not defy the natural sequence of events of the world itself. Poetry that is surrealistic, like Eliot's, on the other hand, contradicts nature by distorting our fragmented world of experience, rearranging objects or events formerly separated by space, time, and notions of causality.

Eliot's verse approaches the surreal, then, because the archetypal surrealist figure is, in fact, the metaphor, through which two ordinarily incongruent or disparate experiences are wrenched out of their customary context in reality and fused into a new combination, or two usually separate and isolated objects are either juxtaposed or metamorphose into each other. As Breton indicates, the ability to reach the unconscious consists essentially of the power to create metaphor: "it is the marvelous faculty of attaining two widely separate realities without departing from the realm of our experience; of bringing them together and drawing a spark from their contact."[77] When the reader encounters such an image presented concretely in the poem and attempts to imagine it, he will be jarred by its unnaturalness and his preconception of the relationships between objects and events in the everyday world will be destroyed. Once liberated from the conscious world of Appearance, these previously isolated components of reality form a new whole which stirs his unconscious and provides him with an experience of that unifying, subliminal region. This is the primal process, and primitive experience, of metaphor for Eliot and the Surrealists.[78]

The metaphorical perceiving and expressing of one object or experience in terms of another has always been a property of poetry. But the Surrealists are the first poets to emphasize the essence of metaphor, unification, in their work through the disparateness of the elements being united. Previously, there has always been a readily recognizable rational and emotional relationship between the elements of a poetic figure that makes the experience of metaphor stimulating, satisfying, or comforting rather than disconcerting. Governing the conceit of Metaphysical verse is the logic of the argument of the poem, or of some theological principle or scientific theory. The reader experiences an intellectual delight in puzzling out the relationships that the logic dictates between objects, events, and experiences ordinarily independent of each other. Motivating the symbol of Romantic poetry is the rational and spiritual force of pantheism. Natural objects are often subtlely personified in order to suggest a living spirit behind Nature. The reader is emotionally reassured by these animate images that the material world shares and will be responsive to the feelings and concerns of a human being. Even the correspondences and analogies of French Symbolist verse, more daring and elusive than those of previous poetry, are still based on exotic or sensual relationships which make them not so much startling as teasing or fascinating.

Surrealist verse, on the other hand, exaggerates the metaphoric process by relating objects and experiences that are not customarily associated with each other, either by artistic or intellectual tradition, or by the laws of nature or logic. Unlike Romantic poetry, for instance, man-made artifacts rather than natural objects are endowed with animate qualities. Lacking any precedent that would make these relationships understandable, the reader finds them enigmatic and shocking. In addition to this qualitative property of joining the entirely dissimilar, the Surrealist image tends to have a particular syntactic structure that emphasizes the disparateness of its elements. Most often it will be a verbal metaphor, as in lines 1 and 2 of Aragon's "Les Débuts du fugutif," [79] or line 7 of Desnos's "Tu prends la première rue à droite," [80] or line 2 of his "Vie d'Ebène"; [81] or the metaphor is adjectival, as in line 1 of Eluard's "L'objectivité poétique n'existe que. . . ." [82] Such a syntactic structure makes the surreal image as startling as possible, because the incongruent elements appear directly adjacent to each other. The shock is further augmented by the logic of the syntax, which instantaneously asserts identity: the syntax implies that the noun performs the incongruent activity of the verb, or possesses the incongruent property of the adjective.

Less frequently, the Surrealist image is a prepositional metaphor (*of, with, in, to, on*), as in line 13 of Desnos's "La Ville"; [83] or the metaphor is constructed with the verb *to be,* as in line 9 of Desnos's "Au petit jour." [84] In these metaphors, the shock is somewhat less severe, because the logical distance of the syntax is greater: the elements are separated by prepositions. Also, these prepositions imply qualification (*of, with*) or relationship (*in, to, on*) rather than identity. Even the verb *to be,* however, places some distance between the two elements. Although it asserts identity, *to be* concretizes this assertion in a word that separates the two elements. This concrete logical assertion does not juxtapose the elements as quickly as the implied logic of the verbal or adjectival metaphor. Eliot's own verse also displays verbal ("daffodil bulbs . . . / Stared"), adjectival ("lipless grin"), and prepositional metaphors, like "smooths the hair of the grass" (54) of "Rhapsody on a Windy Night," in which the vegetable turns into the human. The modern poems in English and French in which Eliot perceives surrealistic effects also contain these types of metaphor.

9. THE VISUAL

The surreal image is also delivered as a simile, although this kind of poetic figure appears least frequently of all. The Surrealists do use similes at times to emphasize the disparateness of the objects that they are uniting. *Like* or *as* promises the reader a logical relationship which is eventually frustrated by the second element of the figure. Thus these images are similes only in structure, not in conception, and their effect is metaphorical, the shock of violating the natural world by uniting two ordinarily disparate objects, as in lines 15 and 16 of Soupault's *Westwego*,[85] or line 1 of Desnos's "Coeur en bouche."[86] But Surrealist poets use *like* or *as* most often when the metaphorical union they wish to express is based upon the coincidental similarity of visual properties. Lines 14 and 15 of Eluard's "Mourir," for instance, rely upon the similarity of the actual depth of a grave and the visual depth of a rectangular mirror.[87] An image from Benjamin Peret's "Mille Fois" depends upon the visual resemblance of an egg yoke in the middle of its white to a lamp and the glow that surrounds it.[88] In these images, one object metamorphoses into the other in the reader's imagination because of the coincidental similarity of visual form.

For Breton, these illogical visual superpositions, as well as unnatural visual collocations, achieve absolute metaphor, "the spontaneous, extralucid, insolent rapport which establishes itself under certain conditions between one thing and another."[89] *Like* as a logical connective is either eliminated, or its rational connotation ignored, so that a physical transformation can take place in the reader's mind: "I demand that he who still refuses, for instance, to *see* a horse galloping on a tomato should be looked on as a cretin. A tomato is also a child's balloon—surrealism, I repeat, having suppressed the word 'like'."[90] But Breton admits that the most effective of the "analogical tools"[91] for establishing metaphoric relationships is, nevertheless, the word *like,* not used in its logical capacity, however, but simply as a syntactic enticement to induce the reader to fuse two incongruent objects in what must inevitably be some nonrational way, that is, visually: "the word *like* is the most exalting at our command when it is pronounced familiarly. Through it the human imagination fulfills itself."[92]

The simile is actually the ideal figure for presenting a metaphor depicting the visual similarity of otherwise incongruent objects. Although an affiliation is asserted between the elements, they are at first virtually independent of each other, isolated on either side of *like* or *as*. Because these two connectives attribute equal importance to each element, one element is not subservient to the other, as in the prepositional metaphors. *Like* and *as* simply assert identity, instead of a particular kind of relationship or qualification. Further, the reader is not directed by the logic of the syntax to imagine any definite, nonvisual aspect of the objects, such as the specific activity of a verbal metaphor, or the specific property of the adjectival metaphor. Consequently, the reader is given a chance to encounter the first object by itself and unmodified—in its full integrity as an object—and thus tends to recall it as a complete visual image. When he encounters the second object, also separate and whole, he is inclined to superimpose its visual image onto the previous visual image, and a metaphoric fusion occurs based on visual similarity. With verbal or adjectival metaphors, on the other hand, the reader may be able to visualize the noun, but he has no chance to visualize, alone and in its entirety, the object implied by the verb or adjective. Thus he conceives of the relationship between the two elements in terms other than, or in addition to, visual properties, such as the laws of logic or nature. He attempts to imagine the noun *performing* the activity of the verb or *displaying* the property of the adjective. Since the juxtaposition involves disparate elements, what it suggests is physically impossible. Unable to visualize the image easily, if at all, therefore, the reader will have a sense only of the illogical and the unnatural. The reader's awareness of incongruity will tend to dominate over any feeling of union suggested by the figurative construction, because the only possible basis of comparison, visual similarity, has been disrupted by nonvisual concerns.

The metaphor of coincidental visual similarity, therefore, may very well be the archetypal Surrealist image. A visual relationship defies natural laws by dislocating reality and joining together ordinarily disparate objects. Yet a coincidental similarity has no basis in logic, providing an entirely nonrational and nonemotional means of uniting otherwise disparate experience. The metaphor of coincidental visual similarity will thus be both startling and unifying, the two characteristics of unconscious experience. Significantly, although Breton seldom uses *like* or *as,* he often depicts coincidental visual similarities in his verbal, adjectival, and prepositional metaphors. He wishes to achieve both the shock of incongruity and a sense of relationship at the same time. As would be expected, his success depends upon how much time, syntactically, the reader is given to visualize the elements of the metaphor. For instance, in the prepositional metaphor of line 1 of

L'Union libre, the reader seems to have just enough time to picture a head of hair as a fire.[93] But in the verbal metaphor of lines 7 and 8 of "A ta place je me méfierais," the reader requires considerably more time to notice the visual similarity that is being implied between random pats of butter on a slice of bread and falling yellow leaves in the air.[94] He feels the incongruence of the elements much more strongly than their unification.

Like the Surrealists, Eliot will also use the simile to express a metaphorical relationship based upon coincidental visual similarity. In "the light of the door / Which opens on her like a grin" (17–18) of "Rhapsody on a Windy Night," for instance, the curve of the light coming out of a half-opened door recalls the curve of a smiling mouth with the flash of teeth. Occasionally, he will use verbal metaphors to express less direct visual similarities, as in his antiromantic transformation of the moon into an old whore: "She winks a feeble eye" (52) and "A washed-out smallpox cracks her face" (56). Most of Eliot's metaphors, in fact, regardless of syntactic structure, are usually inspired by some coincidental visual resemblance, and he frequently emphasizes this resemblance, that is, facilitates its recognition by the reader, through the use of *like* or *as.* Many of the passages from contemporary English verse that Eliot praises for their exemplary poetic quality also consist of metaphors based on the coincidental similarity of visual properties delivered as similes. The sense of relationship in Eliot's poetry and in the passages he quotes, therefore, tends to be somewhat stronger than in Surrealist poetry, even though Eliot and these other poets are also uniting disparate objects and incongruent experience.

Because of this visual discipline inherent in his formation of metaphor and in his taste in poetry, Eliot's images and those of the strain of surrealism that he detects in modern verse appear to resemble Surrealist painting even more than Surrealist poetry. Surrealist paintings often portray metaphors of coincidental visual similarity by superimposing objects in the painted environment on the basis of their shape or configuration. Max Ernst's *The Elephant of Celebes* (1921), for instance, transforms the inanimate into the animate by depicting a piece of mechanical equipment so that it suggests an elephant. The foreground is dominated by a round dark green tank resting on the ground upon two stubby columns that look like an elephant's fat legs. A flexible tube protruding from the front of the tank in a semicircle suggests a trunk. In René Magritte's *The Red Model* (1935), the inanimate metamorphoses into the human again through visual resemblance. The upper half of a pair of shoes is laces and leather, the bottom half the flesh and toes of the foot that usually wears them. Salvador Dali's *Mae West* (1934–36) merges the face of the movie star with a drawing room. Her hair is simultaneously the drapery of the entry; her chin and neck are portrayed as the steps into the room; her lips are converted into a sofa; her nose is located where the fireplace should be and has a clock on top of it; and her eyes are blended with paintings inside of gold frames hung on the wall. Based on coincidental visual similarity, the images in these paintings give the same sense of relationship between disparate objects that is usually communicated by the metaphors presented as similes in Eliot's poetry and the passages that he quotes.

Other Surrealist paintings, however, portray metaphors of visual *dis*similarity, juxtaposing objects of a given scale with other objects whose relative scale in the same painted environment has been increased or decreased. The room of Magritte's *Personal Values* (1952), for example, contains a bed upon which rests a comb that leans against the wall and nearly reaches to the ceiling. In the center of the floor stands a glass that is as tall as the wardrobe. The bar of soap lying on the floor next to it is just as long as the wardrobe is wide. The visual juxtapositions of this painting emphasize incongruence, whereas the visual metamorphoses of the previous paintings emphasize relationship. Like Magritte, Eluard begins his poem "L'Amoureuse" with a metaphor of visual dissimilarity that juxtaposes objects of varying relative scales: in line 1 his lover is said to be positioned on top of his eyelids.[95] As would be expected, since incongruence is the effect of this metaphor instead of relationship, the image is expressed as a verbal metaphor instead of a simile.

Both Eliot and the Surrealist painters had a theoretical justification for using visual metaphor as the fundamental tool for probing the unconscious. The Surrealists learned from Freud that the unconscious impulses which govern the formation of their metaphors usually appear in the form of visual images, or in terms of certain words. The visual nature of dream imagery was also recognized by psychologists upon whom Freud based his work. As Otto Fenichel summarizes, preconscious thinking is carried out more through pictorial, concrete images. . . . The object and the idea of the object, the object and a picture or model of the object, the object and a part of the object are equated. . . . In dreams, symbols appear . . . as a characteristic of archaic pictorial thinking, as a part of visualizing abstract thoughts.[96]

Eliot himself discovered from his own experience that unconscious "feelings" will be found "inhering for the writer in particular words or phrases or images" (SE 8). Eliot's idea of the objective correlative, in fact, tends to emphasize the visual aspect of poetic imagery. The concept is, after all, based on Gourmont's theory that language originates in sensory images which are stored in a visual memory and then recalled at some future time by association with other images to emerge in the form of poetic figures. This visual orientation was reinforced for Eliot by Logical Positivism's assertion that language adheres to perceptual experience only when it names or presents objects, rather than describing them further or analyzing them. The objective correlative approximates immediate experience by expressing ideas and emotions through particular objects. Simply to name such objects in language, regardless of any further description of them beyond sensory experience, will automatically recall first a visual image. Eliot believed, therefore, that any poetry that attempts to express the unconscious mind has to be primarily visual: "the less 'realistic' literature is, the more visual it must be." When we read Dante, we must "visualize" constantly. "Dreams, to be real, must be seen."[97] Dante's 'dream' is the mythic structure of the Christian religion assuming its allegorical form in The Divine Comedy.

Eliot's association of Dante's allegory with poetry that is primarily visual and expressive of the unconscious mind can be further illuminated by considering Angus Fletcher's more recent argument that surrealist art is fundamentally allegory, as he defines the allegorical mode through psychoanalytic and anthropological theory. Fletcher bases his contention upon the stylistic similarity of the two kinds of art:

The term "surrealism" . . . implies obsessional and dream imagery, unexpected even shocking collocations of heterogeneous objects, psychological emblems (usually Freudian), hyperdefinite draftsmanship, distortions of perspective—with all these working together to produce enigmatic combinations of materials. Above all, discontinuity and unnatural groupings seem to characterize surreal art. Objects quite "real" in themselves become "nonreal," i.e. surreal by virtue of their mutual interrelations, or rather, through their apparent lack of rational interrelations, or rather, through their apparent lack of rational interrelation when combined within single frames. This deliberately enigmatic, teasing, strange style is to be found . . . in early allegories as well.[98]

In addition, Fletcher's theoretical framework specifies that allegory and surrealism are related because they both compulsively distort reality in unnatural ways in order to express a particular obsessive idea or meaning. But, although medieval and Renaissance allegories may resemble Surrealist art stylistically, Surrealist art still may not necessarily be allegorical. Fletcher's theoretical framework is not sufficiently oriented to the affective dynamics of both types of art to explain how fundamentally different they really are.

This important distinction is, however, implicit in Fletcher's observations on an allegorical painting and on a Surrealist work. Of the *Madonna and Child with Saints* of Girolamo dai Libri (1474– 1555), Fletcher notes that "the religious allegory is so traditional that one fails to note how fantastic is the collection of pictorial elements."[99] By contrast, Fletcher observes, "because his iconography is unfamiliar, Ernst's *Woman, Old Man and Flower* [1923–24] must force the viewer to accept a shocking discontinuity of elements."[100] Because Christian iconography is available to the viewer before he sees the medieval painting, he is able to 'read' it allegorically, rationally translating image into meaning as he is affected emotionally by its embodiment in a visual image. Since he is handling the painting on this conscious level and can justify its incongruous groupings of figures and objects, and their unnatural relative sizes, he is not shocked: the painting never penetrates to his unconscious. In the Surrealist painting, on the other hand, a culturally shared system of symbols and ideas explaining the unnatural configurations on the canvas is unavailable to the viewer. Consequently, it is impossible for him to deal with the painting in any conscious, simply rational and emotional, way. The image remains for him a physical impossibility rather than an embodiment of meaning, and he is jolted unconsciously by the incongruities which contradict his sense of reality.

Fletcher's description of surrealism as allegory in reverse, as an allegorical artistic structure in search of its corresponding meaning, still does not sufficiently distinguish between the two modes. As Fletcher observes, with surrealism "we are dealing with a decapitated allegory, whose aim is indeed, as Tzara and Breton insisted, an automatic search for a new absolute, a new dogma,"[101] but an absolute that had no relation to our conscious world of experience, thus a dogma that in no way resembles the rational meanings with which we translate allegorical paintings, indeed, hardly 'dogma' at all. Surrealism is certainly a "decapitated allegory" because the head, the meanings that prevent the images from penetrating to our unconscious mind, do not, and cannot, exist, if the Surrealist painting is to be successful. As Breton stipulates in his first "Manifesto of Surrealism", "surrealism is based on the belief in the superior reality of certain forms of previously neglected associations, in the omnipotence of dream, in the disinterested play of thought,"[102] and those "previously neglected associations" come only from the "superior reality" of the unconscious in its psychological and metaphysical dimensions.

Significantly, Eliot, as a twentieth-century man unfamiliar with much of the iconography and dogma that governs medieval allegory, reads *The Divine Comedy* at times as if it were a Surrealist work. Even Breton admits that such an experience is possible: "if one is to judge them only superficially by their result a good number of poets could pass for Surrealists, beginning with Dante and, in his finer moments, Shakespeare."[103] Conscious meanings with which Eliot could translate the allegorical action are not necessary, because, when they are missing, the visual images with their inherent Christian structure will penetrate directly to the unconscious, the source of religious experience:

> What we should consider is not so much the meaning of the images, but the reverse process, that which led a man having an idea to express it in images. . . . [F]or a competent poet, allegory means *clear visual images*. And clear visual images are given much more intensity by having a meaning—we do not need to know what that meaning is, but in our awareness of the image we must be aware that the meaning is there too. (*SE* 204)

This passage indicates, at the same time, a basic difference between Eliot's and the Surrealists' respective conceptions of the unconscious. For Eliot, unconscious experience is more closely related to our conscious life. Eliot found a structure in the unconscious which operated at once as feeling, below the level of consciousness, and yet could easily be 'analyzed' and converted into separate rational and emotional aspects once brought into our conscious mind. For the Surrealists, unconscious experience suggested no such structures.

10. THEORY AND PRACTICE

The artistic technique prescribed by Eliot's poetic actually coincides with Surrealist theory and practice. Eliot believes that a poem is constructed of concrete images derived from sensory experience, but these images are not arranged by the poet to portray the everyday world from which they were taken. Rather, they coalesce and metamorphose according to the impulses of the poet's own mind. Poetry achieves its effect, Eliot specifies, either by the "cumulative succession of images each fusing with the next," or by the "rapid and unexpected combination of images apparently unrelated, which have their relationship enforced upon them by the mind of the author."[104] We can be certain that Eliot is referring to the unconscious, because, when discussing the virtues of Metaphysical verse, he resorts once again, as he did with tradition, to a description of the poet's mind as a medium, rather than a personality, that produces objective correlatives, "forming new wholes." This time, however, Eliot emphasizes the heterogeneity of the images, the experiences and objects to be fused in a poem: "a poet's mind . . . is constantly amalgamating disparate experience." Considering Eliot's example of such an amalgamation, falling in love and reading Spinoza illustrate the unity of emotion and thought that comprises immediate experience, and the additional unity supplied by the noise of a typewriter or the smell of cooking illustrate the joining of incongruous sensory experiences characteristic of the unconscious mind. "The ordinary man's experience is chaotic, irregular, fragmentary" (*SE* 247) because he lives only in the everyday world of consciousness, where dissimilar objects remain separate and isolated. Breton's definition of the Surrealist image that results from the liberation of the unconscious also emphasizes the technique of joining disparate objects and experiences, and in specific ways similar to Eliot's objective correlative. The most effective Surrealist image, Breton explains,

> is the one that is arbitrary to the highest degree, the one that takes the longest time to translate into practical language, either because it contains an immense amount of seeming contradiction, . . . or because it

very naturally gives to the abstract the mask of the concrete, or the opposite, or because it implies the negation of some elementary physical property.[105]

Like the Surrealists, Eliot desires this rapid combination of disjunctive images because only a poem so constructed will stir the unconscious. As Eliot observes of *Anabasis* (1924) by St.-Jean Perse, its "obscurity" is the result of the "suppression of 'links in the chain,' of explanatory and connecting matter." Confronted by a series of naturally inconsistent and enigmatic images, the reader feels an initial confusion, since he cannot rationally and consciously relate them to his ordinary world of experience: thus the "sequence of images coincides and concentrates into one intense impression of barbaric civilization." Such a method leaves the reader in an overwhelmed and defenseless state, so that he cannot prevent the poem from entering his unconscious mind: the reader must permit the "images to fall into his memory successively without questioning the reasonableness of each at the moment; so that, at the end, a total effect is produced."[106] A discursive poem, by contrast, will be comfortably understood and will even be emotionally moving, but hardly startling, for it functions according to the familiar, fragmentary sequentiality of the everyday world and is engaged by the reader only at the conscious level. Eliot's poetry is notorious for its disjointedness, not only from strophe to strophe, as in "Prufrock" or "Gerontion," and from stanza to stanza, as in the quatrain satires, but also within strophes and stanzas, and at times from line to line. Sudden shifts of speaker, time-frame, scene, subject, diction, tone, and theme are common. *The Waste Land* is only the most extreme example of Eliot's forging an artistic whole out of disjunctive elements, especially at the level of the poetic figure.[107]

Eliot and the Surrealists specify a similar artistic method because their respective definitions of the unconscious are similar. The unconscious for Breton, a combination of the Freudian personal unconscious (psychological) and the Hegelian Absolute (metaphysical), is a variation of Eliot's unconscious, where Bradley's immediate experience (metaphysical) is continuous with the collective-historical (psychological) and the material (physiological). Both Eliot and Breton rely upon the metaphysical unconscious for a definition of how the psychological unconscious functions, and thus derive the technique of fusing incongruous images from Idealism. Eliot observes of Donne's verse, for instance, that "these odd changes of key, these sudden changes and strange juxtapositions . . . combine to make a unique emotional whole,"[108] a unity characteristic of the 'whole' that is immediate experience. More explicitly, Eliot notes in the prose of Rimbaud that the "juxtaposition of images" evinces a special kind of "sincerity (as if rising immediately and unreflecting from the core of the man's feeling)."[109] This 'core of feeling', judging from Eliot's adverbs, is at once the metaphysical and the psychological unconscious, which tends to join together experiences ordinarily kept apart by our conscious mind, as immediate experience unites objects that diverge in time and space to form our world of Appearance. Likewise, Breton defines the functioning of the psychological unconscious in terms of the unifying Absolute. In the "Second Manifesto of Surrealism" (1930), Breton states: "everything tends to make us believe that there exists a certain point of the mind at which life and death, the real and the imagined, past and future, the communicable and the incommunicable, high and low, cease to be perceived as contradictions."[110] Dialectical thinking, the strategy of Eliot's mind, inspires Surrealism as well, for Breton entertains "a persistent hope in the *dialectic*" of Hegel "for the resolution of the antinomies which overwhelm man."[111]

It is not surprising, therefore, to find both Eliot and Breton insisting that the more heterogeneous the objects or experiences united in an image, the deeper into the unconscious the poet has traveled. Eliot makes the point in connection with Rimbaud, who appears on Breton's list, in the first "Manifesto," of writers of the past or outside of the movement proper who nevertheless display a surrealistic quality.[112] Eliot observes that the aesthetic effect of the *Illuminations* is created by an "instant and simple impression, a unity all the more convincing because of the apparent incongruity of images."[113] Breton makes the same point in the first "Manifesto" by quoting a statement by Pierre Reverdy, who also appears on Breton's list of unofficial Surrealists:[114]

> The image is a pure creation of the mind.
> It cannot be born from a comparison but from a juxtaposition of two more or less distant realities.
> The more the relationship between the two juxtaposed realities is distant and true, the stronger the image will be—the greater its emotional power and poetic reality.[115]

The similarities in Eliot's and Breton's respective definitions of the unconscious lead to other theoretical coincidences as well.

When Breton speaks of the unifying tendency of the unconscious, he describes it in terms that recall Eliot's definition of immediate experience, the primal union of the external, objects and events, and the internal, the emotions and thoughts that originally accompanied them. Breton asserts that the unconscious can overcome "the opposition of the mental representation and the physical perception, both of them produced from the dissociation of a single primordial faculty of which the primitive and the child bear the trace, which lifts the malediction of an uncrossable barrier between the external and the internal world."[116] Like Eliot, Breton further characterizes this unconscious unity as if it were a result of the primitive mental habit that Lévy-Bruhl defined as mystical participation, which perceives relationships between ordinarily disparate objects: Breton seeks "everything that adventurously breaks the thread of discursive thought and suddenly ignites a flare illuminating a life of relations fecund in another way. Everything indicates that men of an earlier time possessed the secret of these relations."[117] For Breton, the poet can recover this primitive unity by following the dictates of his unconscious through the very faculty that Eliot felt reveals the subliminal mind, the auditory imagination. And like Pound, who specified that an Image was not to be a literal description of objective reality, Breton also seeks a primarily mental event that only coincidentally happens to be expressed most effectively as a visual image: "it always seemed to me that verbo-auditive automatism creates for the reader the most exalting visual images. . . . I believe . . . in the triumph *auditorily* of what is unverifiable visually."[118]

Despite all of these essential similarities, however, Eliot avoided any direct contact with the Surrealist Movement itself. His personal aloofness can probably be attributed in part to his associating Surrealism with Dada, out of which it grew. For Eliot, Dadaism was artistic "chaos,"[119] "a deliberate school of mythopoeic nihilism,"[120] as it certainly was for the Dadaists themselves. Eliot chose to treat the Dadaist phenomenon in terms of his theory of tradition, condemning it, not because it was novel, but because it was novel in the wrong way. For Eliot, tradition never signifies stultification or conformity; it simply provides a background from which an artist can diverge and through which his originality can be recognized: "culture is traditional, and loves novelty";[121] "tradition is ever lapsing into superstition, and the violent stimulus of novelty is required" (*CC* 184). Because Eliot believes that French canons of taste are particularly restrictive, he surmises that French culture is "too uniform, monotonous"; thus, Dadaism becomes the "diagnosis of a disease of the French mind," valuable only to that "small public formidably well instructed in its own literary history, erudite and stuffed with tradition to the point of bursting."[122]

Consequently, when he reviewed *Vingt-cinq poèmes*[123] by Tristan Tzara, one of the founders of Dada, Eliot was at once understanding and critical; his tone is more witty than ironic. Quoting the nonsensical, aurally playful lines 4 and 5 of "Le Géant blanc lépreux du paysage," Eliot observes that the passage should be taken "very seriously" as a "symptom of 'experiment,'" but should not be offered to beginning writers, and Eliot's summary remark indicates why: Tzara's poetry does not seem to possess "very deep roots in the literature of any nation."[124] For Eliot, "the good New grow[s] naturally out of the good Old" (*CC* 184); conservative verse is always second-rate verse, and good verse cannot grow out of nothing any more than it can grow out of bad verse, which will inevitably be conservative—immune to imagination and originality. In its desire to break with tradition, both good and bad, Dadaist verse coincides in Eliot's mind with *vers libre;* and Eliot concludes that "the division between Conservative Verse and *vers libre* does not exist, for there is only good verse, bad verse, and chaos" (*CC* 189).

Certainly Eliot must have perceived the automatism initially counselled by Surrealist polemic as just another method of producing the artistic chaos that Dadaism coveted. Eliot valued the realm of unconscious experience as much as the Surrealists, but he believed that esthetic purpose and unconscious feelings are compatible. The Surrealists, on the other hand, felt that esthetic concerns impinge on the freedom of the unconscious. Because the goal of the Surrealists was, above all, the liberation of the unconscious, they at first denied reason, at least theoretically, and in practice as much as not, any role in the artistic process. They wanted to produce objects whose creation was dictated exclusively by the unconscious. The Surrealists believed, in turn, that the unconscious could be reached through an art work only when it consisted entirely of the unmolested content of the subliminal mind. By contrast, Eliot felt that a poem could stir the unconscious, not only when the verse contained subliminal material, but also when the structure and content observed certain characteristics of the unconscious. The Surrealists' artistic program, therefore, emphasizes ways to liberate the subliminal and preserve its authenticity, such as automatic writing, even at the expense of esthetic concerns, while Eliot's poetic theory stresses how the unconscious initiates the creative process and is incorporated into a work of art.

Because Eliot's goal was always the creation of a work of art, he recognized from the beginning that the esthetic requirements of a poem could not be satisfied solely by the unconscious: "the way in which poetry is written is not any clue to its value" (UPUC 146). The conscious mind of the poet would have to exert sufficient control over the eruptions of or descents into the unconscious in order to make them into a work of art. The poet must consider what effect a given poetic structure will have upon the reader, who begins his reading at the conscious, rather than unconscious, level of attention. Artistic control must be exerted over unconscious material, however, not to violate it through logical analysis, but to arrange it into a larger esthetic whole, requiring at times passages supplied by the conscious mind. The "critical labour" that Eliot specifies is involved in composing a poem consists primarily of assembling, connecting, and accommodating rather than rewriting: "the labour of sifting, combining, constructing, expunging, correcting, testing" (SE 18). Eliot's method of composition was, in fact, to preserve passages of poetry probably written during moments when he was in touch with his unconscious to be incorporated later into a larger artistic structure, "doing things separately and then seeing the possibility of fusing them together, altering them, and making a kind of whole of them."[125] Perhaps because Eliot perceives primitive myth and ritual to be a part of his subliminal mind, he is more likely to insist upon the artistic control of the unconscious than the Surrealists, because for him subliminal experience itself provides the potential organization of a poem. Equating Surrealism with automatic writing late in his life, Eliot observes that Surrealism appeared to offer a "method of producing works of art without imagination";[126] yet Eliot always relied upon the method of descending into the unconscious as a prerequisite for the writing of poetry.

For the Surrealists, however, automatic writing was, finally, only one way of unleashing the unconscious. Whereas previously any product of automatism was in itself considered to be an 'endowed' object worthy of attention, by 1930 Breton had redefined the role of automatism as simply one element, if the integral, catalytic one, in the creative process. He suggested that Surrealists be more observant, more self-aware, in their subliminal investigations by exercising some control over the formation of the objects dictated by the revelations of their unconscious. He also implied that in many instances of Surrealist art the conscious had been playing a part all along, as in those poems and paintings that did not consist of automatic texts and graphic configurations but instead attempted to present dreams previously experienced.[127] Yet the Surrealists never did decide with any conclusiveness the value for them of rationally guiding irrational phenomena, and this methodological dilemma continued to prove a constant source of tension within the movement, as it had been during the 1920s.

Eliot's formulation of the esthetic act, conscious manipulation of unconscious content, perhaps describes the way Surrealists actually created their art better than the exaggerated claims of their early pronouncements. That the images of Surrealist poetry often focus upon or develop a theme suggests some conscious control. The titles of Surrealist paintings often supply the theme their images portray. One can create surreal images as much by consciously and rationally combining disparate objects and experiences as by recording those incongruent images emerging from the unconscious. In the end, can one ever be totally *unconscious* and still be capable of creating any object at all, or objects as complicated as Surrealist works of art? Surely some cooperation between the conscious and unconscious must be taking place. Simply the absence or presence of conscious and rational control in artistic creation cannot be the difference between Eliot and the Surrealists, therefore, but instead how *much* control and toward what *end*. Eliot employed more control than most Surrealists in order to achieve more complex works of art than most of them. His themes are more subtle and his structures more ambitious. Yet his imagery and forms retain a subliminal quality.

Naturally, then, Eliot's poetry will differ from Surrealist art according to the one important way in which their concepts of the unconscious differ. Although Eliot and Breton adopted similar definitions of the metaphysical unconscious, they defined the psychological unconscious somewhat differently. For Breton, it is the Freudian personal unconscious, while for Eliot it is the collective-historical unconscious. Both kinds of unconscious are not mutually exclusive. Freud, in fact, postulated a version of the collective-historical in conjunction with the personal. But the Surrealists usually discovered their own subjective fantasies and private obsessions in the unconscious, while Eliot found the entire history of the human mind. For Freud and the Surrealists, the Oedipal urge may be a universal phenomenon. But the various neuroses it causes, though they continually reappear throughout history, will not be present in every individual. For Eliot, on the other hand, the religious impulse and the death-rebirth pattern are common to all men of every time, place, and personality. The dialectical function of the unconscious, according to Eliot, not only fuses disparate objects of the everyday world of the present, but also unites experience of the present with that of the past.[128]

Eliot relied upon history both for artistic order and unconscious communication. Ritualistic structures persisting throughout the evolution of man provided Eliot with a form for the longer poem and at the same time permitted him to reach the collective-historical unconscious of his readers. Incorporating quotations from older literary works into his poems enabled Eliot not only to align his work with a literary tradition, but also to relate his personal experience to similar experiences of humanity throughout history, and to discover the permanent feelings and desires of human nature. The result in *The Waste Land,* as Paul Ray notes,[129] is a surrealistic literary experience: a contemporary situation metamorphoses into a historical event, or into a previous literary tableau. Such juxtapositions simulate the unifying tendency of the unconscious, whose associations have no temporal limits. Eliot himself found the simultaneous existence of antiquity and contemporaneity throughout *Ulysses* to be surreal, affecting him at an unconscious level; Joyce's novel "has given me all the surprise, delight, and terror that I can require."[130] Because Pound's collective-historical *Cantos* are a "final concentration of the entire past upon the present,"[131] they also attain a surrealistic effect by juxtaposing divergent historical periods.

Although the Surrealists have no exact equivalent of Eliot's collective-historical unconscious, they did not completely reject history like the Dadaists, who renounced a civilization that could produce a world war. Like Eliot, who thinks of literary history in terms of a tradition of great writers of the past whom he admires and often names, Breton conceives of a tradition of surrealistic writers of the past whom he arranges in his theoretical writings in a list.[132] Just as Eliot quotes from the works of the literary past in his poems, so the Surrealists will occasionally allude to their precursors in their art. Eliot contends that an artist must rely upon works of the past for a definition of what poetry and painting are, and the Surrealists do depend upon our sense of tradition for the effectiveness of their art. Surrealist poems and paintings resemble artistic history enough to raise the reader's or viewer's customary expectations of an art work, though Surrealist works often strive to contradict these expectations at the same time in order to deliver a subliminal shock. But an artist must have a historical sense in order to create a poem or painting that *recognizably* departs from the past. And certainly Eliot never wanted to mimic tradition, because he defines originality as an extension of the past, an alteration bold enough to change our very perception of artistic history (*SE* 5). As the visual images of Surrealist painting closely resemble Eliot's surreal metaphors, so the use of history and artistic tradition in Surrealist painting again closely resembles Eliot's surreal use of the past.

In an earlier movement in Italy related to Surrealism that the Surrealists claimed as one of their predecessors, Metaphysical Painting (*pittura metafisica*), Giorgio de Chirico, later to become a member of the Surrealist circle in Paris, presents in the same painting objects from the past and the present, the serenity of history enigmatically clashing with the contemporary world. In a series of paintings done around 1913, De Chirico will place a modern steam locomotive, a cannon, or an industrial smokestack in the background of an open courtyard bounded by arches of Classical architecture, desolate except for a Classical sculpture of a reclining nude or an equestrian monument in the foreground, as in *The Weariness of the Infinite, Ariadne,* or *The Chimney.* These paintings depend for their surreal effect upon a juxtaposition of the past and present that Eliot achieves when he quotes or alludes to works of the remote past in poems depicting the contemporary world.

The Surrealists proper were never quite so explicit in their use of history. Rather than employing pictorial 'quotation', like De Chirico, the Surrealists usually preferred to make allusions to history in their paintings and objects. Ernst's *The Virgin Spanking the Infant Jesus Before Three Witnesses: A. B., P. E., and the Artist* (1926) alludes to Francesco Parmigianino's Mannerist *The Madonna of the Long Neck* (1535–40), from which it derives its structure and style. In both paintings an ill-proportioned Virgin dominates the foreground in red and blue, with a relatively small, oval head and large, long, massive legs bending at the knee and thrust forward toward the viewer. Again in both paintings the Infant is also disproportionately long-limbed and precariously balanced on the Virgin's lap, but in Ernst's version, instead of her right hand at her breast, it is raised above her head, ready to descend on the Child, now lying face down. The children to the left of the Madonna and Child in Parmigianino's work, one looking at the Holy figures, another at the viewer, a third past the viewer, and a fourth with eyes closed, are replaced by a window, again at the left, through which Paul Eluard faces the Madonna with his eyes either closed or averted, Breton looks away, and Ernst at the viewer. A freestanding colonnade in the background is, in turn, replaced in Ernst's painting by a narrow wall, also supporting nothing. In the Surrealist work the viewer is shocked not merely by the blasphemy of the image of Mary spanking Jesus. Recalling all the previous Madonna and Child paintings that he has seen, the viewer is startled to find the tradition metamorphosing before his eyes into some image other than tenderness and compassion. Finally, the viewer cannot help but recall the historical model upon which Ernst's painting is based and be surprised to see the same structure and style depicting such divergent content.

Man Ray's 'object', *The Enigma of Isidore Ducasse* (1920), a photograph of which appeared on the first page of the first issue of *La Révolution surréaliste* (December 1924), alludes to, indeed virtually consists of a sculptural quotation of, a line from Comte de Lautréamont's *Maldoror* (1869): "beautiful as the chance meeting of a sewing machine and an umbrella on a dissecting-table." To create the object, Man Ray wrapped a sewing machine in an army blanket and tied it up.[133] The object later appears in his painting *La Rue Férou* (1952), being pulled in the back of a cart by a man up an alley, Man Ray 'quoting' his own previous work of art. In both instances a surreal effect is achieved by transforming a verbal image from a literary work of the past into a concrete object or visual image in the present. Lautréamont's phrase is an appropriate inspiration for a Surrealist work of art because the movement adopted the image as the archetypal automatic creation.

Perhaps of all the Surrealists, however, Dali, who learned his draftsmanship from a study of the Rennaissance masters, makes the most striking use of the past. This hyperrealistic technique is essential to the surreal effect of his paintings. From his knowledge of art history, the viewer expects that, when he encounters this realistic style, he will also see the voluptuous neoclassical nudes and pastoral scenery usually depicted by it. Instead, he is surprised by

what appear to be only the flaccid remnants of the once majesti-
cally idealized human form in Renaissance art strewn across
bizarre landscapes. In addition, this technique makes these unnatural dream images seem real, and thus all the more shocking.
Such is the effect of *Autumn Cannibalism* (1936–37) or *Soft Con-
truction with Boiled Beans: Premonition of Civil War* (1936).

11. POEMS AND PAINTINGS

The very nature of Eliot's poetic theory led him to consider all
poetry in Surrealist terms: "a degree of heterogeneity of material
compelled into unity by the operation of the poet's mind is omni-
present in poetry" (*SE* 243). Like Breton, Eliot sees surrealistic
qualities present in poetry throughout history: of "the high speed,
the succession of concentrated images, each magnifying the original fancy" of Marvell's "Coy Mistress," Eliot observes that "when
this process has been carried to the end and summed up, the
poem turns suddenly with that surprise which has been one of the
most important means of poetic effect since Homer" (*SE* 254).
Even Coleridge's Romantic maxim comes to signify for Eliot the
presence of unconscious experience in poetry; in Marvell's poem
"there is the making the familiar strange, and the strange familiar,
which Coleridge attributed to good poetry" (*SE* 259).

Eliot's prescription for the modern poem conforms as well to
his idea of the unconscious and the surrealistic effects it dictates.
Because "our civilization comprehends great variety and complexity," the contemporary poet "must become more and more comprehensive" in order to fuse this vast array of disparate experience
into the unity characteristic of immediate experience; "more allu-
sive" in order to indicate how the collective-historical unconscious
shapes the present; "more indirect," that is, more metaphoric
rather than discursive, joining together objects and experiences
otherwise kept apart by the isolating boundaries of logic and natural law, "in order to force, to dislocate if necessary, language into
his meaning" (*SE* 248). If language is a direct translation of sensory experience, as Eliot believed, then to "dislocate" language
could only result in a surrealistic dislocation of reality.

Eliot customarily praises those modern poets whose verse displays surrealistic effects, as demonstrated, for instance, by his ap-
proving remarks on Marianne Moore, focusing on one poem in
particular: "Those Various Scalpels." In this poem Moore depicts

the sophisticated sensibility of a woman by describing each of several of her physical attributes with a rapid succession of beautiful, exotic, and sensuous images that one would not expect to be applied to the appearance of a human being. The vast range of reference of these images, their "very wide spread of association," and the suddenness with which they are juxtaposed prevents the reader from totally digesting any one of them rationally and emotionally. The result is a "bewilderment consequent upon trying to follow so alert an eye, so quick a process of association,"[134] that is, a stunning and exhilarating confusion, a blurred whole of geographical, historical, and perceptual experience:

>   your
>   eyes, flowers of ice
>
> and
> snow sown by tearing winds on the cordage of disabled
>   ships; your raised hand,
>   an ambiguous signature: your cheeks, those rosettes
>   of blood on the stone floors of French châteaux,
>
>   .   .   .   .
>   your
>   other hand,
>
> a bundle of lances all alike, partly hid by emeralds from
>   Persia
>   and the fractional magnificence of Florentine
>   goldwork—
>
>   .   .   .   .
>   your dress, a
>   magnificent square
>   cathedral tower of uniform
>   and at the same time, diverse appearance—a
>   species of vertical vineyard rustling in the storm
>   of conventional opinion.[135] (8–14, 17–23, 29–34)

Eliot finds in Moore's technique of rapid and unexpected combinations of concrete images the same quality of metamorphosis, one object transforming into another, characteristic of Surrealist art. The effect of her "swiftly dissolving images," Eliot explains, is partially the result of the "transformation changes from one image to another, so that the second image is superposed before the first has quite faded."[136] Moore's juxtapositions are based upon other sensuous qualities in addition to the visual, and her metaphors are primarily prepositional or appositional, emphasizing incongruence. "Those Various Scalpels" is, in fact, similar to Breton's *L'Union libre,* in which he describes his wife through a succession of disparate images having a remote visual or sensuous resemblance to a given part of her body. In line 15, for instance, her shoulders are compared to champagne, and in line 17, her wrists to matches.[137]

Eliot also praises *Anabasis* by St.-Jean Perse. In this long poem, Perse relates the history of an Oriental civilization, its social and political attitudes and institutions, through a medley of recurring motifs, including time, eyes, a river, birds, insects, and horses. He often forms shocking metaphors and juxtapositions of images out of disparate objects and experiences which must have delighted Breton as well as Eliot:

> Eternity yawning on the sands.
>
> .   .   .   .
>
>   And the linen ex-
> posed to dry
>   scatters! like a priest torn in pieces. . .
>
> .   .   .   .
>
>   And man inspired by wine, who wears his
>   heart savage and buzzing like a swarm of black flies,
>
> .   .   .   .
>
>   A child sorrowful
>   as the death of apes—one that had an elder sister of great beauty
>   —offered us a quail in a slipper of rose-coloured satin.
>
> .   .   .   .
>
>   our
> eyelids sewn with needles!
>
> .   .   .   .
>
>   these sandsmokes that rise over dead river
> courses, like the skirts of centuries on their route. . . .[138]

Perse's metaphors are usually delivered as similes, with *like* or *as* emphasizing either a visual similarity between the elements or their incongruence. That Eliot translated *Anabasis* into English dramatically indicates his admiration for the poem and its technique.[139] Breton was fond of Perse also. In Breton's list of unofficial Surrealists in the first "Manifesto" appears the line, "Saint-Jean-Perse is Surrealist at a distance."[140]

When offering two passages of contemporary poetry distinguished for their "beauty" (*CC* 185–86) in "Reflections on *Vers Libre*" (1917), Eliot chose from the verse of T. E. Hulme and Ezra Pound.[141] Eliot admired the poems of Hulme so much that he used them, along with Elizabethan drama, to teach the appreciation of poetry. During his experience as an Extension lecturer, Eliot recalls that the poems of Hulme "only needed to be read aloud to have immediate effect" (*SE* 21). Poetry that communicates immediately is for Eliot poetry that can reach the unconscious before consciousness retards its progress into the mind through its isolated faculties of rational analysis and emotional response. Such modifiers as 'immediate' and 'immediately' do not pun on 'immediate experience', but indicate the continuity of the psychological unconscious, communication with which can only be instantaneous, with the metaphysical unconscious, the totality of experience contained in an instant. Eliot quotes Hulme's "The Embankment," which concludes with a remarkable surrealist image, at once contradicting the natural order of the world and joining together three ordinarily disparate objects, a blanket with the sky, and then with a human being. At the same time, the abstract is fused with the concrete, the desire to know the Truth of the universe being satisfied when the heavens are wrapped around oneself as a blanket for warmth:

> Oh, God, make small
> The old star-eaten blanket of the sky,
> That I may fold it round me and in comfort lie. (5–7)

The other poems published along with "The Embankment" that must also have prompted Eliot to refer to Hulme as a "real poet"[142] achieve surrealistic effects as well. In "Autumn," the inanimate, the moon and the stars, metamorphose into the human, a farmer and children, according to visual similarity of form and configuration. The poet

> saw the ruddy moon lean over a hedge
> Like a red-faced farmer.
> . . . .
> And round about were the wistful stars
> With white faces like town children. (3–4, 7–8)

The poetic action of "Above the Dock" also depends upon a transformation of one object into another, again on the basis of visual association, as we perceive the moon through the ropes of a mast as a balloon lodged in the branches of a tree:

Above the quiet dock in midnight,
Tangled in the tall mast's corded height,
Hangs the moon. What seemed so far away
Is but a child's balloon, forgotten after play.[143]

The metamorphosis of the moon into a face or a balloon depends
upon the round shape that these objects coincidentally share, like
the transformation of the earth into an egg in Dali's *Geopoliticus
Child Watching the Birth of the New Man* (1943). In this painting the
continents of the planet are depicted as a yellow viscous substance
dripping off of a large white egg apparently made of stone lying on
its side. Hulme's metaphor also anticipates one of Breton's, based
on the same visual similarity, according to which "a tomato is also
a child's balloon."[144]

In both of Hulme's poems, only after the initial unconscious
shock of perceiving two objects simultaneously fades, do we
analyze the whole of our esthetic experience into its conscious
components. We feel the *emotion* of whimsy at the *thought* of comparing the heavens to people and earthly objects; the awe and
gratitude when thinking that the beauty of these cosmic splendors
can readily be appreciated by something as diminutive and ephemeral as ourselves, the images having brought them within the
range of everyday experience; and finally, regret, a 'wistfulness',
that such beauty is ultimately separate from our world, and thus
can easily be neglected, "forgotten" in the drudgery of practical
concerns, such as transpire in a shipping yard in the daytime.

The second passage of contemporary verse that Eliot praises in
"Reflections on *Vers Libre*" comes from Pound's "Near Perigord,"
Section III, ending again, like "The Embankment," in a surrealist
image, suddenly uniting the abstract with the concrete, a woman's
distracted emotional state with broken mirrors, and fusing two
physically isolated objects, a woman and a mirror, defying the
natural world: "all the rest of her a shifting change, / A bundle of
broken mirrors." Eliot quotes this same passage again in *Ezra
Pound: His Metric and Poetry* (1917) and in his "Introduction"
(1928) to Pound's earlier *Selected Poems* as an example of Pound's
poetic ability. Eliot also presents "A Girl" in these two essays as one
of Pound's finer creative moments. The first stanza consists of a
surreal transformation in process, a girl metamorphosing into a
tree. These lines portray that inclination to identify with one's sur-

roundings characteristic of the unifying childhood imagination, what Eliot would have recognized as mystical participation:

> The tree has entered my hands,
> The sap has ascended my arms,
> The tree has grown into my breast—
> Downward,
> The branches grow out of me, like arms. (1–5)

By the second stanza, the metamorphosis has already been completed:

> Tree you are,
> Moss you are,
> You are violets with wind about them.
> A child—*so* high—you are,
> And all this is folly to the world. (6–10)

The transformation depicted in Pound's poem, according to which a child thinks that she is both a girl and a tree at the same time, is similar to the metamorphoses portrayed in two Surrealist works of art. Magritte's painting *Discovery* (1927) is a half-length portrait of a nude young woman who is at once flesh and wood: her left cheek, arm, and thigh, and her right shoulder, breast, and hip are a light brown wood grain, while the rest of her body is in tan flesh tones. Eluard's poem "L'Amoureuse," in which the beloved merges with the body and consciousness of the poet, depicts the process of transformation in a way similar to Pound's first stanza. Each successive line presents another part of the body becoming the woman. The poem begins with the woman perched on the poet's eyelids, and from there she gradually blends with his hair, hands, eyes, and shadow (1–6).[145]

Eliot objects to the concluding line of "A Girl," despite its thematic necessity, not because it is "'wrong'" or of poor quality, but simply because it is in the conventional poetic mode, departing from an otherwise consistently surreal development: "the phrasing is not 'completed'; for the last line is one which half a dozen other men might have written."[146] It approaches that aspect of ordinary verse that Eliot praises Pound for avoiding: "slightly veiled and resonant abstractions." By contrast, "Pound's verse is always definite and concrete, because he always has a definite emotion behind it" (*CC* 170), a definite feeling because it is created by a fusion of two concrete objects, approximately the unity of unconscious immediate experience.

For Eliot, a surreal metaphoric vision, in which one disparate object is transformed into another, is the primal poetic act, and almost every time that he quotes Pound's verse, he choses lines displaying this tendency. In a passage from "Dance Figure," for instance, a series of surreal transformations based upon visual similarity occur:

Thine arms are as a young sapling under the bark;
Thy face as a river with lights.

White as an almond are thy shoulders;
As new almonds stripped from the husk. (CC 179)

Twice Eliot quotes the following image of a Provençal city from the version of the original "Canto II" appearing in the American edition of *Lustra*, in which darkness, a sensory but nonmaterial phenomenon, suddenly becomes a man-made physical object:

It juts into the sky, Gordon that is,
Like a thin spire. Blue night pulled down about it
Like tent-flaps or sails close-hauled.[147]

Even those personifications that Eliot quotes from Pound fuse animate and inanimate objects, rather than abstractions, such as "the waves' deep laughter."[148] One personification from "Laudantes Decem Pulchritudinis Johannae Templi" depicts a triple metamorphosis partly based on visual association: "The lotus that pours / Her fragrance into the purple cup" (CC 171), in which a flower becomes human; a smell, liquid; and petals, a drinking vessel.

Nothing could have been less surreal than if Pound had said, for instance, "O my Luve's like a red, red rose." When Burns wrote that line in the late eighteenth century, there was already a tradition of comparing women to flowers, so that the reader would have been accustomed to such a juxtaposition. Since there is no visual similarity between a rose and a woman, no metamorphosis can occur in the reader's imagination. The reader resorts to dealing with the image rationally and discovers the underlying logic of the simile: both women and roses are pretty, organic, and ephemeral. Abstractions such as beauty and transience are the basis of the comparison, whereas a concrete physical property, visual form, is the basis of Pound's. Juxtaposing a woman's pale, bare shoulder and a white, husked almond, or the naked arm under her clothing and the raw wood of a branch without its bark, is historically unprecedented and logically incongruent. In either case the two objects are related simply by a coincidental similarity in shape and color: shoulders and almonds are oval, and arms and branches are long, thin, cylindrical, and crooked, bending at the elbow or joint. Breton's prepositional metaphors of lines 44 and 49 of *L'Union libre*[149] are similarly based merely upon the coincidental visual resemblance between a hip and a skiff, or a buttock and a swan's back, enabling a surreal transformation to occur.

Eliot's own verse abounds with surreal images, all of which conform to some characteristic specified by Breton in his definition appearing in the first "Manifesto." The "lipless grin" and 'staring daffodils' of "Whispers of Immortality" and "Till human voices wake us, and we drown" of "Prufrock," in Breton's words, "imply the negation of some elementary physical property." In "Morning at the Window" (1914–15), "the damp souls of housemaids / Sprouting despondently at area gates" (3–4) gives "to the abstract the mask of the concrete" by speaking of the emotional state of a woman as a flower. Likewise, when Prufrock wonders, "Would it have been worth while / To have bitten off the matter with a smile" (90–91), his preoccupations become as concrete as "cakes and ices" (79). And "Rhapsody on a Windy Night" portrays what happens when the poet 'dissolved' "the floors of memory" (5). Also in "Rhapsody" occurs the image "Midnight shakes the memory / As a madman shakes a dead geranium" (11–12), which "provokes laughter," as does "He laughed like an irresponsible foetus" (7) of "Mr. Apollinax" (1915). The opening lines of "Prufrock" contain an image which begins with the high romantic and then descends into the morbidly mundane—"presenting itself as something sensational, it [the image] seems to end weakly (because it suddenly closes the angle of its compass)"—"the evening is spread out against the sky / Like a patient etherised upon a table" (2–3). The same poem contains images in which "one of the terms is strangely concealed," such as "I am pinned and wriggling on the wall" (58), in which there is no mention of the laboratory specimen inspiring the metaphor. Likewise, in the more famous passage, "The yellow fog that rubs its back upon the window-panes . . ." (15–22), the cat is never mentioned.

Images "of a hallucinatory kind" (Breton)[150] are also plentiful.

In the fragment "The Wind Sprang up at Four O'Clock" (1924), "the surface of the blackened river / Is a face that sweats with tears" (7–8). Even the poet suggests the unconscious origin of the image: "Is it a dream or something else. . . ?" (6). Judah Stampfer observes that in "The Hollow Men" (1925), whose imagery this fragment recalls, Eliot "projects surrealistic figures with somber stage-craft."[151] Indeed, if the setting of this poem is a fusion of Dante's *Purgatorio* and *Inferno* with the jungle of Conrad's *Heart of Darkness,* then as "death's dream kingdom" (20) it certainly takes place in the collective-historical unconscious, the source of religious insight and the repository of primitive experience, where one would find a ritualistic effigy, "headpiece filled with straw" (4). As one of Eliot's most intensely religious poems, the purgatorial *Ash Wednesday* contains, not surprisingly, some of his most hallucinatory images. Whatever the symbolic import of the passage of Section II in which three leopards devour the protagonist, leaving him as a heap of bones, its esthetic power derives from the shocking dreamlike circumstance of being a spectator to one's own destruction, and surviving it. Unconscious experience expresses itself in such images of Section III as "a slotted window bellied like the fig's fruit" (108), representing sexual desire, as the protagonist simultaneously descends and ascends the purgatorical stairway, his face a "shape twisted on the banister" (98).

What is most remarkable about Eliot's surreal images is that they often anticipate similar images in Surrealist paintings. This long hallucinatory passage from *The Waste Land,*

> bats with baby faces in the violet light
> Whistled, and beat their wings
> And crawled head downward down a blackened wall
> And upside down in the air were towers
> Tolling reminiscent bells, that kept the hours
> And voices singing out of empty cisterns and exhausted wells
> (380–85)

resembles the nightmarish quality of many Surrealist paintings, not only because it contains eerie violet light, sinister creatures like bats, and contradictions of such laws of nature as gravity, but also because the human shockingly metamorphoses into the animal, as bats with baby faces, or into the inanimate, as cisterns and wells singing. The effect recalls Magritte's *Collective Invention* (1935), in which the ocean and horizon form the background, and in the foreground on the beach lies a creature whose head and torso are those of a fish and whose belly and legs those of a woman, or Ernst's *Ubu Imperator* (1923), in which a large machine resembling a spinning-top has been positioned so that holes and protuberances represent eyes, nose, and mouth, and has been given similarly mechanical arms, but with hands of flesh. Mario Praz has noted that such desolate landscapes appearing in *The Waste Land* as the one depicted in the lines

> Who are those hooded hordes swarming
> Over endless plains, stumbling in cracked earth
> Ringed by the flat horizon only (369–71)

resemble paintings of Yves Tanguy, in which a vast foreground recedes gradually to the horizon line with slender curvaceous objects of a rocklike surface deposited randomly amid the emptiness, sometimes piled upon one another to suggest an anthropomorphic form. Praz also notes that Eliot's image "A woman drew her long black hair out tight / And fiddled whisper music on those strings" (378–79) resembles Dali's *Nightmare of the Soft Violoncello,* also known as *Daddy Longlegs of the Evening . . . Hope!* (1940),[152] in the foreground of which a nude female humanoid, draped over a tree, holds a bow to a similarly limp violinlike instrument at her side.

But in two instances, images from Eliot's poetry directly parallel later Surrealist paintings, in both subject and effect. In "Sweeney Erect," Eliot's description of the hysterical woman is conducted so that her face and her vulva are not merely juxtaposed but are presented simultaneously and become the same part of anatomy:

> This withered root of knots of hair
>   Slitted below and gashed with eyes,
> This oval O cropped out with teeth. (13–15)

Physical attributes of the face alternate and blend with those of the genitals so that the reader is unable to distinguish one from the other. Magritte achieves the same effect in *The Rape* (1934), a visual metaphor in which a woman's torso becomes her face: the outline of the head, chin, and neck are preserved, with long hair extending down to the nape, but the eyes are breasts, the nose a navel, and the mouth the pubis. There is even a thematic resemblance between the poem and the painting: as rape transforms a woman into a sexual object, substituting her physical existence for her psychic identity, so Eliot portrays the earthy Sweeney who perceives all women, even the hysteric, in sexual terms. The other image of Eliot's that directly anticipates a Surrealist painting is from "Morning at the Window":

> The brown waves of fog toss up to me
> Twisted faces from the bottom of the street,
> And tear from a passer-by with muddy skirts
> An aimless smile that hovers in the air
> And vanishes along the level of the roofs. (5–9)

That smile hovering in the air returns in Man Ray's *The Lovers or Observatory Time* (1932–34), where a large pair of lips floats in the sky over the landscape.

12. ROMANTICISM, *SYMBOLISME,* AND THE SURREAL

These surreal images of Eliot and his contemporaries are in marked contrast to the typical Romantic image—the symbol—reflecting a difference in esthetic theory between Romantics and Moderns regarding the role of the unconscious in artistic creation. When Eliot avails himself (*SE* 257) of Coleridge's dialectical definition of the Imagination [153] in order to describe Metaphysical verse because it is, coincidentally, an apt description of immediate experience, he, in effect, implicitly denies a large part of Coleridge's romantic poetic theory. An explicit denial occurs when Eliot rejects Coleridge's distinction between Imagination and Fancy—"the difference between imagination and fancy amounts in practice to no more than the difference between good and bad poetry" (*UPUC* 77)—perceiving in Coleridge's definition of Fancy, as he did with Imagination, yet another description of the unconscious: "fancy may be 'no other than a mode of memory emancipated from the order of space and time' [*sic* [154]]; but it seems unwise to talk of memory in connexion with fancy and omit it altogether from the account of imagination" (*UPUC* 77–78). Eliot ironically cites John Livingston Lowes's source investigation, *The Road to Xanadu: A Study of the Ways of the Imagination,* [155] as proof of the role of subliminal memory in the creation of a work of art, demonstrating "the importance of instinctive and unconscious, as well as deliberate selection." Eliot concludes that "the mind of any poet would be magnetised in its own way to select automatically . . . the material—an image, a phrase, a word—which may be of use to him later" (*UPUC* 78). Eliot's desire to retain the Fancy in the creative act distinguishes him as a surrealistic modern from the romantic Coleridge, who wishes to banish the faculty. In fact, Coleridge's description of the operation of Fancy is virtually indistinguishable from accounts of the unconscious in artistic endeavor by Eliot and Breton: "Fancy is the arbitrary bringing together of things that lie remote, and forming them into a unity. The materials lie ready formed for the mind, and the fancy acts only by a sort of juxtaposition."[156] "The Fancy brings together images which have no connection natural or moral, but are yoked together by the poet by means of some accidental coincidence."[157]

In the end, Coleridge's conception of poetic creation gives the subliminal mind only a restricted scope; he did not consider the Imagination and the unconscious synonymous, and he did not view the Fancy as a creator of the marvellous, but as an inferior faculty, or use, of the conscious mind, to be avoided if the finest poetry was to be produced. Whereas Eliot admires the occasional shocking, incongruous images of the Metaphysicals, as opposed to their rationally belabored conceits, Coleridge disapproves of their influence on Shakespeare's dramatic contemporaries, composing as an example of one of Fancy's reprehensible products what the twentieth-century reader will recognize as an exquisite surreal image:

> What had a grammatical and logical consistency for the ear, what could be put together and represented to the eye, these poets [Jonson, Beaumont, Fletcher, Massinger] took from the ear and eye, unchecked by any intuition of an inward impossibility, just as a man might fit together a quarter of an orange, a quarter of an apple, and the like of a lemon and of a pomegranate, and make it look like one round diverse colored fruit.[158]

Coleridge is also uncomplimentary to Jean Paul Richter, the one Romantic most attune to the possibility of unconscious creation, chastising him for what a surrealist would admire: "his wit did not consist in pointing out analogies in themselves striking, but such as excited your wonder that they should ever be made, so that you admired not the thing combined but the act of combination."[159] Coleridge's organic method of creation is ultimately a conscious endeavor, the creative process being guided by the mind according to a conceptual framework. Contrasting Shakespeare with his contemporaries tainted by Fancy, Coleridge observes that "nature, who works from within by evolution and assimilation according to a law," cannot follow the caprices of Fancy; "nor could Shakespeare, for he too worked in the spirit of nature, by evolving the germ within by the imaginative power according to an idea—for as the power of seeing is to light, so is an idea in the mind to a law in nature."[160]

To be sure, Coleridge and other Romantics were interested in the content of the unconscious mind and in the role that unconscious thought processes might play in artistic creation.[161] But the subliminal is usually subordinated to a creative faculty, the Imagination, that transforms these unconscious feelings into readily recognizable esthetic material that closely conforms, metaphysically speaking, to our everyday sense of reality. Thus, although Coleridge knows that the unconscious defies the laws of nature, he cannot conceive of a work of art doing so in any drastic fashion, even when it is treating subliminal material. For instance, Wordsworth's "Ode on the Intimations of Immortality," he observes, is intended for readers who have been accustomed "to venture at times into the twilight realms of consciousness, and to feel a deep interest in modes of inmost being, to which they know that the attributes of time and space are inapplicable and alien, but which yet can not be conveyed save in symbols of time and space."[162] As a consequence, the predominant mode of the poem of unconscious experience in the Romantic era is the dream vision, depicting a more coherent variety of dream having recognizable plot and character, corresponding to the natural objects serving as symbols in Romantic nature poetry. Modern surreal poets, on the other hand, allow the unconscious a more dominant role in artistic creation and attempt to portray the content of the unconscious directly in their works of art. The resultant poetic figure is the metaphor, which achieves a subliminal combination of the ordinarily separate, conscious entities of emotion, idea, and object that defies the natural order and seeks to stir unconscious feeling; whereas for Coleridge and the Romantics, the characteristic poetic figure is the symbol, in which "idea" combines with "image"[163] and stirs the emotions, creating a nonrational but not unconscious esthetic experience.

Likewise, Eliot's early poetic cannot be considered *symboliste* either. The French Symbolists sought a transcendent realm, separate from the phenomenal world, to which their symbols beckoned. By contrast, the writer of surrealist orientation seeks the marvelous in the everyday world, creating metaphors that unite unconscious experience with perceptual reality. As Jean Pierrot observes of early twentieth-century proto-surrealist poets in France:

> We find that fantasy, the free play of imagination, is gradually moving closer and closer to reality. For an imaginative content cut off from life, elaborated in a world different from that of reality, a universe of legend, these writers are gradually substituting a fusion between the imaginary and the real, between dream and life, which was to lead to the surrealist type of fantasy in which the strange and wonderful can appear at the very heart of the most familiar and humdrum reality.[164]

As Marcel Raymond elaborates, for the proto-surrealist and later the Surrealists themselves:

> The boundaries were to be erased between inward life and the external world, between the self and the things which are said to be external. . . . [T]hey are encouraged to perceive strangeness, mystery, the fantastic, in reality itself. . . . [I]t is in things and events themselves that the wonder can be discovered.[165]

Combining literary with intellectual history, Raymond continues to explain that

> the opposition, traditional since romanticism, between the idea and life, the dream and life, can no longer subsist in the same terms. . . . Once again, a kind of mystical kinship is revealed among all things; everything tends to merge. . . ; a harmony is revealed between the inside and the outside . . . ; a hidden unity, capable of annihilating all objects and living beings, can gradually be perceived beyond the phenomena which appeal to the senses and beyond the images which compose dreams.[166]

This opposition between the Idea and life is the late nineteenth-century literary world's oversimplification of Hegelian Idealism, whereby the Absolute is held to be in transcendent contradistinction to the world. With the early twentieth century, when the possibility of the dialectic moving through the world is once again entertained, when the world can be thought of as in the process of approaching the Absolute, then does metaphor supersede the symbol, and the surreal the symbolist. Then, as Anna Balakian observes, "transcendence is replaced by metamorphosis,"[167] both esthetically and philosophically.

NOTES

CHAPTER I. SKEPTICISM

1. "Eeldrop and Appleplex," part 1, *Little Review*, 4 (May 1917): 8.

2. Fei-Pai Lu studies comprehensively this aspect of Eliot's thought process in *T. S. Eliot: The Dialectical Structure of His Theory of Poetry* (Chicago: Univ. of Chicago Press, 1966) but does not consider how dialectical thinking governs Eliot's awareness and use of history.

3. See Lyndall Gordon, *Eliot's Early Years* (New York: Oxford Univ. Press, 1977), p. 43. See also Eliot's review of Wilhelm Wundt's *Elements of Folk Psychology, International Journal of Ethics* 27 (Jan. 1917): 252–53, where he defends Hegel against Wundt's attack.

4. *Syllabus of a Course of Six Lectures on Modern French Literature* (Oxford: Oxford Univ., 1916), as reprinted by Ronald Schuchard in "T. S. Eliot as an Extension Lecturer, 1916–1919," *Review of English Studies*, n.s., 25 (1974): 165.

5. *A Sermon, Preached in Magdalene College Chapel* (Cambridge: Cambridge Univ. Press, 1948), p. 5.

6. Said in an interview with Donald Hall, "The Art of Poetry I: T. S. Eliot," *Paris Review*, no. 21 (Spring/Summer 1959), p. 49.

7. "A Sceptical Patrician," *Athenaeum*, no. 4647 (23 May 1919), p. 361.

8. "Popular Theologians: Mr. Wells, Mr. Belloc and Mr. Murry," *Criterion* 5 (May 1927): 256.

9. "A Sceptical Patrician," p. 362. In *The Education of Henry Adams* (privately printed, 1907; Boston: Massachusetts Historical Society/Houghton Mifflin, 1918), pp. 454–56, Adams is disturbed by Poincaré's prediction in *La Science et l'hypothèse* (1902) that science has alternated, and will continue to alternate endlessly, between discovering the simple and then the complex in nature, and by his observation that mathematics is merely a convenient system of symbols, a manmade tool for coping with the world instead of a truth based upon the nature of reality itself.

10. Among those studies that Eliot read during his years at Harvard and that are not cited later in this essay are E. S. Ames, *The Psychology of Religious Experience* (1910); G. B. Cutten, *The Psychological Phenomena of Christianity* (1909); W. R. Inge, *Studies of English Mystics* (1906); Rufus M. Jones, *Studies in Mystical Religion* (1909); J. B. Pratt, *The Psychology of Religious Belief* (1907); E. T. Starbuck, *The Psychology of Religion*, 2d ed. (1901), and J. H. Woods, *Practice and Science of Religion: A Study of Method in Comparative Religion* (1906). See Gordon, *Eliot's Early Years*, pp. 141–42.

11. "A Sceptical Patrician," p. 362. Eliot is referring to Adams's *Mont-Saint-Michel and Chartres: A Study of Thirteenth-Century Unity* (privately

printed, 1904; Washington, D.C.: American Institute of Architects/New York: Houghton Mifflin, 1913), in which Adams expresses his vision of the Middle Ages, an integration of theology, philosophy, mysticism, society, economics, art, and architecture.

12. Grover Smith, *T. S. Eliot's Poetry and Plays: A Study in Sources and Meaning*, 2d ed. (Chicago: Univ. of Chicago Press, 1974), p. 317.

13. "Style and Thought," *Nation* 22 (Mar. 1918): 768.

14. "A Prediction in Regard to Three English Authors," *Vanity Fair* 21 (Feb. 1924): 29.

15. See Valerie Eliot, "Introduction," *T. S. Eliot, The Waste Land: A Facsimile and Transcript of the Original Drafts, Including the Annotations of Ezra Pound* (New York: Harcourt, Brace, Jovanovich, 1971), p. ix. The influence of Bradley on Eliot's thought and poetry has been studied by Hugh Kenner, *The Invisible Poet: T. S. Eliot* (New York: McDowell, Obolensky, 1959), pp. 40–69; E. P. Bollier, "T. S. Eliot and F. H. Bradley: A Question of Influence," *Tulane Studies in English* 12 (1962): 87–111; Lewis Freed, *T. S. Eliot: Aesthetics and History* (La Salle, Ill.: Open Court, 1962), and *T. S. Eliot: The Critic as Philosopher* (West Lafayette, Ind.: Purdue Univ. Press, 1979); Eric Thompson, *T. S. Eliot: The Metaphysical Perspective* (Carbondale, Ill.: Southern Illinois Univ. Press, 1963); J. Hillis Miller, *Poets of Reality: Six Twentieth-Century Writers* (Cambridge, Mass.: Harvard Univ. Press, 1965), pp. 131–89; George Whiteside, "T. S. Eliot's Dissertation," *Journal of English Literary History* 34 (Sept. 1967): 400–424; John J. Soldo, "Knowledge and Experience in the Criticism of T. S. Eliot," *Journal of English Literary History* 35 (June 1968): 284–308; Anne C. Bolgan, "The Philosophy of F. H. Bradley and the Mind and Art of T. S. Eliot: An Introduction," in S. P. Rosenbaum, ed., *English Literature and British Philosophy* (Chicago: Univ. of Chicago Press, 1971), pp. 251–77, and *What the Thunder Really Said: A Retrospective Essay on the Making of The Waste Land* (Montreal: McGill-Queen's Univ. Press, 1973); Mowbray Allan, *T. S. Eliot's Impersonal Theory of Poetry* (Lewisburg, Pa.: Bucknell Univ. Press, 1974); and Piers Gray, *T. S. Eliot's Intellectual and Poetic Development, 1909–1922* (Sussex: Harvester Press, 1982). An exclusively philosophical approach is adopted by Richard Wollheim, "Eliot and F. H. Bradley: An Account," in Graham Martin, ed., *Eliot in Perspective: A Symposium* (London: Humanities Press, 1970), pp. 169–93. Wollheim studies Bradley's thought in *F. H. Bradley*, 2d ed. (Baltimore: Penguin Books, 1969). See also Hiralal Haldar, *Neo-Hegelianism* (London: Heath Cranton, 1927), pp. 214–56, and John H. Muirhead, *The Platonic Tradition in Anglo-Saxon Philosophy: Studies in the History of Idealism in England and America* (London: George Allen and Unwin, 1931), pp. 219–304.

The following summary of Bradley's philosophy is a distillation of ideas presented in *Appearance and Reality: A Metaphysical Essay*, 2d ed. (1897; Oxford: Clarendon Press, 1930); *Essays on Truth and Reality* (Oxford: Clarendon Press, 1914); *Ethical Studies*, 2d ed. (Oxford: Clarendon Press, 1927); *Principles of Logic*, 2d ed., 2 vols. (Oxford: Oxford Univ. Press, 1922); and *Collected Essays*, 2 vols. (Oxford: Clarendon Press, 1935). *The Presuppositions of Critical History*, ed. Lionel Rubinoff (Chicago: Quadrangle, 1968), is a useful edition of Bradley's essay published in 1874 and later included in *Collected Essays*.

16. Bradley, *Appearance and Reality*, p. 406.

17. Ibid., pp. 404, 414, 152.

18. *Dictionary of Philosophy,* ed. Dagobert D. Runes (Totowa, N.J.: Littlefield, Adams, 1962), p. 2.

19. American New Realism established itself with the publication of "The Program and First Platform of Six Realists" by E. B. Holt, Walter T. Marvin, W. P. Montague, Ralph Barton Perry, Walter B. Pitkin, and E. G. Spaulding, *Journal of Philosophy* 7 (July 1910): 393–401. Their position was elaborated in *The New Realism: Cooperative Studies in Philosophy* (New York: Macmillan, 1912). A rival group, the Critical Realists, consisting of Durant Drake, Arthur O. Lovejoy, J. B. Pratt, A. K. Rogers, George Santayana, Roy W. Sellars, and C. A. Strong, differentiated themselves from the New Realists with *Essays in Critical Realism: A Cooperative Study of the Problem of Knowledge* (New York: Macmillan, 1920). See Herbert W. Schneider, *Sources of Contemporary Philosophical Realism in America* (New York: Bobbs-Merrill, 1964, and W. H. Werkmeister, *A History of Philosophical Ideas in America* (New York: Ronald Press, 1949), pp. 369–518. Eliot makes specific references to their epistemological theories in *KE* 113, 118–20.

Ralph Barton Perry's *Present Philosophical Tendencies: A Critical Survey of Naturalism, Idealism, Pragmatism, and Realism Together with a Synopsis of the Philosophy of William James* (New York: Longmans, Green, 1912) provides a lively view of the intellectual history of the period from a New-Realist perspective. More objective accounts of early twentieth-century philosophy are John Passmore, *A Hundred Years of Philosophy,* 2d ed. (New York: Basic Books, 1966), and Frederick Copleston, *A History of Philosophy,* vol. 8, *Modern Philosophy: Bentham to Russell* (Westminster, Md.: Newman Press, 1966). Bruce Kuklick focuses upon philosophical activity at Harvard University during the period of Eliot's years of attendance in *The Rise of American Philosophy: Cambridge, Massachusetts, 1860–1930* (New Haven: Yale Univ. Press, 1977).

20. Bradley, *Appearance and Reality,* pp.322–23.

21. Ibid., p. 321

22. "Views and Reviews," *New English Weekly* 7 (6 June 1935): 151.

23. "Introduction" to Charlotte Eliot, *Savonarola: A Dramatic Poem* (London: R. Cobden-Sanderson, 1926), p. viii.

24. "The Modern Dilemma; Religion and Science: A Phantom Dilemma," *Listener* 7 (23 Mar. 1932): 429.

25. This summary of Royce's thought is a distillation of ideas originally introduced in *The Religious Aspect of Philosophy* (Boston: Houghton Mifflin, 1885) and later elaborated in *The World and the Individual,* 2 vols. (New York: Macmillan, 1899, 1901), *The Philosophy of Loyalty* (New York: Macmillan, 1908), and *The Problem of Christianity,* 2 vols. (New York: Macmillan, 1913).

26. *Josiah Royce's Seminar, 1913–1914: As Recorded in the Notebooks of Harry T. Costello,* ed. Grover Smith (New Brunswick, N.J.: Rutgers Univ. Press, 1963), p. 78.

27. Ibid., p. 121.

28. Bradley, *Appearance and Reality,* p. 402.

CHAPTER II. MYSTICISM

1. Herbert Howarth, *Notes on Some Figures Behind T. S. Eliot* (Boston: Houghton Mifflin, 1964), pp. 20, 2, 4.

2. As quoted by Valerie Eliot in her "Note" to *Poems Written in Early Youth* (New York: Farrar, Straus and Giroux, 1967), pp. v–vi.

3. See Howarth, *Notes on Some Figures,* pp. 23–27, and Gordon, *Eliot's Early Years,* pp. 5–6.

4. Charlotte Eliot, *Savonarola,* p. 80.

5. Ibid., p. 1.

6. "The Significance of Charles Williams," *Listener* 36 (19 Dec. 1946): 895.

7. "The Silurist," *Dial* 83 (Sept. 1927): 259. Perhaps for this reason both Gordon in *Eliot's Early Years* and Fayek M. Ishak in *The Mystical Philosophy of T. S. Eliot* (New Haven, Conn.: College and University Press, 1970) have studied Eliot's intellectual and poetic development strictly in terms of mystical experience and religious vision.

8. See Smith, *Eliot's Poetry and Plays,* pp. 255, 336; T. S. Matthews, *Great Tom: Notes Towards the Definition of T. S. Eliot* (New York: Harper and Row, 1974), pp. 130, 142–43; Gordon, *Eliot's Early Years,* pp. 55–57; and Helen Gardner, *The Composition of Four Quartets* (New York: Oxford Univ. Press, 1978), p. 36.

9. Martz, "T. S. Eliot: The Wheel and the Point," *The Poem of the Mind: Essays on Poetry, English and American* (New York: Oxford Univ. Press, 1969), pp. 109–14. See also Leonard Unger, "The Rose Garden," *T. S. Eliot: Moments and Patterns* (Minneapolis: Univ. of Minnesota Press, 1966), pp. 69–91.

10. Martz, "The Wheel and the Point," p. 113, and Helen Gardner, "The Landscapes of Eliot's Poetry," *Critical Quarterly* 10 (1968): 324.

11. Address at the centennial celebration of Mary Institute, *From Mary to You,* Centennial Issue (Dec. 1959), p. 135.

12. "Mystic and Politician as Poet: Vaughan, Traherne, Marvell, Milton," *Listener* 3 (2 Apr. 1930): 590.

13. See Gordon, *Eliot's Early Years,* pp. 141–42. Eliot mentions *Varieties of Religious Experience* in SW 170, and James's pragmatic view of religion in his review of *Group Theories of Religion and the Religion of the Individual* by Clement C. J. Webb, *International Journal of Ethics* 27 (Oct. 1916): 117, and in "Popular Theologians," p. 258; Underhill is mentioned in "Beyle and Balzac," *Athenaeum,* no. 4648 (30 May 1919), p. 393.

14. The manuscript of "Silence" is in the Berg Collection of the New York Public Library. Gordon's interpretation of this poem (*Eliot's Early Years,* pp. 15–16) is more accurate than the one offered by Eloise Knapp Hay in *T. S. Eliot's Negative Way* (Cambridge, Mass.: Harvard Univ. Press, 1982), p. 72. The tranquility of the poem does not connote, nor does it originate from, emptiness, as Hay alleges, and the terror that Eliot experiences will continue to be for him, throughout his life, a central component of religious experience, as it has always been for others. A similar mystical experience, characterized again as a sensation of silence, is recorded in "Fragment: Bacchus and Ariadne; Second Debate between the Body and Soul," dated February 1911.

15. Howarth, *Notes on Some Figures,* pp. 126–27. Eliot acknowledges Babbitt's influence on him in *Irving Babbitt: Man and Teacher,* ed. Frederick Manchester and Odell Shepard (New York: Putnam's, 1941), p. 104, and "Ezra Pound," *Poetry* 68 (Sept. 1946): 329. John Margolis, *T. S. Eliot's Intellectual Development, 1922–1939* (Chicago: Univ. of Chicago Press, 1972), passim, studies Babbitt's influence on Eliot.

16. See Babbitt, *The Masters of Modern French Criticism* (Boston:

Houghton Mifflin, 1912) and *Rousseau and Romanticism* (Boston: Houghton Mifflin, 1919).

17. *A Sermon,* p. 5.

18. Gordon, *Eliot's Early Years,* p. 38. Staffan Bergsten briefly considers the philosophical relationship between Eliot and Bergson in *Time and Eternity: A Study in the Structure and Symbolism of T. S. Eliot's Four Quartets* (Stockholm: Bonniers, 1960); pp. 13–15.

19. "A Commentary," *Criterion* 13 (Apr. 1934): 451–52.

20. *Syllabus,* p. 167.

21. Underhill, *Mysticism: A Study in the Nature and Development of Man's Spiritual Consciousness* (London: Methuen, 1911), pp. 30–32.

22. This summary of Bergson's thought is a condensation of *Essai sur les données immédiates de la conscience* (1889), tr. F. L. Pogson, *Time and Free Will: An Essay on the Immediate Data of Consciousness* (New York: Macmillan, 1910); *Matière et mémoire* (1896), tr. Nancy M. Paul and W. Scott Palmer, *Matter and Memory* (New York: Macmillan, 1911); "Introduction à la métaphysique," *Revue de métaphysique et de morale* (Jan. 1903), tr. T. E. Hulme, *An Introduction to Metaphysics* (New York: Macmillan, 1913); *L'Évolution créatrice* (1907), tr. Arthur Mitchell, *Creative Evolution* (New York: Henry Holt, 1911).

23. Bergson, *Creative Evolution,* p. 268.

24. In *Les Deux Sources de la religion et de la morale* (1932), tr. R. Ashley Audra and Cloudesley Brereton, with W. Horsfall Carter, *The Two Sources of Morality and Religion* (New York: Henry Holt, 1935). Ironically, Underhill, in the twelfth edition of her book, published two years earlier than the original French edition of Bergson's book, expressed her belief that she had found "a better philosophic background to the experience of the mystics than the vitalism which appeared, twenty years ago, to offer so promising a way of escape from scientific determinism" (p. viii). As she explains, "the ideas of Bergson and Eucken no longer occupy the intellectual foreground. Were I now writing it for the first time, my examples would be chosen from other philosophers, and especially from those who are bringing back into modern thought the critical realism of the scholastics" (p. 43). Early studies exploring the relationship between the Vitalists and religion include E. Hermann, *Eucken and Bergson: Their Significance for Christian Thought* (London: James Clarke, 1912), and Lucius Hopkins Miller, *Bergson and Religion* (New York: Henry Holt, 1916). K. W. Wild will revive the issue in *Intuition* (Cambridge: Cambridge Univ. Press, 1938).

25. F. O. Matthiessen, *The Achievement of T. S. Eliot: An Essay on the Nature of Poetry,* 3d ed. (New York: Oxford Univ. Press, 1958), p. 183, and Gordon, *Eliot's Early Years,* p. 41.

26. Other conservative French writers with whom Eliot would become familiar between 1910 and 1916 are mentioned in *Syllabus,* pp. 167–68. By 1915, as Ronald Schuchard demonstrates in "Eliot and Hulme in 1916: Toward a Revaluation of Eliot's Critical and Spiritual Development," *Publications of the Modern Language Association* 88 (1973): 1083–94, Eliot's classicism was again reinforced, as he himself would later recall (*CC* 17), by Hulme's antiromantic position (see also "A Commentary," *Criterion* 16 [July 1937]: 668). But Eliot's repudiation of Bergson was formulated long before his acquaintance with Hulme's thought, and certainly Eliot's classicism gained impetus from only a select portion of it. At the same time that Eliot began criticizing Bergson's philosophy, Hulme was publishing his translation of *An Introduction to Metaphysics,*

having already advocated Bergson in published articles and defended him against detractors. Hulme's enthusiasm for Bergson appears never to have abated.

27. "Introduction," *Savonarola*, p. vii.

28. Ibid., p. ix.

29. Ibid., p. x. Eliot again associates Bergson directly with nineteenth-century Romanticism in "Three Reformers," *Times Literary Supplement*, no. 1397 (8 Nov. 1928), p. 818.

30. *A Sermon*, p. 5.

31. "A Sceptical Patrician," p. 361.

32. Babbitt, *Masters of Modern French Criticism*, pp. 252–53.

33. "Views and Reviews," *New English Weekly* 7 (6 June 1935): 151.

34. Schleiermacher, *On Religion: Speeches to its Cultured Despisers*, tr. John Oman (London: Routledge and Kegan Paul, 1893), p. 93.

35. Ibid., p. 101.

36. "A Commentary," *Criterion* 5 (May 1927): 190.

37. Howarth, *Notes on Some Figures*, p. 207. Kristian Smidt, in *Poetry and Belief in the Work of T. S. Eliot*, 2d ed. (London: Routledge and Kegan Paul, 1961), p. 19, states that Eliot heard Eucken lecture during his brief stay in Germany in July and August of 1914 for Marburg University's summer program for foreign students. See also Gordon, *Eliot's Early Years*, p. 65, and Howarth, *Notes on Some Figures*, p. 214.

38. "A Commentary," *Criterion* 4 (Apr. 1926): 390.

39. "Introduction," *Savonarola*, p. x.

40. "Mr. Middleton Murry's Synthesis," *Criterion* 6 (Oct. 1927): 343, 344.

41. "Mr. Read and Mr. Fernandez," *Criterion* 4 (Oct. 1926): 754–55.

42. "Three Reformers," p. 818.

43. "A Prediction in Regard to Three English Authors," p. 98.

44. Ibid., p. 29.

45. "Mr. Middleton Murry's Synthesis," p. 343.

46. "Mr. Read and Mr. Fernandez," p. 757.

47. "Eeldrop and Appleplex," Part I, p. 11.

48. "Mr. Middleton Murry's Synthesis," pp. 345–46.

49. Babbitt, *Masters of Modern French Criticism*, p. 383.

50. Underhill, *Mysticism*, pp. 47, 44, 45–46.

51. Bradley, *Appearance and Reality*, p. 443.

52. Ibid., p. 442.

53. Quoted by Matthiessen, *Achievement of T. S. Eliot*, p. 183.

54. See Smidt, *Poetry and Belief*, pp. 165–81, and Gordon, *Eliot's Early Years*, pp. 40–41. Gray, *Eliot's Intellectual and Poetic Development*, pp. 38–89, believes that "Preludes" III and IV and "The Love Song of J. Alfred Prufrock" are also Bergsonian.

55. Underhill, *Mysticism*, p. 49. Bollier, "T. S. Eliot and F. H. Bradley," pp. 93–94, tentatively suggests a relationship between the philosophical skepticism that Eliot constructed from Bradley's thought and mysticism but does not develop the point further. Ishak, *Mystical Philosophy*, pp. 47–48, 130, also notes in passing a mystical potential in Bradley's philosophy, but his study relies primarily upon the perspective of Far Eastern religions for its interpretation of Eliot's thought and poetry.

56. James, *The Varieties of Religious Experience: A Study in Human Nature* (New York: Longmans, Green, 1902), p. 416.

57. Ibid., p. 426.

58. Underhill, *Mysticism,* p. 4.

59. Ibid., p. 15.

60. Inge, *Christian Mysticism* (London: Methuen, 1899), p. 25.

61. Ibid., p. 31.

62. Ibid., pp. 28, 33, 255.

63. Bradley, *Appearance and Reality,* p. 394.

64. Ibid., pp. 395–96.

65. Ibid., p. 469.

66. Ibid., p. 452.

67. Ibid., p. 465–66. This implicit denial of the transcendent in Idealism seems to be the provocation of Underhill's complaint in *Mysticism,* p. 15, that it is ultimately deficient as a philosophical explanation for mysticism, providing only "a diagram of the heavens, not a ladder to the stars."

68. Review, *Group Theories of Religion, International Journal of Ethics,* p. 117.

69. Bradley, *Appearance and Reality,* p. 401.

70. Bradley, *Ethical Studies,* 2d ed. (London: Oxford Univ. Press, 1927), pp. 317–18.

71. *SE* 327 (1931), and *UPUC* 135 (1933).

72. "Preface to the Seventh Edition," *Elements of Metaphysics* (London: Methuen, 1924), p. xiii.

73. Inge, *Christian Mysticism,* p. 31.

74. Because Miller attributes to Eliot, Bradley's position that "God is merely one part of the all-embracing system of relations which makes up the collective mind," he concludes, falsely, that "Eliot can only become a Christian when he ceases to be an idealist" (*Poets of Reality,* p. 179). Eliot, in fact, departed from Bradley but not from a number of other Idealists, on this point. In addition to "Spleen" (1910) and "Conversation Galante" (1909), several early manuscript poems use the term Absolute to refer to the Divine. See, for instance, in the Berg Collection of the New York Public Library, "Suite Clownesque" and "He said this universe is very clever."

75. Bradley, *Appearance and Reality,* p. 469.

76. Ibid., p. 462.

77. Ibid., p. 470.

78. Ibid., p. 462.

79. Ibid., p. 141.

80. Inge, *Christian Mysticism,* p. 12.

81. James, *Varieties of Religious Experience,* pp. 416, 417.

82. Taylor, *Elements of Metaphysics,* p. 408.

CHAPTER III. THE UNCONSCIOUS

1. Inge, *Christian Mysticism,* pp. 26, 30–31.

2. James, *Varieties of Religious Experience,* p. 426.

3. Underhill, *Mysticism,* pp. 61–62.

4. Ibid., pp. 62–63.

5. "A Commentary" (Apr. 1934), p. 452.

6. Gordon, *Eliot's Early Years,* p. 141.

7. Underhill, *Mysticism,* p. 71.

8. O'Neil, *The Beginnings of Modern Psychology* (Baltimore: Penguin Books, 1968), p. 117.

9. Edward L. Margetts, "The Concept of the Unconscious in the History of Medical Psychology," *Psychiatric Quarterly* 27 (1953): 115–19; see also Henry Ellenberger, "The Unconscious Before Freud," *Bulletin of the Menninger Clinic* 21 (1957): 3–4, 14.

10. Quoted by Underhill in the 12th ed. of *Mysticism* (1930), p. 52.

11. Ibid., pp. 51–52.

12. Lancelot L. Whyte, *The Unconscious Before Freud* (New York: Basic Books, 1960), pp. 140–43, 154–57, and Henri F. Ellenberger, *The Discovery of the Unconscious: A History and Evolution of Dynamic Psychiatry* (New York: Basic Books, 1970), pp. 207–8, 209–10. Gray notes that Laforgue had a concept of the unconscious as the Absolute of Idealism, which he acquired from Hartmann (*Eliot's Intellectual and Poetic Development*, p. 8). Although Gray continues to observe that Eliot employed the same imagery in his early poetry ("Preludes" I and II, "Conversation Galante," "Portrait of a Lady") that Laforgue used to express the unconscious, Gray does not pursue further the ramifications for Eliot's thought of his early encounter of this association of the unconscious with Idealist philosophy. Gray proceeds to analyze Eliot's conception of the unconscious in terms of Bergson's theories of memory, resulting in a kind of personal psychological unconscious. Then Gray claims that Eliot rejected the concept of the unconscious entirely along with Bergson when he came under the influence of Bradley (pp. 38–89).

13. *Royce's Seminar*, pp. 173–74; KE 57–83.

14. Eliot's review of Wundt's *Elements of Folk Psychology* reveals a knowledge of Wundt's earlier work as well, which treated this issue.

15. Taylor, *Elements of Metaphysics*, pp. 313–33. See also the previous chapter, "The Logical Character of Psychological Science," pp. 294–312.

16. *Brett's History of Psychology,* ed. R. S. Peters, 2d ed. (London: Allen and Unwin, 1962), pp. 651–53; D. B. Klein, *A History of Scientific Psychology: Its Origins and Philosophical Backgrounds* (New York: Basic Books, 1970), p. 411; and J. C. Flugel, *A Hundred Years of Psychology,* 3d ed., rev. D. J. West (London: Duckworth, 1964), pp. 130–31.

17. *Royce's Seminar,* pp. 174–75.

18. *Brett's History,* ed. Peters, pp. 696–99; Klein, *Scientific Psychology,* pp. 223, 243, 261, 307; Flugel, *Hundred Years of Psychology,* pp. 213–27; and Robert Thomson, *The Pelican History of Psychology* (Baltimore: Penguin, 1968), pp. 156–67.

19. See also *Royce's Seminar,* p. 173, where Eliot again draws the distinction between the Absolute, as God, and other kinds of objects and half-objects. Gordon's discussion of half-objects (*Eliot's Early Years,* p. 52) mistakenly implies that illusions, hallucinations, and superstitions are for Eliot the same kind of mental experience as a vision of God. In fact, however, illusions and hallucinations, according to Eliot, are caused merely by physiological malfunctions. Superstitions are early primitive notions out of which our idea of causality developed; superstitions are just as suspect as causality because they are merely an idea about the differentiated world, an interpretation, and thus not directly revelatory of immediate experience or Reality. Finally, the Absolute transcends both illusion-causing physiology and the idea-producing intellect, for they are fragments of it, to be reconciled and subsumed in its unity.

20. Review of *Theism and Humanism, International Journal of Ethics* 26 (Jan. 1916): 288.

21. "Mr. Read and Mr. Fernandez," p. 755.

22. "On Our Knowledge of Immediate Experience" (1909), *Essays on Truth and Reality*, pp. 172, 173.

23. Ibid., pp. 172–73.

24. Freed, *The Critic as Philosopher*, pp. 22, 115, implies, wrongly, that the foregoing passages in which Eliot and Bradley discuss unconsciousness support a similar position. Eliot in fact departs from Bradley on the issue of the relationship between immediate experience and the psychological unconscious.

25. Bradley, *Essays on Truth and Reality*, p. 174.

26. Ibid., pp. 173, 174.

27. E. E. Evans-Pritchard, in *Theories of Primitive Religion* (Oxford: Clarendon Press, 1965), offers a cogent presentation, comparison, and evaluation of, among others, the more important theories of primitive religious experience either argued or assumed by the anthropologists and Classicists of the late nineteenth and early twentieth centuries upon which Eliot depended for his conception of the primitive mind. See also the comprehensive survey of Jan de Vries, *The Study of Religion: A Historical Approach*, tr. Kees W. Bolle (New York: Harcourt, Brace and World, 1967).

28. See *Royce's Seminar*, p. 74.

29. *Les Règles de la méthode sociologique* (Paris: Felix Alcan, 1895; 2d ed., rev., 1901); tr. Sarah A. Solovay and John H. Mueller, ed. George E. G. Catlin, *The Rules of Sociological Method* (Chicago: Univ. of Chicago Press, 1938).

30. "Représentations individuelles et représentations collectives," *Revue de métaphysique et de morale* (1898).

31. Review of *Group Theories of Religion, International Journal of Ethics*, p. 117.

32. Durkheim, *The Elementary Forms of the Religious Life*, tr. Joseph W. Swain (London: Allen and Unwin, 1915) from *Les forms élémentaires de la vie religieuse: Le Système totémique en Australie* (Paris: Felix Alcan, 1912).

33. Durkheim, *Elementary Forms of the Religious Life*, p. 439.

34. Ibid., pp. 441–42.

35. Ibid., p. 441.

36. Ibid., p. 442.

37. Ibid.

38. Ibid.

39. Ibid., p. 444.

40. Ibid., p. 445.

41. Ibid., p. 446.

42. William Harmon, "T. S. Eliot, Anthropologist and Primitive," *American Anthropologist* 78 (1976): 797–811, overstates Lévy-Bruhl's influence on Eliot by not taking into account the entire system of thought into which Eliot accommodated certain of Lévy-Bruhl's theories with appropriate modifications.

43. *Royce's Seminar*, p. 74.

44. Lévy-Bruhl, *Les Fonctions mentales dans les sociétés inférieures* (Paris: Felix Alcan, 1910), tr. Lilian A. Clare, *How Natives Think* (London: Allen and Unwin, 1926).

45. *How Natives Think*, pp. 76–77, as revised by Peter Riviere in Jean Cazeneuve, *Lucien Lévy-Bruhl* (New York: Harper and Row, 1972), p. 42.

46. Review of *Group Theories of Religion, International Journal of Ethics*, p. 116.

47. *Royce's Seminar*, p. 74.

48. Ibid., p. 119.
49. Ibid., p. 120.
50. Ibid., p. 135.
51. Ibid., p. 119.
52. Ibid., p. 135.
53. Ibid., p. 138.
54. Ibid., pp. 135–36.
55. Recent essays considering the possibility of a sociology and an anthropology in view of epistemological reservations similar to Eliot's, with emphasis upon the comparative study of religions, and also critical of Lévy-Bruhl's distinction between a prelogical and a logical mentality are collected in *Rationality*, ed. Bryan R. Wilson (London: Basil Blackwell, 1970). For a critique of Durkheim's *Rules* observing an orientation similar to Eliot's, see Paul Q. Hirst, *Durkheim, Bernard and Epistemology* (London: Routledge and Kegan Paul, 1975).
56. Lévy-Bruhl, *How Natives Think*, p. 36; Cazeneuve, *Lucien Lévy-Bruhl*, p. 36.
57. *Royce's Seminar*, p. 119.
58. Lévy-Bruhl, *How Natives Think*, p. 38; Cazeneuve, *Lucien Lévy-Bruhl*, p. 38.
59. See "Beyle and Balzac," p. 392.
60. Review of *Group Theories of Religion*, *International Journal of Ethics*, p. 116.
61. Review of *Group Theories of Religion*, *New Statesman* 7 (29 July 1916): 405.
62. In *Royce's Seminar*, p. 74, Eliot mentions Müller, Tylor, Lang, and King; in his review of *Elements of Folk Psychology*, of course, Wundt; in "War-Paint and Feathers," *Athenaeum*, no. 4668 (17 Oct. 1919), p. 1036, Rendell Harris, Spencer and Gillen, and Codrington; in *SE* 49 (1920), Wundt, Tylor, and Robertson Smith; in "A Prediction in Regard to Three English Authors," p. 29, Mannhardt, Tylor, Robertson Smith, Rendell Harris, Hartland, Elliot Smith, Codrington, Spencer and Gillen, and Hewett; and in "The Ballet," *Criterion* 3 (Apr. 1925): 441, Spencer and Gillen, and Hewett.
63. *Royce's Seminar*, pp. 74–75.
64. "A Prediction in Regard to Three English Authors," p. 29.
65. This brief summary of Frazer's work is based in part on the survey of the third edition of *The Golden Bough* by John B. Vickery in *The Literary Impact of "The Golden Bough"* (Princeton: Princeton Univ. Press, 1973), pp. 38–67, on *The New Golden Bough*, ed. Theodore H. Gaster (New York: Criterion Books, 1959), and on Frazer's one-volume abridged edition (New York: Macmillan, 1922). For a comprehensive analysis of Frazer's work in its contemporary context, see Stanley Edgar Hyman, *The Tangled Bank: Darwin, Marx, Frazer, and Freud as Imaginative Writers* (New York: Atheneum, 1962), pp. 189–291, 436–40.
66. Review of *Group Theories of Religion*, *International Journal of Ethics*, p. 116.
67. *Royce's Seminar*, pp. 76, 78.
68. "A Prediction in Regard to Three English Authors," p. 29.
69. Ibid.
70. "London Letter," *Dial* 71 (Oct. 1921): 453.
71. "A Prediction in Regard to Three English Authors," p. 29.
72. "A Commentary," *Criterion* 3 (Apr. 1925), 342.

73. Matthew Arnold was particularly affected by Renan's *Life of Jesus* (1863), as is readily apparent in *Literature and Dogma* (1873) and *God and the Bible* (1875), having praised the book warmly in "The Function of Criticism at the Present Time" (1864). Indicative of how influential was Frazer's thesis that Christianity evolved out of primitive mystery cults, Norman P. Williams felt compelled to attempt a refutation on behalf of the orthodox Anglican community in "The Origins of the Sacraments," *Essays Catholic and Critical,* ed. Edward G. Selwyn (London: Society for Promoting Christian Knowledge, 1926), pp. 365–423. In the course of his discussion Williams considers, along with Frazer, the related work of K. Reinhardt, Gilbert Murray, Jane Harrison, Alfred Loisy, F. Cumont, Adolf von Harnack, T. R. Glover, W. Bousset, and W. H. R. Rivers.

74. Vickery, *Literary Impact of "The Golden Bough"* pp. 243–44. In *The Golden Bough* (abridged edition), pp. 414–15, 419–20, Frazer prefers what he sees as the Greco-Roman (though in his case Victorian) ideal of the subordination of the individual to family, community, and state through public service to the pursuit of individual spiritual salvation encouraged by "Oriental" religions which he finds to have dominated Europe until the Renaissance.

75. For a discussion of the theories of religion posited by the leading psychoanalytic psychologists of the early twentieth century, and their relationship to late nineteenth-century psychology and anthropology, see G. Stephen Spinks, *Psychology and Religion: An Introduction to Contemporary Views* (London: Methuen, 1963), as well as De Vries, *Study of Religion.*

76. "A Commentary" (Apr. 1934), p. 452, and Gordon, *Eliot's Early Years,* p. 141.

77. "The Modern Dilemma; The Search for Moral Sanction," *Listener* 7 (30 Mar. 1932): 445.

78. Review of *Group Theories of Religion, International Journal of Ethics,* p. 116.

79. Rank, "The Myth of the Birth of the Hero: A Psychological Interpretation of Mythology," tr. F. Robbins and Smith E. Jelliffe, appeared in *Journal of Nervous and Mental Disorders* during 1914.

80. Two of the essays in *Ritual: Four Psychoanalytic Studies,* tr. Douglas Bryan (New York: International Universities Press, 1946) originally appeared in *Imago* during 1914–15.

81. Relevant essays appeared in *Contributions to Psycho-Analysis,* tr. Ernest Jones (Boston: R. G. Badger, 1916).

82. Jung, *Wandlungen und Symbole des Libido* (Vienna: Deuticke Verlag, 1912); tr. Beatrice M. Hinkle, *Psychology of the Unconscious* (New York: Moffatt Yard, 1916; London: Kegan Paul, 1917). Later revised in 1952 and translated in 1956 as *Symbols of Transformation.*

83. Freud, *Totem und Tabu* (Vienna: Hugo Heller, 1913); tr. A. A. Brill, *Totem and Taboo* (New York: Moffatt, Yard, 1918; London: Kegan Paul, Trench, Trubner, 1919). The subsequent authorized translation by James Strachey was published in 1950.

84. Wundt, *Elemente der Völkerpsychologie* (Leipzig: A. Kröner, 1912), tr. Edward L. Schaub, *Elements of Folk Psychology* (London: Allen and Unwin; New York: Macmillan, 1916).

85. Review of Wundt, *Elements of Folk Psychology,* pp. 253, 252, 253–54.

86. Stephen Spender, in *T. S. Eliot* (New York: Penguin Books, 1976), pp. 101–2, quotes Freud's description, from *Civilization and Its Discon-*

tents (1930), tr. James Strachey (New York: Norton, 1961), p. 17, of the architectural history of Rome as an analogy of our unconscious mind to illustrate the poetic, prophetic consciousness of Tiresias in *The Waste Land* that ranges over all phases of human development. Jung had previously employed the architectural history of a building as a metaphor for the unconscious in "Mind and the Earth" (1927), *Contributions to Analytical Psychology*, tr. H. G. and Cary F. Baines (New York: Harcourt Brace, 1928), pp. 118–19.

87. Spender, *The Destructive Element: A Study of Modern Writers and Beliefs* (London: Jonathan Cape, 1935), pp. 145–47.

88. Drew, *T. S. Eliot: The Design of His Poetry* (New York: Scribner's).

89. Martin, *Experiment in Depth: A Study of the Work of Jung, Eliot, and Toynbee* (London: Routledge and Kegan Paul, 1955).

90. Fabricius, *The Unconscious and Mr. Eliot: A Study in Expressionism* (Copenhagen: Nyt Nordisk Forlag, 1967).

91. "London Letter," *Dial* 73 (Sept. 1922): 330.

92. "Introduction" to S. L. Bethell, *Shakespeare and the Popular Dramatic Tradition* (Durham, N.C : Duke Univ. Press, 1945), p. ix.

93. "London Letter" (Sept. 1922), p. 330.

94. "A Commentary" (Apr. 1925), p. 342.

95. "London Letter" (Sept. 1922), p. 330.

96. "The Hawthorne Aspect," *Little Review* 5 (Aug. 1918): 51.

97. "A Commentary" (Apr. 1925), p. 342.

98. "Hooker, Hobbes, and Others," *Times Literary Supplement,* no. 1293 (11 Nov. 1926), p. 789.

99. Inge, *Christian Mysticism*, p. 35.

CHAPTER IV. PRIMITIVE EXPERIENCE

1. "Tarr," *Egoist* 5 (Sept. 1918): 106.

2. "War-Paint and Feathers," p. 1036.

3. "A Commentary," *Criterion* 6 (Dec. 1927): 481.

4. "A Commentary," *Criterion* 5 (June 1927): 283.

5. Review of *Theism and Humanism*, p. 287.

6. "The Beating of a Drum," *Nation and Athenaeum* 34 (6 Oct. 1923): 11.

7. Review of *Elements of Folk Psychology*, p. 254.

8. In "War-Paint and Feathers," Eliot mentions Harrison and Cooke; in *SE* 49 (1920), Harrison, Cornford, Cooke, and Murray; in "A Prediction in Regard to Three English Authors," Harrison, Cornford, and Cooke.

9. Harrison, *Prolegomena to the Study of Greek Religion* (1903; 1908), 3d ed. (Cambridge: Cambridge Univ. Press, 1922), p. vii.

10. *Royce's Seminar*, p. 76.

11. Review of *Group Theories of Religion*, *New Statesman*, p. 405.

12. Harrison, *Themis: A Study of the Social Origins of Greek Religion* (1912), 2d ed. (Cambridge: Cambridge Univ. Press, 1927), p. xii.

13. Ibid., p. 477.

14. Ibid., p. xii.

15. Ibid., p. xiii.

16. Ibid., p. xxii.

17. Ibid., pp. 45–46.

18. Ibid., p. 341.

19. Ibid., pp. 362–63.

20. Cornford, *The Origin of Attic Comedy* (London: Edward Arnold, 1914); ed. Theordore H. Gaster (Garden City, N.Y.: Doubleday, 1961), p. 165.

21. Ibid., p. 184–85.

22. Ibid., p. xxx.

23. Cornford, *From Religion to Philosophy: A Study in the Origins of Western Speculation* (London: Edward Arnold, 1912).

24. Tracing the evolution of primitive ritual still further by means of a structuralist methodology, Dan O. Via, Jr., in *Kerygma and Comedy in the New Testament: A Structuralist Approach to Hermeneutic* (Philadelphia: Fortress Press, 1975), finds in certain books of the New Testament, the Gospel of Mark, and the letters of Paul, the same structure that Cornford found in Greek comedy, thus lending further support to Frazer's contention that Christianity's heritage lies in primitive fertility cults.

25. Murray, *The Classical Tradition in Poetry* (London: Oxford Univ. Press, 1927), pp. 239–40.

26. Cornford, "The Unconscious Element in Literature and Philosophy" (1921), *The Unwritten Philosophy and Other Essays*, ed. W. K. C. Guthrie (Cambridge: Cambridge Univ. Press, 1967), pp. 6, 9.

27. "The Beating of a Drum," p. 11.

28. Ibid., p. 12.

29. *The Sacred Dance: A Study in Comparative Folklore* (Cambridge: Cambridge Univ. Press, 1923).

30. "The Beating of a Drum," p. 12.

31. *Royce's Seminar*, p. 78.

32. "Introduction," *Savonarola*, p. viii.

33. *Royce's Seminar*, p. 76. Gordon's reading of this passage is contrary to what it appears to mean in the context of the seminar and of Eliot's later writings. He did *not* criticize the anthropologists "for giving no explanation of religious ritual 'in terms of need'" (p. 58), but precisely *because* they explained them according to need.

34. "Introduction," *Savonarola*, p. viii.

35. "The Beating of a Drum," p. 12.

36. Ibid. Eliot is quoting from S. H. Butcher's *Aristotle's Theory of Poetry and Fine Art*, presumably the 4th ed. (New York: St. Martin's Press, 1907).

37. "The Ballet," pp. 441–42. Howarth, *Notes on Some Figures*, pp. 307–8, provides a discussion, though not entirely precise and complete, of the relationship between ritual, rhythm, and the nervous system expressed by Eliot in this passage.

38. Gordon, *Eliot's Early Years*, pp. 52, 58, misleadingly implies that mystical visions and hallucinations are for Eliot equivalent experiences. Eliot does believe that both religious visions and hallucinations have their origin in physiology. But for Eliot, as for William James, hallucinations are a malfunction of our physiology, as the visions of hysterics in psychiatric clinics are an inverted mysticism resulting from mental disease. The religious impulse, on the other hand, is a normal function of our physiology for Eliot which, at more intense and heightened moments, will produce mystical visions. As Eliot observes of an analogous kind of experience, hallucination is simply the "disease" of memory (*KE* 50).

39. "Marianne Moore," *Dial* 75 (Dec. 1923): 597.

40. Review of *The Growth of Civilisation,* and *The Origin of Magic and Religion* by W. J. Perry, *Criterion* 2 (July 1924): 490–91.

41. "The Ballet," p. 441.

42. "London Letter," *Dial* 71 (Aug. 1921): 214.

43. See "London Letter" (Aug. 1921) and (Oct. 1921), and "A Commentary," *Criterion* 3 (Oct. 1924) and 3 (Jan. 1925). Charles Spencer provides an interesting account of the Ballets Russes in *The World of Serge Diaghilev* (New York: Henry Regnery, 1974). See also Richard Buckle, *Diaghilev* (New York: Atheneum, 1979).

44. "Dramatis Personae," *Criterion* 1 (Apr. 1923): 305–6.

45. "Introduction," *Savonarola,* pp. xi–xii.

46. "The Beating of a Drum," p. 12.

47. "Introduction," *Savonarola,* pp. x–xi.

48. "Dramatis Personae," p. 305.

49. "London Letter" (Aug. 1921), p. 214.

50. "A Commentary" (Jan. 1925), p. 161.

51. "Dramatis Personae," p. 305.

52. Eliot's historical and theoretical analysis of satiric humor shares a number of premises with the later, more elaborate study of Robert C. Elliott, *The Power of Satire: Magic, Ritual, and Art* (Princeton: Princeton Univ. Press, 1960).

53. "The Beating of a Drum," p. 11.

54. Ibid., pp. 11, 12. Eliot's evolutionary account of the Fool will later be corroborated by Enid Welsford's *The Fool* (London: Faber and Faber, 1935), which considers the Fool in its various guises as mascot, scapegoat, poet, clairvoyant, and buffoon. A recent symposium is *The Fool and the Trickster,* ed. Paul V. A. Williams (Totowa, N.J.: Rowman and Littlefield, 1979).

55. "War-Paint and Feathers," p. 1036.

56. "Tarr," pp. 106, 105.

57. "Contemporary English Prose," *Vanity Fair* 20 (July 1923): 51, 98.

58. "Tarr," p. 105.

59. "London Letter," *Dial* 70 (June 1921): 689, 688.

60. "London Letter," *Dial* 72 (May 1922): 513.

61. "London Letter" (June 1921), pp. 687–88.

62. Ibid., p. 688.

63. Ibid.

64. Grover Smith, *Eliot's Poetry and Plays.*

65. Jones, *The Plays of T. S. Eliot* (Toronto: Univ. of Toronto Press, 1960).

66. Carol Smith, *T. S. Eliot's Dramatic Theory and Practice: From Sweeney Agonistes to The Elder Statesman* (Princeton: Princeton Univ. Press, 1963).

67. *Dynamo* (New York: Duell, Sloan and Pearce, 1943), p. 83.

68. "The Rock" (letter), *Spectator* 152 (8 June 1934): 887.

69. See "Poetry and Drama" (1951), *PP* 75–95. Eliot's drama is sympathetically assessed by Katherine Worth in "Eliot and the Living Theatre," *Eliot in Perspective: A Symposium,* ed. Graham Martin (London: Humanities Press, 1970), pp. 148–66.

70. "Dramatis Personae," p. 306.

71. "The Ballet," p. 442.

72. "A Commentary," *Criterion* 4 (June 1926): 419. Eliot was not entirely against the medium of film as such, but objected, in part, to the way

[1942], *PP* 22–23). Feeling, in which
s ultimately more important than con-
nd assents: Virgil's *Georgics,* Lucretius's
's *Divine Comedy* "were not designed to
tual assent, but to convey an emotional
cretius and Dante teach you, in fact, is
liefs" ("The Social Function of Poetry,"
54). Thus, "much has been said every-
ous belief; not so much notice has been
nsibility. The trouble of the modern age
lieve certain things about God and man
ut the inability to *feel* towards God and
unction of Poetry," *PP* 15). In turn, then,
stian Society* (New York: Harcourt Brace,
ould primarily train people to be able to
ough it could not compel and would not
re profession of belief" (p. 26).
Belief," *Enemy,* no. 1 (Jan. 1927), p. 16.

Eliot: A Memoir,* ed. Donald Adamson (New

a: Christianity and Communism," *Listener*

a," *Christian Register* 102 (19 Oct. 1933):

holly other" was first introduced by Rudolf
John W. Harvey, *The Idea of the Holy,* 2d ed.
s, 1950), pp. 25–30, and then employed by
(1918; 1921), tr. Edwyn C. Hoskyns, *The
n: Oxford Univ. Press, 1933), p. 250 et pas-
riss (1947), tr. G. T. Thomson, *Dogmatics in
1949), pp. 35–41. For Otto, the phrase sig-
s experience, of our sense of the Deity, that
on or rational comprehension, and available
ess. Although Barth uses the term to separate
God from human speculation and the tem-
serve his transcendence, he goes on to assert
lly and ethically in his acts as 'given' to man
the other hand, because God's existence is
ments about him must be treated as myths;
lds 'categories' and 'structures' of thought and

ST POETIC

ug. 1921), p. 216.
of Surrealism" (1930), in André Breton, *Mani-
ichard Seaver and Helen R. Lane (Ann Arbor:
1969), p. 152.
ealism" (1924), *Manifestoes,* p. 40.
Egoist 5 (June/July 1918): 84.
vement is studied by Sarane Alexandrian, *Sur-

in which it was currently being used. Although the movies did lack the element of live performance that the theater had, Eliot realized that the as yet untapped potential of the cinema for "eluding realism" was significant ("Dramatis Personae," p. 306). Fabricius, *Unconscious and Mr. Eliot,* pp. 30–40, and Bolgan, *What the Thunder Really Said,* pp. 55–59, in fact, compare Eliot's poetic technique, particularly in *The Waste Land,* to Sergei Eisenstein's avant-garde cinematic theory and practice, which was both experimental and 'unrealistic.'

73. "The Beating of a Drum," p. 12.

74. "Introduction," *Savonarola,* p. xi.

75. "A Commentary" (June 1926), p. 419.

76. "The Poetic Drama," *Athenaeum,* no. 4698 (14 May 1920), p. 635.

77. "Introduction" to Ezra Pound, *Selected Poems* (1928), 2d ed. (London: Faber and Faber, 1949), p. 8.

78. This distinction between the dramatic monologue and its subgenre, the internal monologue, is a refinement of Robert Langbaum's discrimination between Browning's and Eliot's poems in *The Poetry of Experience: The Dramatic Monologue in Modern Literary Tradition* (New York: Random House, 1957), pp. 189–92. Kenner, *Invisible Poet,* pp. 40–56 passim, implies a similar distinction.

79. Genesius Jones, in *Approach to the Purpose: A Study of T. S. Eliot's Poetry* (London: Hodder and Stoughton, 1964), finds ritualistic elements in Eliot's earlier poetry as well.

CHAPTER V. MYTHIC CONSCIOUSNESS

1. For a general and informed discussion of the nature of myth, the uses to which man puts it, and its relationship to ritual, see G. S. Kirk, *Myth: Its Meaning and Functions in Ancient and Other Cultures* (Cambridge: Cambridge Univ. Press; Berkeley: Univ. of California Press, 1970), and *The Nature of Greek Myths* (Baltimore: Penguin Books, 1974).

2. See Cornford, *From Religion to Philosophy.*

3. Harrison, *Prolegomena,* p. vii.

4. "Tarr," p. 105.

5. "Notes on Current Letters: The Romantic Englishman, the Comic Spirit, and the Function of Criticism," *Tyro,* no. 1 (Spring 1921), p. 4. Eliot's mode of analysis of specific occurrences of myth in literature and society anticipates contemporary mythic criticism beginning with Maud Bodkin's *Archetypal Patterns in Poetry: Psychological Studies of Imagination* (London: Oxford Univ. Press, 1934), codified by Northrop Frye in *Anatomy of Criticism: Four Essays* (Princeton: Princeton Univ. Press, 1957), and operative in Roland Barthes's dissection of aspects of popular culture, *Mythologies* (1957), tr. Annette Lavers (New York: Hill and Wang, 1973). Recent collections of such criticism include *Myth: A Symposium,* ed. Thomas A. Sebeok (Bloomington, Ind.: Indiana Univ. Press, 1958); *Myth and Mythmaking,* ed. Henry A. Murray (New York: Braziller, 1960); Northrop Frye, L. C. Knights, et al., *Myth and Symbol: Critical Approaches and Applications* (Lincoln: Univ. of Nebraska Press, 1963); *Myth and Literature: Contemporary Theory and Practice,* ed. John B. Vickery (Lincoln: Univ. of Nebraska Press, 1966); *Myth, Symbol, and Culture,* ed. Clifford Geertz (New York: Norton, 1974).

6. "Tarr," p. 105.

7. "The Romantic Englishman, the Comic Spirit, and the Function of Criticism," p. 4.

8. "Ulysses, Order, and Myth" (Nov. 1923), *Selected Prose,* ed. Frank Kermode (New York: Harcourt Brace Jovanovich; Farrar, Straus and Giroux, 1975), pp. 177–78.

9. "John Donne," *Nation and Athenaeum* 33 (9 June 1923): 332.

10. "Ulysses, Order, and Myth," *Selected Prose,* p. 175.

11. "London Letter" (Oct. 1921), pp. 452–53.

12. "The Poetic Drama," p. 635.

13. "Introduction," *Savonarola,* p. xi.

14. "The Ballet," p. 443.

15. This account of Eliot's view of the self as a process of consciously unifying disparate points of view differs from Bolgan's more elaborate interpretation of Eliot's view of the self, for which she adopts the concept "soul-making" (*What the Thunder Really Said,* p. 92) from Keats, upon which she bases her study. Bolgan's ingenious, evolutionary account of philosophy and literary theory from Kantian to Hegelian and then to Anglo-American Idealism, and from the Romantics through Yeats, presents Eliot's thought in the context of a wider intellectual tradition. But by using the ideas and terminology of this tradition to explain Eliot's own concepts, Bolgan at times appears to stray from Eliot's more restricted and idiosyncratic thought. Eliot relied upon only a very few of these philosophers and poets, and only certain aspects of their ideas, to formulate his own system, and combined philosophical concepts with anthropological, psychological, and mystical theory. Of the two passages that Eliot quotes from Keats's letters with praise, the one criticizes Wordsworth for not thinking "deeper" in his poetry, and the other specifies that artists do not have "a proper self" at all (*UPUC* 101). To say that Eliot conceived of the self as a process of reconciliation, a "significant-self-in-becoming," between the "empirical" or "phenomenal" self, and the "noumenal" or "transcendent" self, as Idealists mean these terms, seems to lead us astray of Eliot's idea of self, a strictly conscious, empirical, spatial-temporal construction, subsequent to the disintegration of the noumenal immediate experience, or finite center, and therefore essentially separate from it. As Eliot asserts, quoting Bradley, "a soul, or a self . . . is always the 'creature of an intellectual construction'; it is never simply given, but depends upon a transcendence of immediacy" (*KE* 150). That Eliot wished to reach the unconscious through poetry and mystical experience does not mean that he viewed immediate experience or the Absolute as a Real Self to which he wished to bring his temporal personality in line, or that a Real Self could be formed from such a synthesis. As Bolgan herself quotes Eliot (*What the Thunder Really Said,* p. 171), "the distinction is not between a 'private self' and a 'public self' or a 'higher self'" (*SE* 402). The creation of any kind of 'self' is, in fact, contrary to Eliot's literary, philosophical, and religious ambitions. The lack of any resemblance to a self or a personality, the synthesis of all selves, of all history and human experience in a single whole, is the appeal immediate experience and the Absolute had for Eliot. To encounter immediate experience is, therefore, to lose all sense of self, even the very notion of 'self', entirely, in a single act of humility and sacrifice. When one returns to the fragmented world of experience, and to one's self, from a mystical moment, one then applies the previous experience of wholeness, of 'selflessness', to the world of Appearance, to one's

still exist" ("The Music of Poetry"
thought and emotion are united i
scious intellectual formulations a
On the Nature of Things, and Dant
persuade the readers to an intellec
equivalent for the ideas. What L
what it feels like to hold certain b
Adelphi 21 [July/Sept. 1945]: 1
where about the decline of religi
taken of the decline of religious s
is not merely the inability to be
which our forefathers believed,
man as they did" ("The Social F
according to *The Idea of a Chri*
1940), "a Christian education v
think in Christian categories, th
impose the necessity for insinc

23. "A Note on Poetry and
24. Ibid., pp. 16–17.
25. Robert Sencourt, *T. S.*
York: Dell, 1971), p. 132.
26. "The Modern Dilemm
7 (16 Mar. 1932): 383.
27. "The Modern Dilemn
pp. 675–76.
28. The concept of "the v
Otto in *Das Heilige* (1917), tr
(New York: Oxford Univ. Pre
Karl Barth in *Der Romanbrie*
Epistle to the Romans (Londo
sim, and *Dogmatik im Grund*
Outline (London: SCM Press
nified that aspect of religiou
is mystery, beyond percepti
only as an emotional awarer
completely the existence o
poral world in order to pre
that God is defined rationa
in the Bible. For Eliot, o
unknowable, specific state
naturalistic description yie
feeling.

CHAPTER VI. A SURREAL

1. "London Letter" (*A*
2. "Second Manifesto
festoes of Surrealism, tr.
Univ. of Michigan Press,
3. "Manifesto of Sur
4. "Contemporanea,
5. The Surrealist M

s
f
n
le
Pl
(P
co
ma
gior
sibi
mod
critic
sider
frame

El
his co
scious
ticism
(the my
(1931)
lief," of
which tr
two cont
third. Sk
Notes Tow
Faber, 19
tion of the
makes pos
"what I wa
deliberately
with frontie

realist Art, tr. Gordon Clough (New York: Praeger, 1970); Ferdinand Al-
quié, The Philosophy of Surrealism, tr. Bernard Waldrop (Ann Arbor: Univ.
of Michigan Press, 1965); Anna Balakian, The Literary Origins of Surrealism: A New Mysticism in French Poetry (1947; rpt. New York: New York
Univ. Press, 1965), Surrealism: The Road to the Absolute, 2d ed. (New York:
Dutton, 1970), and André Breton: Magus of Surrealism (New York: Oxford
Univ. Press, 1971); Roger Cardinal and Robert Short, Surrealism: Permanent Revelation (London: Studio Vista, 1970); Michel Carrouges, André
Breton and the Basic Concepts of Surrealism, tr. Maura Prendergast (Univer-
sity, Ala.: Univ. of Alabama Press, 1974); Mary Ann Caws, André Breton
(The Hague: Mouton, 1966) and The Poetry of Dada and Surrealism: Ara-
gon, Breton, Tzara, Eluard, and Desnos (Princeton: Princeton Univ. Press,
1970); Wallace Fowlie, Age of Surrealism (Bloomington, Ind.: Indiana
Univ. Press, 1960); Herbert S. Gershman, The Surrealist Revolution in
France (Ann Arbor: Univ. of Michigan Press, 1969); Malcolm Haslam, The
Real World of the Surrealists (New York: Rizzoli Internatl., 1978); Marcel
Jean, The History of Surrealist Painting, tr. Simon Watson Taylor (New York:
Grove Press, 1960); Georges Lemaitre, From Cubism to Surrealism in
French Literature (Cambridge, Mass.: Harvard Univ. Press, 1941); J. H.
Matthews, An Introduction to Surrealism (University Park, Pa.: Pennsyl-
vania State Univ. Press, 1965), André Breton (New York: Columbia Univ.
Press, 1967), Surrealist Poetry in France (Syracuse, N.Y.: Syracuse Univ.
Press, 1969), Toward the Poetics of Surrealism (Syracuse, N.Y.: Syracuse
Univ. Press, 1976), and The Imagery of Surrealism (Syracuse, N.Y.: Syracuse Univ. Press, 1977); Maurice Nadeau, The History of Surrealism, tr.
Richard Howard (New York: Macmillan, 1965); Gaeton Picon, Surrealists
and Surrealism (New York: Rizzoli, 1977); Marcel Raymond, From Baudelaire to Surrealism (London: Methuen, 1970); William S. Rubin, Dada and
Surrealist Art (New York: Abrams, 1968); Uwe M. Schneede, Surrealism,
tr. Maria Pelikan (New York: Abrams, 1974); Robert Short, Dada and Surrealism (London: Octopus Books, 1980); and Patrick Waldberg, Surrealism (London: Thames and Hudson, 1965).

For the influence of Janet on Breton, see Philippe Soupault, Profils
Perdu (Paris: Mercure de France, 1963), quoted by Matthews, Imagery of
Surrealism, p. 1, and Balakian, André Breton, pp. 28–34.

6. For an account of Surrealist activity before 1924, see Robert Short,
"Paris Dada and Surrealism," Journal of European Studies 9 (1979): 75–98.

7. In the Criterion, F. S. Flint, "French Periodicals," 3 (July 1925),
601–2, and 4 (Apr. 1926): 405–7, is harshly dismissive of Surrealism;
Montgomery Belgion, "Meaning in Art," 9 (Jan. 1930): 201–16, and
"French Chronicle," 12 (Oct. 1932): 80–90, criticizes the Surrealists'
theoretical basis of their reliance upon automatism to produce a work of
art; Michael Roberts, 13 (Apr. 1934): 506, and review of Herbert Read,
ed., Surrealism 16 (Apr. 1937): 551–53, finds Surrealism to be a re-
affirmation of Romantic principles; Roger Hinks, "Art Chronicle: Surrealism," 16 (Oct. 1936): 70–75, assesses the social consequences of
Surrealist theory, deciding that Surrealist art is a symbolic expression of
dialectical materialism; and Brian Coffey, review of Breton, Position politi-
que du surrealisme, and David Gascoyne, A Short Survey of Surrealism
15 (Apr. 1936): 506–11, explores the relationship between Surrealist
theory and the movement's political stance. Eliot did publish Hugh Sykes
Davies, "Banditti: From the Biography of Petron," 13 (July 1934): 577–
80, a portion of his novel Petron, which eventually became, according to

Paul Ray, *The Surrealist Movement in England* (Ithaca, N.Y.: Cornell Univ.
Press, 1971), p. 89, "one of the showpieces of English surrealism."

8. Paul Ray, *Surrealist Movement*, pp. 265–69. Ray concludes that
Eliot "is not a surrealist by any definition" (p. 265), nor was he influenced
by them," but "both he and they found a common source elsewhere,
probably in Freud's analyses of dream-images" (p. 269). Neither Freud,
nor for that matter Charcot or Janet, was their common source, but instead the unconscious itself. For that reason, the distinctive qualities of
Eliot's poetic theory and practice so resemble Surrealist theory and art, as
Ray himself suggests, that Eliot *can* be considered 'surrealistic' in kind
from an esthetic standpoint without violating definitions. Jacob Korg, in
"Modern Art Techniques in *The Waste Land*," *Journal of Aesthetics and Art
Criticism* 18 (June 1960), displays a confusion similar to Ray's when he
observes that, "though its principles and those of Eliot's are in nearly all
respects exactly opposed to each other, the fact remains that *The Waste
Land* is in some ways an unmistakably Surrealist poem" (p. 461). On the
other hand, Louis Simpson has expressed the opinion that "a case can be
made for Eliot's poems being surrealist, if we admit that surrealist writing
may have logical connections," in *Three on the Tower: The Lives and Works
of Ezra Pound, T. S. Eliot, and William Carlos Williams* (New York: Morrow,
1975), p. viii.

9. See especially Thompson, *T. S. Eliot*, pp. 62–79; Freed, *Aesthetics
and History* and *The Critic as Philosopher*, passim; and Mowbray Allan,
Eliot's Impersonal Theory, pp. 59–170.

10. See Valerie Eliot, "Introduction," *The Waste Land: A Facsimile and
Transcript*, pp. ix–x; Howarth, *Notes on Some Figures*, p. 214; Gordon,
Eliot's Early Years, pp. 65–67; Noel Stock, *The Life of Ezra Pound*, 2d ed.
(New York: Discus, 1974), pp. 187–88, 241, 245–46; and E. J. H. Greene,
T. S. Eliot et la France (Paris: Boivin, 1951), p. 146.

11. Pound, *The Natural Philosophy of Love* (New York: Boni and Live-
right, 1922).

12. For an account of Gourmont's career and his influence on Pound
and Eliot see Greene, *Eliot et la France*, pp. 143–70, and Glenn S. Burne,
"Remy de Gourmont: A Scientific Philosophy of Art," *Western Humanities
Review* 13 (Winter 1959); 71–79; and "T. S. Eliot and Remy de Gourmont," *Bucknell Review* 8 (Feb. 1959): 113–26, both incorporated into
Remy de Gourmont: His Ideas and Influence in England and America (Carbondale, Ill.: Southern Illinois Univ. Press, 1963). Burne's *Remy de Gourmont: Selected Writings* (Ann Arbor: Univ. of Michigan Press, 1966) is also
helpful.

13. Burne, *Remy de Gourmont: His Ideas and Influence*, p. 135. By arguing that Bradley is the sole source of ideas that Eliot felt he shared with
Gourmont, Freed, in *The Critic as Philosopher*, pp. 136–49, oversimplifies
a richer and more subtle relationship.

14. As a great admirer of Hartmann's *Philosophy of the Unconscious*,
Laforgue too had a conception of the unconscious, but like Gourmont's
it also differs from Eliot's, being the metaphysical Spirit animating and
directing the course of Nature as propounded by German Romantic
Idealists. See A. G. Lehmann, *The Symbolist Aesthetic in France, 1885–
1895* (New York: Macmillan, 1950), pp. 115–20, and Warren Ramsey,
Jules Laforgue and the Ironic Inheritance (New York: Oxford Univ. Press,
1953), pp. 22–23, 82–89, et passim.

15. In his brief discussion of Gourmont's subjective idealism and

behaviorism, Mowbray Allan (*Eliot's Impersonal Theory*, pp. 38–41) mistakenly implies that Gourmont's rapprochement of idealism and materialism overcomes the subjectivity inherent in his use of physiology.

16. "Marianne Moore," p. 595.

17. "John Donne," p. 332.

18. "Turgenev," *Egoist* 4 (Dec. 1917): 167.

19. "Style and Thought," p. 769.

20. "A Commentary" (Oct. 1924), p. 2.

21. Freed, *Aesthetics and History*, p. 140, and *The Critic as Philosopher*, p. 54.

22. Bradley, "On Professor James's 'Radical Empiricism,'" *Essays on Truth and Reality*, pp. 152–53.

23. See "Homage à Charles Maurras," *Aspects de la France et du Monde*, 25 Apr. 1948, p. 6. Eliot's relationship with Maurras, and with Benda, is studied by Greene, *Eliot et la France*, pp. 143–210; Howarth, *Notes on Some Figures*, pp. 175–89; Margolis, *Eliot's Intellectual Development*, pp. 42–45, 87–99; James Torrens, "Charles Maurras and Eliot's 'New Life,'" *Publications of the Modern Language Association* 89 (1974): 312–22; and Roger Kojecky, *T. S. Eliot's Social Criticism* (New York: Farrar, Straus and Giroux, 1971), pp. 58–61.

24. "Was There a Scottish Literature?" *Athenaeum*, no. 4657 (1 Aug. 1919), p. 680.

25. Ibid.

26. "Reflections on Contemporary Poetry," *Egoist* 6 (July 1919): 39.

27. "The Three Provincialities," *Tyro*, no. 2 (Spring 1922), p. 13.

28. "A Preface to Modern Literature," *Vanity Fair* 21 (Nov. 1923): 118.

29. "The Method of Mr. Pound" *Athenaeum*, no. 4669 (24 Oct. 1919), p. 1065.

30. "Turgenev," p. 167.

31. "A Brief Introduction to the Method of Paul Valery," p. 14.

32. The psychoanalytic interpretation of Hamlet is customarily associated with Ernest Jones and his *Hamlet and Œdipus* (New York: Norton, 1949). The original version of this study, first published as "The Oedipus Complex as an Explanation of Hamlet's Mystery" in *American Journal of Psychology* (Jan. 1910), began as an exposition of a footnote in Freud's *Interpretation of Dreams* (1900).

33. "Reflections on Contemporary Poetry," *Egoist* 4 (Oct. 1917): 133.

34. "Kipling Redivivus," *Athenaeum*, no. 4645 (9 May 1919), p. 298.

35. "In Memory of Henry James," *Egoist* 5 (Jan. 1918): 2.

36. "American Literature," *Athenaeum*, no. 4643 (25 Apr. 1919), p. 237.

37. "In Memory of Henry James," p. 1.

38. "London Letter" (Sept. 1922), p. 331.

39. Stead, *The New Poetic: Yeats to Eliot* (London: Hutchinson, 1964), pp. 127–30. Freed, *Aesthetics and History*, p. 150, had previously noted the distinction Eliot makes between 'emotion' and 'feeling', citing Bradley as the origin for it.

40. "London Letter" (Aug. 1921), p. 216.

41. Within his overall conceptual framework that a work of art in all of its aspects originates in the unconscious, and that form and content are both subject to subsequent conscious improvement, Eliot draws a further distinction between "creative fiction" and "critical fiction," according to which Jonson's is creative, adding that Jonson was a "conscious critic, but

he was also conscious in his creations." Then Eliot proposes that the "method antithetical" to Jonson's, critical fiction, is exemplified by *Education Sentimentale*. Eliot goes on to stipulate that in creative fiction the characters of Jonson and Shakespeare, and indeed of great drama in general, are created in "simple and positive outlines" while a character of Flaubert's cannot be separated from the "environment" in which he functions (*SE* 131–32). Whether Eliot is thus implying that creative fiction is conscious while critical fiction is unconscious is difficult to say. What Eliot means by calling Jonson a conscious creator in this context is also uncertain, although Eliot is probably expressing the opinion that Jonson and Shakespeare exercise the artist's third point of view in their work to a greater extent than does Flaubert. Since Flaubert is a novelist while Shakespeare and Jonson are dramatists, Eliot may actually, if unwittingly, be drawing some distinction between the writing of a play and the writing of fiction: perhaps he means that a writer must be more detached, observe a more conscious distance, from his work as a dramatist than as a novelist. This discussion does *not* imply, however, as Stead alleges, that Shakespeare's creations are unconscious while Jonson's are conscious, since both dramatists are perceived to be similar in relation to Flaubert at this point, and Eliot makes clear his distinction between Jonson and Shakespeare at the end of the essay along other than conscious versus unconscious lines.

42. Stead, *The New Poetic*, p. 127.

43. "Rhyme and Reason: The Poetry of John Donne," *Listener* 3 (19 Mar. 1930): 503.

44. "John Donne," p. 332.

45. "Introduction," to Josef Pieper, *Leisure the Basis of Culture*, tr. Alexander Dru (London: Faber and Faber, 1952), p. 12. See also *SE* 399 (1927), where Eliot refers to the contemporary philosophy that superceded Bradley's as "crude and raw and provincial (though infinitely more technical and scientific)," and "I" in *Revelation*, ed. John Baillie and Hugh Martin (London: Faber and Faber, 1937), p. 27, where Eliot states that he would include a discussion of Logical Positivism in an analysis of the "situation of belief in the modern world."

46. Eliot describes his philosophical education under the New Realists at Harvard in "Views and Reviews" (6 June 1935), p. 151, where he observes that they "professed considerable respect" for Russell and his "Cambridge friends." According to Russell, in *Our Knowledge of the External World* (Chicago: Open Court, 1914), "the 'new realism' which owes its inception to Harvard is very largely impregnated with its [Logical Atomism's] spirit" (p. 4). Werkmeister, *A History of Philosophical Ideas in America*, explains that the New Realists were influenced primarily by G. E. Moore's "A Refutation of Idealism" (*Mind*, 1903) and Russell's *The Principles of Mathematics* (1903): "English and American realism may best be considered as parallel phenomena which have many points in common and which therefore mutually support each other" although they are essentially "independent of each other as specific cultural movements" (p. 372). Roderick M. Chisholm compares the two in his "Editor's Introduction" to *Realism and the Background of Phenomenology* (New York: Free Press, 1960), pp. 3–36.

47. See Gordon, *Eliot's Early Years*, p. 49, and Bernard Bergonzi, *T. S. Eliot* (New York: Macmillan, 1972), p. 26.

48. In *Philosophical Analysis: Its Development Between the Two World*

Wars (Oxford: Clarendon Press, 1956), p. 1, because the first edition of Russell's *Our Knowledge of the External World* was published in 1914.

49. "On Denoting," *Mind,* n.s. 14 (1905): 479–93, *KE* 126; "Knowledge by Acquaintance and Knowledge by Description," *Proceedings of the Aristotelian Society,* n.s. 11 (1910–11): 108–28, *KE* 105, rpt. in *Mysticism and Logic* (New York: Longmans, Green, 1918), of which "Style and Thought" is a review; and *The Problems of Philosophy* (New York: Henry Holt, 1912), chap. 5, "Knowledge by Acquaintance and Knowledge by Description," *KE* 104–7.

50. Russell's summary statement of the confluence of his and Wittgenstein's thought in the years just before World War I is "The Philosophy of Logical Atomism," *The Monist* (1918–19), rpt. *Logic and Knowledge: Essays 1901–1950,* ed. Robert C. Marsh (New York: Macmillan, 1956), pp. 177–281.

51. Eliot's earliest references to *Principia Mathematica* are in his review of *A Defense of Idealism* by May Sinclair, *New Statesman* 9 (22 Sept. 1917): 596; "Style and Thought," p. 768; and in the letter, "The Perfect Critic," *Athenaeum,* no. 4710 (6 Aug. 1920), p. 190.

52. "A Commentary," *Criterion* 6 (Oct. 1927): 291.

53. "A Commentary" (Dec. 1927), pp. 481, 482.

54. Later Wittgenstein will modify his view of language in *Philosophical Investigations* (1953, posthumous), relying upon a kind of analysis he called "language games" to explore, not the strict one-to-one correspondence between a word and an object, but the various kinds of uses to which we put language in order to express our diverse experiences of and reactions to the world, both intellectual and emotional. For an analysis of Wittgenstein's logical atomism, see G. E. M. Anscombe, *An Introduction to Wittgenstein's Tractatus,* 2d ed. (London: Hutchinson, 1963); Max Black, *A Companion to Wittgenstein's Tractatus* (Ithaca, N.Y.: Cornell Univ. Press, 1964); and James Griffin, *Wittgenstein's Logical Atomism* (Oxford: Clarendon Press, 1964). For this and other aspects of Wittgenstein's thought see David Pears, *Ludwig Wittgenstein* (New York: Viking, 1970), and Anthony Kenny, *Wittgenstein* (Cambridge, Mass.: Harvard Univ. Press, 1973). For Russell's logical atomism, see, in addition to Urmson's study, C. A. Fritz, *Bertrand Russell's Construction of the External World* (London: Routledge and Kegan Paul, 1952); David Pears, *Bertrand Russell and the British Tradition in Philosophy* (New York: Random House, 1968); A. J. Ayer, *Bertrand Russell* (New York: Viking, 1972); Herbert Hochberg, *Thought, Fact, and Reference: The Origins and Ontology of Logical Atomism* (Minneapolis: Univ. of Minnesota Press, 1978); and E. D. Klemke, ed., *Essays on Bertrand Russell* (Urbana: Univ. of Illinois Press, 1970).

55. In addition to Russell, Eliot may have been reminded of the notion that mathematical ideas are experienced as immediately and as emotionally as objects of sense perception by Gourmont, who in *Le Problem du style* observes that for Pascal even geometric propositions became feelings. The severe criticism of German Idealism by the New Realists may also have been refreshed in Eliot's mind by Gourmont, who observes in the same essay that Hegel is an 'ideo-emotive' philosopher, working in the realm of pure ideas, out of touch with concrete reality. But Eliot then goes on to interpret these observations in terms of Bradley's idealism and Babbitt's view of nineteenth-century Romanticism. Gourmont's praise of Schopenhauer and Nietzsche as philosophers in touch with their senses and the world of experience indicates the extent to which Eliot liberates

these ideas from Gourmont's intellectual context and transcends his romantic view of intellectual history. By contrast, Eliot criticizes both Schopenhauer and Nietzsche as exponents of cosmic flux who have made a philosophy out of evolutionary theory through their respective conceptions of a cosmic 'will'. Eliot considers Bergson their heir, and finds Nietzsche's morality to be the inevitable egotistical result of romantic pantheism. Finally, Eliot considers Nietzsche's work, like Bergson's, a confusion of points of view, more literary than philosophical, more emotional stimulus than logical thought, and, in direct contradiction to Gourmont, an example of words and thought having little basis in reality. See Eliot's review of *The Philosophy of Nietzsche* by A. Wolfe, *International Journal of Ethics* 26 (Apr. 1916): 426–27, and *SE* 119–20 (1927).

56. "Prose and Verse," *Chapbook,* no. 22 (Apr. 1921), p. 9.

57. "Tarr," p. 105.

58. "John Donne," p. 332.

59. At the same time that he determined to become a member of the Church of England, Eliot decided that Donne did not truly represent a unity of sensibility but only a tendency toward it, though Eliot did reaffirm his contention, also originally made in "The Metaphysical Poets" (*SE* 247), that Dante and Cavalcanti did. The theoretical principle, however, remains essentially the same, despite a change in illustration. As Eliot observes in "Donne in Our Time," *A Garland for John Donne, 1631–1931,* ed. Theodore Spencer (Cambridge, Mass.: Harvard Univ. Press, 1931), the thought and emotion that are fused in the unified sensibility are inherently related in themselves, just as object, thought, and emotion form an integrated whole in immediate experience. In order to reach this underlying correspondency, a poet must possess, as did the medieval poets, "the assumption of an ideal unity in experience, the faith in an ultimate rationalisation and harmonisation of experience, the subsumption of the lower under the higher, an ordering of the world more or less Aristotelian." With Donne, on the other hand, his "learning is just information suffused with emotion, or combined with emotion not essentially relevant to it." What is expressed is simply the "apparent irrelevance and unrelatedness of things," the world of Appearances. Tellingly, Eliot asserts that Donne's "temper" is the "antithesis of the scholastic, of the mystic, and of the philosophical system maker" (p. 8). As would be expected, Eliot came to believe that the unity of sensibility, dependent as it is upon access to the unconscious, could be achieved only through the psychic possession of a religious structure, specifically the Judao-Christian religion, that would facilitate experience of the subliminal.

In "Baudelaire" (1930), for instance, Eliot assesses Baudelaire's "adjustment of the natural to the spiritual" in terms of sacred romantic love as found in Dante, "the reaching out towards something which cannot be had *in,* but which may be had partly *through,* personal relations" (*SE* 379). Thus the human and the physical are not abandoned, but instead continue to be subsumed in a higher synthesis. Dante and Cavalcanti become, in fact, paradigms of the unified sensibility in the unpublished Clark lectures of 1926, while Donne and Laforgue are perceived as being in quest, but finally falling short, of the ideal of sacred romantic love of Dante. Originally, Dante, Cavalcanti, Guinzelli, and Cino, as well as Donne, Marvell, and Laforgue, were said to possess a unified sensibility (*SE* 247). The change in examples does not, however, imply a change of principle. Both the emotions and the intellect, the erotic and the religious, must be unified. David Spurr, *Conflicts in Consciousness: T. S. Eliot's Poetry and Criticism* (Urbana: Univ. of Illinois Press, 1984), astutely observes the resulting dialectic between the ideal and the real when he notes that "Eliot is the type of Donne striving to emulate the example of Dante" (p. 50). As Eliot in 1926 approaches his religious conversion, he realizes that the believing point of view requires the support of the contemporary institutional embodiment of the religious impulse, the Christian Church—its mythology, dogma, and liturgy—in order to balance successfully the skeptical point of view, both being subsumed under the third point of view of mythic consciousness. Direct participation in the Church gives specific mythic form and intellectual dimensions to experiences that had always seemed at once erotic, mystical, and religious. For discussion of the Clark lectures, see Edward Lobb, *T. S. Eliot and the Romantic Critical Tradition* (London: Routledge and Kegan Paul, 1981), passim; Hay, pp. 98–99; and Ronald Bush, *T. S. Eliot: A Study in Character and Style* (New York: Oxford Univ. Press, 1983), pp. 82–86.

Even Eliot's earliest poems reveal a desire to unite the physical and the spiritual, the intellectual and the emotional, romantic love and religious aspiration. "Convictions" (Berg Collection, New York Public Library) asserts that social propriety and nature impede such a union. "Conversation Galante" (Nov. 1909) expresses frustration over being with a woman who distracts him from, rather than leading him to, the Absolute, her eroticism and intellectual naivete clashing with his philosophical and religious preoccupations. On the other hand, "Entretiens dans un parc" (Feb. 1911; Berg Collection) records the moment in which physical love enters an intellectual and emotional relationship. Disappointment ensues with the woman's indifference to the erotic, while in "Paysage Triste" (Berg Collection), a chance erotic encounter with a woman must be avoided because of her inferior social position and intellectual background.

In poems where the romantic element is absent, the preoccupation remains the same. In "First Debate Between the Body and Soul" (Jan. 1910; Berg Collection), spiritual aspirations are frustrated by the world of sensory experience. In "Fragment: Bacchus and Ariadne: Second Debate Between the Body and Soul" (Feb. 1911; Berg Collection), a mystical moment is contrasted with the physical world back into which the speaker lapses. Not surprisingly, "Easter: Sensations of April" (Apr. 1910; Berg Collection) reveals a fascination with, almost an envy of, the literal belief of a child in orthodox Christian statements about God, statements in which the speaker finds himself unable to believe literally. Thus, in the second section of "Oh little voices of the throats of men" (McKeldin Library, University of Maryland), the experiences of the everyday world are said to lead only to confusion, yielding little support for religious truth.

Because these early poems are recording a religious struggle, and one frequently expressed through Christian concepts and symbols, Hay's contention that the early Eliot is negative beyond Christian and even religious boundaries seems an inexact oversimplification. Following Eliot's distinction between prose, expressing "ideals," and poetry, dealing with "actuality" (p. 7), Hay wishes to dismiss the ideals of the prose as somehow a false, inessential record of Eliot's mind. We must remember, however, that a man's life, and certainly Eliot's, is the struggle to embody his ideals in his lived reality. The ideals are as much a part of his life as are the failures to realize them recorded in the poetry. Contrary to Hay's contention that the early Eliot is preoccupied only with the negative aspects of Dante (pp. 7,

9, 11–12), Eliot explains in "Dante" (1920) that one must be aware of Dante's Christian vision in its entirety in order to read any part of the *Divine Comedy,* even the *Inferno:* "the examination of any episode in the *Comedy* ought to show that not merely the allegorical interpretation or the didactic intention, but the emotional significance itself, cannot be isolated from the rest of the poem" because "the artistic emotion presented by any episode of the *Comedy* is dependent upon the whole." In short, Dante "does not analyze the emotion so much as he exhibits its relation to other emotions. You cannot, that is, understand the *Inferno* without the *Purgatorio* and the *Paradiso*" (*SW* 165, 167, 168).

Hay insists that Eliot's early negative path was exclusively Buddhist, whereas it seems more likely that he sensed a confluence between Buddha's negative way and that of St. John of the Cross, whose writings are quoted on the index cards recording Eliot's reading at Harvard between 1912 and 1914 when he was also studying Far Eastern philosophy (*Eliot's Negative Way,* p. 98). The quatrain poems, such as "Mr. Eliot's Sunday Morning Service," use blasphemy to mock not religion, or a specific religion, but the vapid, self-congratulatory piety of the religiously naive church-goer. Although Hay dismisses Eliot's contention that blasphemy is "a sign of Faith," "a product of partial belief" (pp. 99–100), he appears to be correct, for the blasphemer must accept the general orientation of a religious mythology to some degree first in order to profane it.

60. Bradley, *Appearance and Reality,* p. 419.

61. "Kidnapping Donne," *Essays in Criticism, Second Series* (Berkeley: Univ. of California Press, 1934), pp. 61–89.

62. Mazzeo, "A Seventeenth-Century Theory of Metaphysical Poetry" and "Metaphysical Poetry and the Poetic of Correspondence," *Renaissance and Seventeenth-Century Studies* (New York: Columbia Univ. Press, 1964), pp. 29–59.

63. Tuve, "The Logical Functions of Imagery," part 2, *Elizabethan and Metaphysical Imagery: Renaissance Poetic and Twentieth-Century Critics* (Chicago: Univ. of Chicago Press, 1947), pp. 249–410.

64. Guss, *John Donne, Petrarchist: Italianate Conceits and Love Theory in The Songs and Sonnets* (Detroit: Wayne State Univ. Press, 1966).

65. Miles, "Twentieth-Century Donne," *Twentieth-Century Literature in Retrospect,* ed. Reuben A. Brower (Cambridge, Mass.: Harvard Univ. Press, 1971), pp. 205–24.

66. Orgel, "Affecting the Metaphysics," *Twentieth-Century Literature in Retrospect,* pp. 225–45.

67. "Donne in Our Time," *A Garland for John Donne,* ed. Theodore Spencer (Cambridge, Mass.: Harvard Univ. Press, 1931), p. 16.

68. Ibid., p. 13.

69. "Mystic and Politician as Poet: Vaughan, Traherne, Marvell, Milton," p. 591.

70. "The Devotional Poets of the Seventeenth Century: Donne, Herbert, Crashaw," *Listener* 3 (26 Mar. 1930): 552.

71. "Andrew Marvell," *Nation and Athenaeum* 33 (29 Sept. 1923): 809.

72. "Studies in Contemporary Criticism, I," *Egoist* 5 (Oct. 1918): 114.

73. Cohen, *A Preface to Logic* (New York: Henry Holt, 1944), p. 83.

74. Fenichel, *The Psychoanalytic Theory of Neurosis* (New York: Norton, 1945), p. 47.

75. "Studies in Contemporary Criticism, I," p. 114.

76. "Andrew Marvell," p. 809.

77. "Max Ernst" (1920), *What is Surrealism?: Selected Writings*, ed. Franklin Rosemont (New York: Monad Press, 1978), p. 8.

78. Many other theories of the metaphoric act have, of course, been proposed since Aristotle. Among the major modern theorists are Owen Barfield, Monroe Beardsley, Max Black, I. A. Richards, Stephen Ullmann, Wilbur Marshall Urban, and Phillip Wheelwright. Two recent symposiums are *On Metaphor*, ed. Sheldon Sacks (Chicago: Univ. of Chicago Press, 1979), and *Metaphor and Thought*, ed. Andrew Ortony (Cambridge: Cambridge Univ. Press, 1979). The important philosophical papers are collected in *Philosophical Perspectives on Metaphor*, ed. Mark Johnson (Minneapolis: Univ. of Minnesota Press, 1981), and recent linguistic theory is reviewed in the course of Samuel R. Levin's study, *The Semantics of Metaphor* (Baltimore: Johns Hopkins Univ. Press, 1977), and more systematically and comprehensively by Paul Ricoeur in *The Rule of Metaphor: Multi-Disciplinary Studies of the Creation of Meaning in Language*, tr. Robert Czerny (Toronto: Univ. of Toronto Press, 1977). The following analysis of metaphor has its origins in, though it does not conform to, that developed in *Rhétorique générale* by Group μ (J. Dubois, F. Edeline, J.-M. Klinkenberg, P. Minguet, F. Pire, H. Trinon) (Paris: Librairie Larousse, 1970), tr. Paul B. Burrell and Edgar M. Slotkin, *A General Rhetoric* (Baltimore: Johns Hopkins Univ. Press, 1981).

Brief portions of this discussion of surrealism and metaphor, and the subsequent discussion of surrealism and the visual, have appeared in slightly different form in my "Pound's Imagism and the Surreal," *Journal of Modern Literature* 12 (July 1985): 185–210.

79. *Le Mouvement perpétuel* (Paris: Gallimard, 1926).

80. From "Inédits," *Robert Desnos*, editions Poètes d'aujourd'hui (Paris: Seghers, 1960), p. 102.

81. From *Les Ténèbres* (1927), *Domaine public* (Paris: Gallimard, 1953), p. 133.

82. From *La Rose publique* (1934), *Choix de poèmes* (Paris: Gallimard, 1951), p. 144.

83. *Calixto, suivi de contrée* (Paris: Gallimard, 1962), p. 47.

84. From *Les Ténèbres, Domaine public*, p. 139.

85. *Westwego* (1922), *Poèmes et poésies (1917–1973)* (Paris: Bernard Grasset, 1973), p. 50.

86. From *Langage cuit* (1923), *Domaine public*, p. 84.

87. From *Le Livre ouvert—I.* (1940), *Choix de poèmes*, p. 246.

88. From *De Derrière les Fagots* (1934), *Benjamin Peret*, editions Poètes d'aujourd'hui (Paris: Seghers), p. 90.

89. "Rising Signs" (1947), *What is Surrealism?*, p. 280.

90. "Exhibition X . . . Y . . ." (1929), *What is Surrealism?*, p. 43.

91. "Rising Signs," *What is Surrealism?*, p. 280.

92. Ibid., p. 282.

93. *L'Union libre* (1931), *Poèmes* (Paris: Gallimard, 1948), p. 57.

94. From *L'Air de l'eau* (1934), ibid., p. 124.

95. From *Mourir de ne pas mourir* (1924), *Choix de poèmes*, p. 58.

96. Fenichel, *The Psychoanalytic Theory of Neurosis*, pp. 47–48.

97. "The Noh and the Image," *Egoist* 4 (Aug. 1917): 103.

98. Fletcher, *Allegory: The Theory of a Symbolic Mode* (Ithaca, N.Y.: Cornell Univ. Press, 1964), p. 379.

99. Ibid.

100. Ibid., p. 380.

101. Ibid., p. 266.

102. *Manifestoes,* p. 26.

103. Ibid.

104. "Prose and Verse," p. 9.

105. Breton, "Manifesto of Surrealism," *Manifestoes,* p. 38.

106. "Preface" (1930), *Anabasis, A Poem by St.-John Perse,* tr. T. S. Eliot, 3d ed. (New York: Harcourt, Brace, 1949), p. 10.

107. For other surrealistic effects in *The Waste Land,* see Korg, "Modern Art Techniques in *The Waste Land,*" pp. 460–63.

108. "Rhyme and Reason: The Poetry of John Donne," p. 503.

109. "The Borderline of Prose," *New Statesman,* 9 (19 May 1917), 158.

110. Breton, *Manifestoes,* p. 123.

111. Breton, "Situation of Surrealism Between the Two Wars" (1943), *What is Surrealism?* p. 246. See also "Surrealist Situation of the Object" (1935), *Manifestoes,* pp. 258–60.

112. Breton, *Manifestoes,* p. 27.

113. "The Borderline of Prose," p. 158.

114. Breton, *Manifestoes,* p. 27.

115. Ibid., p. 20. Reverdy's statement first appeared in *Nord-Sud* (Mar. 1918).

116. Breton, "Situation of Surrealism Between the Two Wars," *What is Surrealism?,* p. 245.

117. Breton, "Rising Signs," *What is Surrealism?,* p. 280. In an interview the Surrealist poet Michel Leiris has told Sidra Stich that, to quote Stich's paraphrase, "nearly everyone associated with the Surrealist Movement was profoundly affected by Lévy-Bruhl's ideas." See *Joan Miro: The Development of a Sign Language* (St. Louis: Washington Univ. Gallery of Art, 1980), pp. 8, 60.

118. Breton, "The Automatic Message," *What is Surrealism?,* p. 108.

119. "Ulysses, Order, and Myth," *Selected Prose,* p. 175.

120. "The Romantic Englishman, the Comic Spirit, and the Function of Criticism," p. 4.

121. "London Letter," *Dial* 70 (Apr. 1921): 451.

122. "Notes on Current Letters: The Lesson of Baudelaire," *Tyro,* no. 1 (Spring 1921), p. 4.

123. *Vingt-cinq poèmes* (Zurich: Collection Dada, 1918). The lines that Eliot quotes from "Le Géant blanc lépreux du paysage" are extant in *Oeuvres complètes* (Paris: Librairie Ernest Flammarion, 1975), p. 87.

124. "Reflections on Contemporary Poetry" (July 1919), p. 39.

125. Interview, "The Art of Poetry, I: T. S. Eliot," p. 58. Certainly much of *The Waste Land,* written during a period of nervous collapse, was composed in this way:

> some forms of ill health . . . produce an efflux of poetry in a way approaching the condition of automatic writing. . . . To me it seems that at these moments, which are characterized by the sudden lifting of the burden of anxiety and fear which presses upon our daily life so steadily that we are unaware of it, what happens is something *negative:* that is to say, not "inspiration" as we commonly think of it, but the breaking down of strong habitual barriers—which tend to reform very quickly. (*UPUC* 144)

Eliot reflects elsewhere that in such a state substantial passages may be written that need little if any editing (*SE* 358). Indicative of how great a role the unconscious played in his poem's composition, Eliot admits later in his *Paris Review* interview that with *The Waste Land* he did not concern himself whether he "understood what I was saying" (p. 105). Interestingly, Eliot proceeds to compare *The Waste Land* to Joyce's *Ulysses* on the basis of this subliminal quality in their composition and effect. More generally with regard to the writing of a poem, Eliot observes that, in contrast to "conscious intention," there are "intentions more in a negative than a positive sense": an author might obey the urge to create with little clear idea of what he wishes to express until the work lies finished before him (p. 97).

126. "Introduction," *Leisure the Basis of Culture,* p. 12.

127. See Breton, "Second Manifesto of Surrealism," *Manifestoes,* pp. 158–64. For an early expression of these views see "Manifesto of Surrealism," p. 10, whose emphasis is otherwise predominantly automatic. Uwe Schneede's discussion, pp. 29–34, of the changing role of automatism in Surrealist theory and practice is discerning.

128. In later years Breton did speak of the unconscious as a "collective myth"; the artist was to surrender his preoccupation with his personality and, in terms of Freud's psychological model, explore the id rather than the ego and superego. But Breton's collective myth is not like Eliot's, a permanent structure of the human mind, but a historically relative method for reaching the unconscious. For the Romantic era it was ruins and the apparitions in gothic novels; for the early twentieth century it is mannequins and the coincidences of Surrealist art. See "Manifesto of Surrealism," p. 16, and "Political Position of Today's Art" (1935), p. 232, in *Manifestoes,* and "Limits Not Frontiers of Surrealism" (1937), in *What is Surrealism?,* pp. 155–58. For the relationship between Surrealism and myth, see Evan Maclyn Maurer, "In Quest of the Myth: An Investigation of the Relationship Between Surrealism and Primitivism" (Ph.D. dissertation, University of Pennsylvania, 1974), and Whitney Chadwick, *Myth in Surrealist Painting, 1929–1939* (Ann Arbor: UMI Research Press, 1980).

129. Paul Ray, *Surrealist Movement in England,* p. 281.

130. "Ulysses, Order, and Myth," *Selected Prose,* p. 175.

131. "The Method of Mr. Pound," p. 1065.

132. See, for instance, Breton, "Manifesto of Surrealism," *Manifestoes,* pp. 26–27; "Surrealism: Yesterday, Today, and Tomorrow," *This Quarter* 5 (Sept. 1932): 17–18, in which the former list is repeated with one omission, and variations in wording, and a second name added; "What is Surrealism?" *What is Surrealism?,* pp. 122–23, in which the second list is repeated.

133. See Arturo Schwarz, *Man Ray: The Rigour of Imagination* (New York: Rizzoli, 1977), p. 161.

134. "Introduction" to Marianne Moore, *Selected Poems* (New York: Macmillan, 1935), pp. xi, x.

135. Moore, *Poems* (London: Egoist Press, 1921).

136. "Marianne Moore," p. 595.

137. Breton, *Poèmes,* p. 57.

138. *Anabasis, A Poem by St.-John Perse,* pp. 29, 33, 37, 45, 49, 63.

139. For echoes of Perse's imagery and technique in Eliot's poetry see Howarth, *Notes on Some Figures,* pp. 166, 289, 367. Howarth conjectures that Eliot may have read Perse during his student year in Paris, for Perse was published at that time in a journal with which Eliot was familiar.

Howarth also claims that Eliot translated *Anabasis* during the mid-1920s; the first edition of the translation was published in 1930. Likewise, Smith, *Eliot's Poetry and Plays,* p. 123, states that Eliot began translating in 1926.

140. Breton, *Manifestoes,* p. 27.

141. The poems and passages that Eliot selects are actually Imagist in nature, and Imagism in theory and practice is generically surreal. With regard to Pound, see my "Pound's Imagism and the Surreal," *Journal of Modern Literature* 12 (July 1985): 185–210, where a portion of the following discussion of Pound's poems appears in slightly different form. Hulme, in turn, as a proto-Imagist theoretician, believed that "thought is prior to language and consists in the simultaneous presentation to the mind of two different images" ("Notes on Language and Style," ed. Herbert Read, as reprinted in *Further Speculations,* ed. Sam Hynes [Lincoln, . Neb.: Univ. of Nebraska Press, 1962], p. 84. This article originally appeared in Eliot's *Criterion* for July 1925). Hulme thought, like Gourmont, that language originated as metaphors expressing immediate sensory experiences. Because these metaphors tend to become abstractions with frequent use over time, language must be revived periodically through the creation of new metaphors. For Hulme, also, the primary perceptual experience is visual and can be communicated only through metaphor; hence, the high value he places upon an imagistic verse: "poetry is not a counter language, but a visual, concrete one. . . . Visual meanings can only be transferred by the new bowl of metaphor" ("Romanticism and Classicism," *Speculations: Essays on Humanism and the Philosophy of Art,* ed. Herbert Read [London: Kegan Paul, Trench, Trubner, 1924], p. 134). Hulme becomes a propagandist for the surreal when he endorses metaphor as a poetic technique for purposes beyond merely the renewal of language. Relishing the effect of metaphoric expression for its own sake in ways strikingly similar to Breton, and Eliot, Hulme announces that "literature [is] a method of sudden arrangement of commonplaces. The *suddenness* makes us forget the commonplace." Poetic statements, Hulme insists, "always must have analogies, which make an other-world through-the-glass effect," which "give a sense of wonder, a sense of being united in another mystic world," which "overawe the reader" ("Notes on Language and Style," *Further Speculations,* pp. 93, 87, 88). As Hulme made clear in "Bergson's Theory of Art," *Speculations,* pp. 143–96, his esthetic and linguistic theories derive from Bergson. In *Time and Free Will,* p. 105, Bergson explains that an intuition of duration, the unified absolute below the level of consciousness and impervious to scientific study, would be like experiencing a perceptual metaphor: if "I retain the recollection of the preceding oscillation together with the image of the present oscillation, . . . either I shall set the two images side by side, . . . or I shall perceive one *in* the other, each *permeating* the other and organizing themselves like the notes of a tune, so as to form what we shall call a continuous or qualitative multiplicity with no resemblance to number. I shall thus get the image of pure duration" (my emphasis). Hulme's 'through-the-looking-glass other-world' is really Bergson's duration, which shares with Eliot's and Breton's unconscious this metaphoric quality. Eliot observed that the intention of Imagism was to "induce a peculiar concentration upon something visual, and to set in motion an expanding succession of concentric feelings" ("Introduction" to Marianne Moore, *Selected Poems* [New York: Macmillan, 1935], pp. xi–xii).

142. Review of *The New Elizabethans* by E. B. Osborn, *Athenaeum*, no. 4640 (4 Apr. 1919), p. 134.

143. "The Complete Poetical Works of T. E. Hulme," *New Age* 10 (23 Jan. 1912): 307; rpt. in Ezra Pound, *Ripostes* (London: Stephen Swift, 1912; reissued Elkin Matthews, 1915), a volume which Eliot mentions in "A Note on Ezra Pound," *Today* 4 (Sept. 1918): 7, and again in "The Method of Mr. Pound," p. 1065.

144. "Exhibition X . . . Y . . . ," *What is Surrealism?* p. 43.

145. Eluard, *Choix de poèmes*, p. 58.

146. "Introduction," Ezra Pound, *Selected Poems*, p. 14.

147. "A Note on Ezra Pound," p. 7.

148. Ibid., p. 6.

149. Breton, *Poèmes*, p. 58.

150. Breton, *Manifestoes*, p. 38.

151. Stampfer, *John Donne and the Metaphysical Gesture* (New York: Funk and Wagnells, 1970), p. 93.

152. Praz, *Mnemosyne: The Parallel Between Literature and the Visual Arts* (Princeton: Princeton Univ. Press, 1970), pp. 201–3, 206–7. See also Paul Ray, *Surrealist Movement in England*, p. 267.

153. *Biographia Literaria*, ed. John Shawcross (Oxford: Clarendon Press, 1907), II. 12.

154. Ibid., I. 202: "time and space."

155. (Boston: Houghton Mifflin, 1927).

156. Coleridge, "Conversations with Henry Crabb Robinson," *Coleridge's Miscellaneous Criticism*, ed. Thomas M. Raysor (Cambridge, Mass.: Harvard Univ. Press, 1936), p. 387.

157. Coleridge, *Table Talk, Miscellaneous Criticism*, p. 436.

158. "Lectures of 1818," *Miscellaneous Criticism*, pp. 42–43. Hence, the reason why surrealistic verse was not written in the Romantic era.

159. Coleridge, *Miscellaneous Criticism*, p. 387.

160. Ibid., p. 43.

161. In *A History of Modern Criticism: 1750–1950*, vol. 2, *The Romantic Age* (New Haven: Yale Univ. Press, 1955), Rene Wellek discusses the unconscious in Herder, Schelling, and Schlegel, pp. 45–50, and Jean Paul Richter, pp. 101–2, as well as Wordsworth, pp. 139–40, and Coleridge, p. 163. Other useful discussions of the topic appear in Walter Jackson Bate, *From Classic to Romantic: Premises of Taste in Eighteenth-Century England* (Cambridge, Mass.: Harvard Univ. Press, 1946), pp. 115–17, 164–66; M. H. Abrams, *The Mirror and the Lamp: Romantic Theory and the Critical Tradition* (New York: Oxford Univ. Press, 1953), pp. 167–77, 187–225 *passim*; and Robert Langbaum, *The Poetry of Experience*, pp. 233–34.

162. Coleridge, *Biographia Literaria*, II. 120.

163. Ibid., II. 12. See J. Robert Barth, *The Symbolic Imagination: Coleridge and the Romantic Tradition* (Princeton: Princeton Univ. Press, 1977).

164. Pierrot, *The Decadent Imagination, 1880–1900*, tr. Derek Coltman (Chicago: Univ. of Chicago Press, 1981), p. 258.

165. Raymond, *De Baudelaire au Surréalisme* (1933), tr. *From Baudelaire to Surrealism* (1950; London: Methuen, 1970), pp. 198, 202, 211.

166. Ibid., pp. 202–3.

167. Balakian, "Metaphor and Metamorphosis in André Breton's Poetics," *French Studies* 19 (1965): 34.

INDEX OF WORKS BY T. S. ELIOT

INDEX OF NAMES AND TERMS